CHARLOTTE BRONTË

CRITICAL ISSUES

Published

George Eliot   *Pauline Nestor*
Virginia Woolf   *Linden Peach*
Charles Dickens   *Lyn Pykett*
Henry James   *Jeremy Tambling*
William Wordsworth   *John Williams*
Charlotte Brontë   *Carl Plasa*

In preparation

Geoffrey Chaucer   *Ruth Evans*
Jane Austen   *Darryl Jones*
James Joyce   *Kiernan Ryan*
D. H. Lawrence   *Rick Rylance*
Joseph Conrad   *Allan Simmons*
John Keats   *John Whale*
Thomas Hardy   *Julian Wolfreys*

Critical Issues Series
Series Standing Order
ISBN 1–4039–2158–X hardcover
ISBN 1–4039–2159–8 paperback
(outside North America only)

You can receive future titles in this series as they are published by placing a standing order. Please contact your bookseller or, in case of difficulty, write to us at the address below with your name and address, the title of the series and the ISBN quoted above.

Customer Services Department, Macmillan Distribution Ltd, Houndmills, Basingstoke, Hampshire RG21 6XS, England

Critical Issues

Charlotte Brontë

Carl Plasa

palgrave
macmillan

First published 2004 by
PALGRAVE MACMILLAN
Houndmills, Basingstoke, Hampshire RG21 6XS and
175 Fifth Avenue, New York, N.Y. 10010
Companies and representatives throughout the world

PALGRAVE MACMILLAN is the global academic imprint of the
Palgrave Macmillan division of St. Martin's Press, LLC and of
Palgrave Macmillan Ltd. Macmillan® is a registered trademark in the
United States, United Kingdom and other countries. Palgrave is a
registered trademark in the European Union and other countries.

ISBN 0–333–92247–6 hardback
ISBN 0–333–92248–4 paperback

This book is printed on paper suitable for recycling and made from fully
managed and sustained forest sources.

A catalogue record for this book is available from the British Library.

Library of Congress Cataloging-in-Publication Data

Plasa, Carl, 1959-
Charlotte Brontë / Carl Plasa.
    p. cm– (Critical issues)
    Includes bibliographical references and index.
    ISBN 0–333–92247–6 (cloth) – ISBN 0–333–92248–4 (paper)
    1. Brontë, Charlotte, 1816–1855–Criticism and interpretation.
2. Women and literature–England–History–19th century. I. Title. II. Critical
issues (Palgrave Macmillan (Firm))

PR4169.P55 2004
823'.8–dc22
                                                            2003067597

10   9   8   7   6   5   4   3   2   1
13   12   11   10   09   08   07   06   05   04

Printed in China

For BJ and the boy
and to the memory of Annoushka

Contents

Acknowledgements

I am grateful to Martin Coyle and John Peck for providing me with the opportunity to write on Charlotte Brontë and for their helpful comments and advice along the way; and to Sean Purchase, for his swift and attentive responses to various portions of the book. I would also like to thank the Arts and Humanities Research Board, which supported this project with a research leave grant covering the Spring semester of the 2001–2 academic session.

Special gratitude goes, as ever, to Betty Jay, whose unstinting patience, insight and sense of proportion were invaluable to the completion of this work.

An earlier version of Chapter 3 appeared in *Journal of Narrative Theory*, 30:1 (2000), 1–28, and of Chapter 4 in my *Textual Politics from Slavery to Postcolonialism: Race and Identification* (Palgrave Macmillan, 2000), pp. 60–81.

Introduction

> There is a conspiracy of silence around the colonial truth, whatever that might be.
>
> Homi K. Bhabha, *The Location of Culture*, p. 123

Under the gaze of their biographers, authors find themselves curiously repositioned, transformed from writing into written subjects. In Charlotte Brontë's case, the original agent of such transformation is Elizabeth Gaskell, whose biography of her fellow-writer appeared in 1857, almost two years to the day after Brontë's death, aged 38, on 31 March 1855. As several critics have noted, one of the recurrent features of Gaskell's study is its emphasis on the culturally and socially isolated conditions in which Brontë lived and wrote.[1] A passage from volume 1, chapter 5 is indicative of this particular aspect of the text. Pondering the nature of Brontë's childhood (and that of her siblings) as it stood in the late 1820s, Gaskell writes:

> Life in an isolated village, or a lonely country-house, presents many little occurrences which sink into the mind of childhood, there to be brooded over. No other event may have happened, or be likely to happen, for days, to push this aside, before it has assumed a vague and mysterious importance. Thus, children leading a secluded life are often thoughtful and dreamy: the impressions made upon them by the world without – the unusual sights of earth and sky – the accidental meetings with strange faces and figures – (rare occurrences in those out-of-the-way places) – are sometimes magnified by them into things so deeply significant as to be almost supernatural. This

ix

peculiarity I perceive very strongly in Charlotte's writings at this time.[2]

If it is indeed true that Gaskell 'may be said to have created, almost single-handedly, the myth of the Brontës',[3] then it is passages such as this on which the 'myth' in part relies, with its blatantly Romantic figuration of its 'secluded' child-subjects as 'thoughtful and dreamy' and endowed with mental powers verging on the 'supernatural'.

Gaskell's exceptionalist vision of Brontë as one amongst a trinity of splendidly isolated geniuses has proved surprisingly resilient, extending its influence well into the twentieth century.[4] Over the last 30 years or so, however, it has been seriously challenged on several fronts. Largely as a consequence of the advent of critical theory, approaches to Brontë's work have become increasingly politicized, with critics seeking to return 'Charlotte's writings', to adopt Gaskell's phrase, to the cultural and historical contexts in which they were originally produced. In the initial stages of this endeavour, the main emphases were Marxist and feminist, with major contributions being made, respectively, in Terry Eagleton's *Myths of Power: A Marxist Study of the Brontës* (1975) and Sandra M. Gilbert and Susan Gubar's *The Madwoman in the Attic: The Woman Writer and the Nineteenth-Century Literary Imagination* (1979). These approaches were supplemented – if not always complemented – in the mid-1980s, by the emergence of readings of Brontë's *oeuvre* from a postcolonial critical perspective, and it is in relation to this latter body of work that this book situates and defines itself. While such work can often be highly illuminating, it has none the less left many possibilities unexplored, privileging some texts while ignoring others, and failing, in particular, to consider the relationships of continuity and transformation which exist between Brontë's earlier and later writings. Despite its undoubted importance, the current postcolonial understanding of Brontë's work requires considerable further broadening and development in order to bring what might be called the genealogy of her colonial imagination into clearer focus.

The catalyst to the postcolonial reassessment of Brontë was Gayatri Chakravorty Spivak's landmark analysis of *Jane Eyre* in 'Three Women's Texts and a Critique of Imperialism', an essay much anthologized in the wake of its first appearance in 1985. In this theoretically dense but rewarding *tour de force*, Spivak characteristically adopts a deconstructive reading strategy, looking to the margins of *Jane Eyre* and the figure of Bertha Mason, the white Creole heiress who is encrypted there as Rochester's allegedly mad first wife. Despite its prestigious position as Brontë's most celebrated novel, *Jane Eyre* is a problematic text for Spivak, encouraging, or perhaps even coercing its readers to identify with its eponymous narrator-heroine by representing her colonial other in purely negative terms: English is to white Creole, Jane to Bertha, the text implies, as human is to bestial/monstrous. For Spivak, it is this kind of hierarchical opposition which signals and enacts the violent complicity between 'nineteenth-century British literature' and 'the imperialist project'.

It is not only *Jane Eyre* which thus blithely 'reproduces the axioms of imperialism',[5] however. Such a process is also troublingly supported in the work of Brontë's Anglo-American feminist critics, as typified, for Spivak, in the highly influential reading of Brontë's novel propounded by Gilbert and Gubar. By seeing Bertha 'only in psychological terms, as Jane's dark double',[6] Spivak contends, these critics repeat the very effacement of Bertha's status as an autonomous subject, caught up in a particular colonial history, which is performed by *Jane Eyre* itself.

Spivak's critique of *Jane Eyre* and her searching reflections on the politics of feminist interpretation have themselves been highly influential, leading a veritable host of critics to deploy, extend, refine and sometimes challenge her insights throughout the course of the late 1980s and the 1990s.[7] Yet there is a sense in which the new critical possibilities opened up by Spivak and her followers for a postcolonial reading of Brontë have subsequently become closed down, or at least not been sufficiently investigated. Postcolonial critics seem just as keen as their feminist predecessors, generally speaking, to fetishize *Jane Eyre* – as if it were the only, or even most significant, juncture in Brontë's writing at which an encounter with colonial history takes place. Although there are, of course, some notable exceptions to this pattern, there remain, nearly 20 years on from Spivak's intervention, remarkably few instances of critics moving debates about Brontë's relationship to colonialism much beyond the charismatic limits of Brontë's best known and best loved novel.[8] Perhaps even more remarkably, there are still no book-length studies which set out to position the full range of Brontë's writings within the archive of nineteenth-century colonial history. This book precisely attempts to undertake such a project, offering the most comprehensive account to date of a crucial but considerably under-researched aspect of Brontë's literary production. While it necessarily devotes the bulk of its attention to Brontë's four novels, the book gives space, also, to the work Brontë produced prior to her emergence as novelist: the Ashanti narratives, the poetry and the Belgian essays. These initial textual productions have largely been slighted by the critical institution and are likely, consequently, to be unfamiliar to most readers. They are, however, of major importance to a postcolonial reading of Brontë. As well as suggesting the extent to which her authorial self-fashioning is bound up with the project of nineteenth-century colonialism, these neglected writings are themselves the sources from which a good deal of the colonial material in Brontë's later works is derived.

The book opens with a chapter on Brontë's early writings, generated and sustained by an imaginative collaboration with her brother, Branwell, which took place between 1829 and 1839. This extraordinary but critically unacclaimed body of work, whose quantity exceeds that of all Brontë's later novels put together, is, amongst other things, a striking blend of fantasy and history. The strangely named spaces into which Brontë first ventures and experiments as writer – Glass Town and later Angria – are purely imaginary constructs. At the same time, though, they are situated in a geographically real location, 'carved', in Juliet Barker's formulation, 'out of the interior of Africa'[9] and, more specifically, the Ashanti region of what is now Southern Ghana. As the chapter argues, the frequently violent and disturbing narratives Brontë unfolds in these spaces are not only the hybrid product of an interplay between fantasy and history, but themselves much concerned with questions of racial hybridity and miscegenation. Such questions are addressed by Brontë on a number of occasions in the course of the Ashanti project, becoming particularly significant in three texts: 'A Leaf from an Unopened Volume' (1834); 'Well, here I am at Roe Head' (1836); and 'Caroline Vernon' (1839). Different as they are from one another, what binds these narratives together is a construction of racial mixing which is itself, appropriately, ambivalent, combining a fear and loathing of the racial other with desire and fascination.

In its second chapter, the book continues to consider the material Brontë produced in the protracted period before the composition of her novels, exploring two new areas. The first and more substantial of these is Brontë's poetry, a relatively small portion of which appeared during her lifetime, in the pseudonymous, self-funded and resoundingly unsuccessful collection which she published, in conjunction with her sisters, Emily and Anne, as *Poems*, in 1846.[10] The second area consists of Brontë's Belgian essays, an eclectic series of short exercises, originally written in French. These were composed in 1842–3 at the Brussels school where Brontë (accompanied by Emily) studied and later taught, under the guidance of Constantin Georges Romain Heger, a figure with whom she was also to become emotionally involved, to her considerable detriment.[11] Each of these elements of Brontë's writing has, if anything, received even less critical attention than the Ashanti narratives. Even so, it is clear that both play significant roles in the evolution of Brontë's colonial imagination, contributing to the sense of continuity and overlap between the earlier and later stages of her career, and containing some valuable insights into her pre-novelistic engagement with the complexities of British colonial history. This chapter examines the nature of this engagement by offering close readings of four of the poems and one of the Belgian essays, a selection spanning the period from 1833 to 1846. What emerges from the analysis of this group of texts is that Brontë is less drawn to the question of colonial history *per se* than to its diverse points of intersection with the imagined subjectivities of those who are caught up in it, whether they be colonizer or colonized, male or female.

With Chapter 3, the book moves out from the writings forming the pre-history of Brontë's novels and on to the novels themselves, beginning with *The Professor*. Although originally completed in 1846, Brontë's first novel was a late arrival on the literary scene, appearing only posthumously, in 1857, following the huge public interest which Gaskell's biography had created in the lives and writings of the Brontës as a whole. At first glance, *The Professor* would seem to mark a decisive break with the overtly colonial orientations of Brontë's earlier work. Yet the departure from the colonial is only a prelude to its return. Taking the notion of contrapuntal reading formulated in Edward W. Said's *Culture and Imperialism* (1994) as its starting point, this chapter traces the modes of this return as they are articulated in terms of the novel's language and, more broadly, its treatment of the question of sexuality. The chapter begins by historicizing *The Professor*'s characteristic figurings of class and gender in terms of slavery, situating them in relation to British colonial and African American histories in order to underline the questionable politics of the novel's rhetorical strategies. It goes on from this to place *The Professor* in the context of contemporary medical discourses and explores the implication of sexuality in questions of nation and race. For William Crimsworth, the novel's first-person narrator and central protagonist, sexuality is indissociable from the foreign and the Oriental and, in this way, poses a constant threat to the stability of his identity as Englishman. As he struggles against his desires, and those of the others around him, Crimsworth rehearses anxieties of racial contamination already addressed in the Ashanti narratives, thus linking the novel back to the very origins from which it would seem, ironically, to have swerved away.

For Gaskell, *The Professor* constitutes 'a very curious link in [Brontë's] literary history ... showing the *promise* of much that was afterwards realized'.[12] This observation presumably refers to the reworking of the novel Brontë was to undertake in *Villette,* some seven years later. Gaskell's comment could also be applied, however, to the relationship between *The Professor* and *Jane Eyre* (1847), the novel which is the focus of Chapter 4. In this text, the language of enslavement and mastery introduced in *The Professor* undergoes a significant development and indeed becomes *Jane Eyre*'s key rhetorical system or colonial tropology. Such a tropology has a double function. On the one hand, it provides Jane with a means by which to define herself and her interactions with others. On the other, the recourse to a metaphorics of slavery enables Brontë to elaborate a radical critique of gender and class relations within early Victorian England. Equally, though, the radical nature of such figurative procedures is itself radically undercut by the gap between enslavement as metaphor and its material embodiment in the form of British colonial oppression in the West Indies, a phenomenon which *Jane Eyre* never openly names. In so far as Brontë's first two novels mobilize untenable analogies between colonial domination and forms of oppression at home, they reveal themselves to share a textual politics whose assumptions solicit interrogation. Yet if there is a repetition of *The Professor* in *Jane Eyre*, there is also difference. Brontë's most famous novel co-opts and exploits the trope of slavery, shaping it to its own feminist design, but at the same time disputes and dismantles its own rhetorical strategies. In this way, it offers a complex reflection on the very identifications (between white woman and black slave) on which it relies.

In Chapter 5, the book shifts the focus from *Jane Eyre* to *Shirley* (1849), setting Brontë's third novel within the historical framework of the Irish Famine of 1845–51. The horrors of this contemporary catastrophe are no more directly named or addressed in *Shirley* than are the horrors of slavery in *Jane Eyre*. The Famine is cryptically present in the novel none the less, its traces detectable, principally, in the conflicts which *Shirley* stages in the contexts of race, class and gender. The Anglo-Irish antagonisms with which the novel begins take the form of a struggle over food, just as class hostilities are represented in terms of a hunger and corporeal wasting which comes, in the end, to affect both worker and master. Similarly, the struggles which the novel dramatizes between men and women are played out at the level of the somatic, as *Shirley*'s middle-class female bodies become transformed into instruments of protest against patriarchy, articulating their complaints by means of self-starvation. Yet if there is something distinctly anorectic about these spectacularly hungry female bodies, the novel itself could be said to have anorectic tendencies of its own. *Shirley*'s middle-class women do not speak their discontent openly, but translate it into a corporeal hieroglyphics, just as the novel's obsessive figurings of race, class and gender in terms of the body and food, eating and hunger, point beyond themselves towards an otherwise unacknowledged history. The Famine's shadowy presence not only subtends the representation of the body in *Shirley*, however, but is also decipherable in the fantasies of transatlantic migration and resettlement which intrude upon the novel from time to time, flouting its overtly regional emphasis. As the chapter suggests in a brief coda, such fantasies themselves bear historical traces, recalling the patterns of diaspora to which the Famine was to lead.

Chapter 6 reads Brontë's last completed novel, *Villette* (1853), as a more complex reimagining of her first, drawing attention to the similarities and differences between the two texts. Like *The Professor*, *Villette* is a novel as much saturated with xenophobia as it is preoccupied with questions of repressed sexuality, though, in this case, the sexuality which interests Brontë is female rather than male, with the enigmatic figure of Lucy Snowe usurping Crimsworth as first-person narrator. Despite the regendering of narrative perspective, however, the dread and hatred of the foreigner circulating in *Villette* does not merely denote an anxiety about that which is culturally or racially other. As for Crimsworth, the foreigners whom Lucy encounters in the course of her narrative are overdetermined figures, operating as surrogates or scapegoats, onto which disavowed desires can be safely exported.

The play of similarity and difference between *Villette* and *The Professor* is also manifest with regard to the evidently perennial Brontëan subject of slavery. In *The Professor*, this is a topic percolating into the novel's metaphors, which jar against its fleeting allusions to the West Indies, as against the racial predicaments of Brontë's contemporary America. Such a tension between figure and ground is yet more sharply realized in *Villette*, as Brontë's ubiquitous slave tropes are silently questioned by the fragmentary but haunting narrative of colonial oppression in Guadeloupe, which begins to surface in the novel's third volume. Where *Villette*'s treatment of slavery most markedly deviates from and enriches *The Professor*'s, however, is in terms of the intertextual relationships it establishes with two other novels, Harriet Beecher Stowe's *Uncle Tom's Cabin* (1852) and Jacques-Henri Bernardin de Saint-Pierre's *Paul and Virginia* (1788). Each of these anti-slavery texts becomes important to *Villette* at different junctures and in different ways. *Uncle Tom's Cabin* features mainly in *Villette*'s second volume, as the institutions of slavery and patriarchy Stowe and Brontë respectively critique are brought into an uneasy transatlantic parallel. *Paul and Virginia*, by contrast, plays a particularly influential role in volume three, providing a narrative of doomed romance and colonial exploitation which *Villette* appropriates and reworks in its own image.

As Said has argued, 'The power to narrate, or to block other narratives from forming and emerging, is very important to culture and imperialism, and constitutes one of the main connections between them.'[13] For many postcolonial critics of Brontë, such narrative power is most conspicuously demonstrated by *Jane Eyre*, viewed, quite rightly, as a novel which articulates one story at the expense of another, with Jane's narrative driving Bertha's into silence. For this book, on the other hand, the simultaneous telling and blocking of stories at work in *Jane Eyre* is also broadly characteristic of the postcolonial criticism which has grown up around Brontë's writings in the last two decades or so. What is now required is a widening of the horizon beyond the critically much fêted *Jane Eyre*, so that new narratives of Brontë's relationship to the question of colonialism can be constructed. Sometimes direct, sometimes devious, often complex, that relationship is always compelling.

1

'Mingled Gold and Iron': Miscegenation in the Ashanti Narratives

> When the blood of your daughter or your son is mixed with that of one of this race ... how shall sickly sentimentalities solace your shame if in the blood of your mulatto grandchild ... there shall be disported primitive appetites, propensities, passions fit only to endow an Ashanti warrior or grace the orgies of an African bacchanalia?
> Robert Lee Durham, cited in Werner Sollors, *Neither Black nor White yet Both*, p. 65

> [There is] an ambivalent driving desire at the heart of racialism: a compulsive libidinal attraction disavowed by an equal insistence on repulsion.
> Robert J. C. Young, *Colonial Desire*, p. 149

> If you knew my thoughts; the dreams that absorb me; and the fiery imagination that at times eats me up ... you would pity and I dare say despise me.
> Charlotte Brontë, letter to Ellen Nussey, 10 May 1836[1]

In a letter of 25 July 1856, Elizabeth Gaskell provides an account of a visit to Haworth Parsonage, undertaken in the course of her researches for *The Life of Charlotte Brontë*, which she was to publish in the following year. As she recalls, the visit proves to be 'very successful' and she leaves the Brontë family residence veritably laden with manuscripts. Some of these turn out, on closer inspection, to be quite remarkable. 'I came away', Gaskell enthuses:

with the 'Professor' the beginning of [Brontë's] new tale 'Emma' –
about 10 pages written in the finest pencil writing, – & by far the
most extraordinary of all, a packet about the size of a lady's travelling writing case, full of paper books of different sizes … all in this
indescribably fine writing. – Mr Gaskell says they would make
more than 50 vols of print, – but they are the wildest & most
incoherent things, as far as we have examined them. . . . They give
one the idea of creative power carried to the verge of insanity.[2]

The 'packet' to which Gaskell proudly refers is indeed an 'extraordinary' one, containing, as it does, the dense and sprawling body
of Brontë's so-called juvenilia or early writings, which she
produced, in partnership with Branwell, between the ages of 13
and 23. Gaskell's encounter with these materials has a direct and
significant effect upon the literary project in which she herself is
engaged. As Bette London summarizes, 'after perusing some of the
manuscripts, [Gaskell] felt compelled to rewrite about forty pages'
of her biography, even as 'she remained … notoriously nonplused'
by the texts she had read, unable, in the end, to give them 'any
serious treatment'.[3]

Gaskell's sense of perplexity in the face of Brontë's experimental
and extravagant first fictions has been frequently shared by other
readers, who have evidently deemed it best to leave this 'wild
weird writing'[4] well alone. Over the last 20 years or so, however,
several critics have set out to examine Brontë's early narratives,
giving them a variety of 'serious treatment[s]'. Christine
Alexander, for example, privileges the texts' formal qualities,
valuing them principally as a way of charting and assessing 'the
development of … Brontë's technique as a writer'.[5] Sally
Shuttleworth considers the early stories in terms of their 'preoccupation with the practices and effects of domination',[6] as played
out, particularly, in the context of gender. For her own part,
London favours an approach which emphasizes the self-reflexive-
ness of the juvenile writings, seeing them, that is, as a series of
engagements with the cultural construction of 'professional
authorship'.[7]

These critical perspectives can all, in their different ways, be
highly illuminating. Yet their common problem is that they tend
to marginalize, if not altogether ignore, what is the strangest and
most striking aspect of Brontë's early writings: their colonial dimension. For as she begins to write, Brontë begins also to travel,
embarking upon a metaphorical journey which takes her to an

imaginary space situated on the coast of Central West Africa, in the kingdom of Ashanti. Brontë's gravitation towards these distant lands is not an accident occurring in an historical void, but directly inspired by detailed contemporary accounts, particularly in *Blackwood's Edinburgh Magazine,* of English colonial interest and activity in the area.[8] Far from being the escapist 'dream world'[9] which Fannie Ratchford once claimed them to be, Brontë's early stories are thus fully implicated (just as much as the rest of her *oeuvre*) in the colonial enterprise with which they are coeval.[10]

Brontë's exploitation of colonialism as a major resource for her own complicated and prolific early textual production is first evidenced in 'A Romantic Tale [or The Twelve Adventurers]' (1829).[11] In this blithely programmatic narrative, the adventurers in question make landfall on the shores of an 'immense continent', and, after triumphing in 'a very fierce encounter'[12] with the Ashanti and the 'King of the Blacks',[13] promptly 'set about building a city'.[14] This city comes to be governed by Arthur Wellesley, Duke of Wellington, the military hero of Brontë's childhood. At first called Glass Town and subsequently classically renamed as Verdopolis, the city rapidly develops into a flourishing colonial centre, remaining Brontë's narrative focus until around the end of 1833. At this point, her attention switches from Glass Town to the newly emergent world of Angria. This realm is dominated, both politically and sexually, by the refulgent yet ruthless figure of Zamorna, Wellington's eldest son. Zamorna's Angrian rule is neither halcyon nor consensual: his is a world under constant threat, both from within and without. The internal dangers take the respective forms of working-class agitation and the quest for power of Alexander Percy, Earl of Northangerland, who is at once Angria's Prime Minister, Zamorna's political rival and the father to Zamorna's third wife, Mary. Such challenges are complemented by the threat posed by the Ashanti themselves. This is principally embodied in the rebellious and intractable figure of Quashia Quamina, who spends his youth as Wellington's adopted son and Zamorna's foster-brother.

While Quamina and the Ashanti ultimately seek the destruction of Zamorna and Angria, they also harbour other dangers. These have less to do with the shedding of white blood than with its adulteration by means of miscegenation. In many instances, racial mixing is an issue relegated to the margins of Brontë's Ashanti narratives. In the poem included in 'A Fragment' (1831), it is a possibility barely imagined beyond the tentative vision of Zamorna slumbering 'in his gorgeous Indian home / On slave-surrounded bed'.[15] In 'A Day Abroad' (1834), miscegenation is intended to be largely comic. In this text, Henry Bramham Lindsay, whom Zamorna has 'not seen ... for ten years',[16] briefly teases his ill-tempered friend with recollections of childhood effeminacy, describing him as 'the most passionate young lady' he knows. As well as feminizing Zamorna, Lindsay playfully changes his sexual orientation, suggesting that his bad moods are attributable to 'love of Quashia'. At the same time, the badinage contains a warning against interracial desire, as Lindsay tells Zamorna, 'Don't act the part of Desdemona ... whatever you do!'[17] Miscegenation is similarly incidental to 'Passing Events' (1836). Here it is evoked, precisely, in passing, in the lines of a song near the narrative's beginning: 'My blood is not the high Castile, / The Moor has breathed his flame / Through every blushing artery / That leads the crimson stream.'[18]

In opposition to this intermittent pattern, there are three major narratives where the question of miscegenation receives a far more sustained and sophisticated treatment: 'A Leaf from an Unopened Volume' (1834), 'Well, here I am at Roe Head' (1836) and 'Caroline Vernon' (1839). In the first two texts, miscegenation represents a possibility from which the white sovereign subject must be defended, lest it be infected, to cite this chapter's first epigraph, with those 'primitive appetites, propensities [and] passions fit only to endow an Ashanti warrior'. This is also the danger faced in 'Caroline Vernon', which at the same time extends the concern with miscegenation into an Orientalist context. As the second epigraph suggests, however, where there is 'repulsion' from there is also 'attraction' towards the racial other, and where there is a threat there is a lure. Miscegenation not only entails a mixing of bloods, in other words, but also provokes an appositely mixed response in Brontë's work. Such an ambivalence is played out, in different ways, in the three texts which define the main focus of this chapter. It is best teased out by a close attention to their language and form.

If 'Literature cannot be the business of a woman's life',[19] as Brontë was once to be famously cautioned by Robert Southey, then her early narratives are doubly transgressive. As well as being stories sparked and driven by the muse of colonialism, they are acts of discursive colonization in their own right, appropriating topics traditionally associated with male authors – travel and adventure, war and violence. At the same time, though, Brontë's concern with miscegenation works to feminize or domesticate the discursively masculine domains upon which she intrudes. Her emphasis is less on colonial conflict as an abstract clashing of nations than as a more intimate tension played out between men and women across the lines dividing white from black.

'A Leaf from an Unopened Volume'

'A Leaf from an Unopened Volume' is a complex text whose brief opening and closing sections are narrated by Zamorna's younger brother, the flamboyantly titled Lord Charles Albert Florian Wellesley. These sections frame the text's much longer central segment, in which the main narrative is elaborated. The textual frame is further distinguished from the tale it encompasses in terms of temporal location and authorial origin. While the text's introductory and concluding parts are set in the present, the main narrative takes place in 'about 1858',[20] roughly a quarter of a century after the date given by Brontë for the text's completion, 'January 17th 1834' (p. 378). The proleptic nature of the events recorded in the main narrative provides an alibi for Lord Charles's claim that he 'could not have been the author of what is here detailed' (p. 323), a privilege accorded, instead, to the mysterious 'midnight visitor' whom he encounters 'One evening', on returning home after a 'dinner party' (p. 324). As Susan Meyer notes, the physical traits of Lord Charles's unexpected guest make him 'unmistakably diabolic':[21] he is 'club-footed on both legs', with 'eyes ... of a fierce, fiery red'. Appearing *ex nihilo*, this 'dusky figure' literally usurps Lord Charles's authorial place, ensconcing himself in 'a small sitting-room', normally 'set apart as a receptacle' for its owner's 'books [and] papers'.

The tale told by this self-declared 'unfortunate author' (p. 324) is as exuberant in the twists and turns of its plot as it is frequently violent in its content. The former are indeed sufficiently labyrinthine as to demand a brief reprise. At the tale's centre are two exotically named figures, Zorayda and Finic, whose outlandish stories are thematically interrelated. What is distinctive about the first of these figures is that, for much of the text, she exists in a condition of genealogical error. Although in reality of exclusively white descent, Zorayda believes herself to be the mixed-race child of a liaison between Quamina and a white woman. It is this misconception of her parental origins which forms the basis for Zorayda's attempted assassination of Zamorna,[22] who, when the main narrative begins, has all but destroyed the Ashanti and executed Quamina, impaling the head of this supposed father upon a stake for good measure.

In the end, the conundrum of Zorayda's racial identity is resolved. As the scene of the assassination attempt unfolds, both Zorayda and the reader come to learn that her true progenitor is not Quamina but another figure, the English-born aristocrat-artist, Sir William Etty. No longer condemned to be a 'daughter of darkness' (p. 372), Zorayda marries Adrian, Zamorna's son, and is assimilated into the very order she had once opposed. Even as 'A Leaf from an Unopened Volume' tells Zorayda's tale, then, it simultaneously engages in the process of untelling an alternative story: the twinned possibilities of interracial desire and rebellious hybridity are raised by Brontë's text only in order to be wished away.

Such possibilities are not quite so easily annulled, however. The denouement to Zorayda's narrative is the prelude to the uncovering of a second tale of miscegenation and rebellion. This arcane postscript to Zorayda's story focuses on the grotesque and stunted figure of Finic, bastard son of an obscure union between Zamorna and Sofala, the Ashanti mistress whose love, it turns out, the former had betrayed in his youth, some 'twenty-five years since' (p. 374). Like Zorayda, Finic is also Zamorna's would-be nemesis and both are leagued with Shungaron, one of Quamina's faithful subjects and Sofala's brother. Finic's story reverses Zorayda's, as the 'harmless fiction' (p. 363) of her mixed-race identity is brutally realized in the shape of a hateful biological truth. Equally, though, the two stories run in parallel. This is most clearly evidenced in the manner in which they are concluded. In Zorayda's case, the threats posed by racial mixing are undone by the narrative volte-face which transforms her from hybrid rebel into docile white woman. This moment of narrative reversal has its correlate in the physical violence with which Zamorna attempts to conceal the history of his own sexual and racial transgressions: Brontë's text ends with Zamorna's order for the execution of Finic and Shungaron alike, whose 'bloody heads', in a makeshift final tableau, are left 'lying severed on a temporary scaffold' (p. 377).

From the perspective of this complicated plot, Lord Charles's initial mystification of his own identity as author of the text's main narrative takes on a new significance. While its intention is to dissociate him from the story proper – his role is to be strictly that of 'an amanuensis' (p. 324) – the effect is quite the opposite, as the disavowal of authorial agency covertly prefigures the annulment of paternal claims which the story dramatizes, with Quamina and Zamorna respectively losing and rejecting the status of father-figure. Lord Charles declares that no 'mortal pen can ... trace events whose birth, course and issue are perhaps as yet but newly inscribed in the Book of Fate' (p. 323). None the less, it appears that such events can be adumbrated in allegorical form. The reconfiguring of interracial filiations which Brontë's text elaborates is already subtly staged in the deferential scene of writing with which it begins.

These oblique connections between writing and race are implied, similarly, in the two closing paragraphs of the 'Introduction'. Here Lord Charles finds himself presented by his 'brother author' (p. 324) with 'a bundle of dirty-looking blurred manuscripts', whose 'contents' he feels 'compelled to put in black and white', as if in the grip of 'some foreign power'. This contrast between the soiled and fuzzy condition in which the original text is received and the cleansed and clearer form into which it will be recomposed is suggestive. The shift from what is defiled and 'blurred' to the salient resolution of what is unequivocally 'black and white' might itself be a metaphor for the trajectory pursued by Brontë's text overall. For 'the narrative which follows', edited and transcribed by Lord Charles, 'despite of [his] own opposing will' (p. 325), is marked by its own internal revisions, as the racial difference between 'black and white' is repeatedly threatened and then reinstated.

The first chapter of the narrative begins with a radically abridged account of 'the twenty-five years during which the sceptre of dominion [is] swayed' (p. 325) over 'Africa's children' (p. 326) by Zamorna. Despite its 'dazzling lustre', Zamorna's 'reign' (p. 325) cannot quite conceal his 'faults', which are said to be both 'great and dark' (p. 326). These defects are already encrypted within the magniloquent prose which struggles to accommodate his 'colossal majesty', as the 'gigantic conquests' of empire become interwoven with the smaller but no less violent subjections of Zamorna's private life. This can be seen, for example, in the language describing Zamorna's grandeur as principally dependent upon 'the energy with which [his] plans' for imperial expansion are 'not only conceived but carried into execution' (p. 325). The latter phrase silently crosses the 'sceptre of dominion' with the spectre of hybridity. It offers, in particular, a precise and prevenient gloss on the fate of Finic, conceived as the child of a mixed-race love and finally 'hurried off' (p. 376) to be beheaded, together with Shungaron, at the 'commands' (p. 377) of his own father.

Throughout the narrative, decapitation is clearly the favoured means by which Zamorna disposes of his enemies. In Quamina's case, this form of death is grimly appropriate to the fate he suffers with respect to his own nation. Following the 'war' with Zamorna, which culminates in 'the bloody extermination of his devoted people', Quamina is initially 'preserved' as a living trophy designed 'to grace [Zamorna's] triumphant return to his own most gorgeous capital' (p. 326). In this way, he acquires the strange status of a figurehead detached from a national body which no longer exists. This anachronistic state is subsequently paralleled by the event of Quamina's personal 'extermination', in which his head is not only disjoined from his body, but also made to serve as the grisly index of Zamorna's power. As Etty and Adrian look down from an 'oriel window' in the artist's studio, this is the vision they see:

> In the midst of the area stood a black scaffold, spread partly with sawdust saturated with blood and forming an elevated support for a lofty stake which rose from the centre, displaying on its summit the ghastly exhibition of a severed human head.   (p. 329)

As befits the 'bloody spectacle' (p. 332) of the decapitation recorded here, the language of Brontë's text is itself somewhat acephalous. In this passage, Quamina's 'severed … head' remains recognizably 'human'. In contrast to this, the humanity of his executioners is itself cut off from representation by dint of a finely honed rhetoric. In the narrator's incisive metonymies, it is 'a sharp axe and a bloody block [which] rid the Emperor of an abhorred rival', just as 'the day of Quamina's execution' is 'terminated' by the cruel indifference of 'A mild, sunny evening' (p. 326). These rhetorical effects also attend the later deaths of Finic and Shungaron, as Zamorna bluntly incites the impersonal agencies of 'axe and scaffold' to 'cure treason and falsehood' (p. 376).

As well as being the sign of a crushing military triumph, Quamina's decapitation accrues to itself a range of meanings relating to the sexual fears and desires aroused in the colonizer by the confrontation with his black counterpart. Most obviously, Quamina's mutilated image serves to gratify the colonizer's fantasy of black castration. It constitutes a symbolic annihilation, that is, of the libidinal powers invested in the black man by the colonizer himself, even as those powers are resiliently figured in the phallic hauteur of the 'lofty stake' on which Quamina's 'head' is mounted. The logic here is circular and ironic: the colonizer must defend himself against the threat of a black male sexuality which is essentially of his own making and in relation to which he feels inadequate.

The classic analysis of the 'Deep and fixed ... hatred' (p. 326) underlying such fantasmal conflicts is given by the anticolonial theorist Frantz Fanon. In *Black Skin, White Masks*, Fanon writes:

> when a white man hates black men, is he not yielding to a feeling of impotence or of sexual inferiority? Since his ideal is an infinite virility, is there not a phenomenon of diminution in relation to the Negro, who is viewed as a penis symbol? Is the lynching of the Negro not a sexual revenge? We know how much of sexuality there is in all cruelties, tortures, beatings. . . . Is the Negro's superiority real? Everyone *knows* that it is not. But that is not what matters. The prelogical thought of the phobic has decided that such is the case.[23]

Yet while Quamina's 'severed ... head' is a trope for black castration, it possesses a certain fetishistic quality. This suggests that it also functions as a means by which the 'phobic' colonizer, whether Adrian or Zamorna himself, can find recompense for his imagined 'sexual inferiority'. This is a point which can be clarified by shifting the theoretical focus from Fanon to Freud. In the canonical Freudian account, the fetish comes into being at the moment when the young male child confronts the threat of castration, which he believes has already been perpetrated upon the maternal body. The task of the fetish is to stand in for what the mother appears to lack. While it is, as Freud somewhat tenderly puts it, 'a memorial' to castration, the fetish at the same time provides 'a token of triumph over' such a possibility and operates as 'a protection against it'.[24] This fetishistic logic is similarly at work, in racialized form, in Brontë's text. Its presence adds another dimension to the 'glance of

fierce satisfaction' (p. 329) which the sight of Quamina's 'severed
... head' elicits from Adrian. Such savage pleasure is not reducible
to a fantasy of black castration: it also arises from the status of the
'head' as compensatory fetish-object, redressing a white male
sexual wound.

Brontë's text extends the range of its beheadings in a significant
passage in chapter 4, as the preferred form of violence used by
colonizer against colonized is turned back upon the colonizer
himself. In narrative terms, this passage is placed between the two
decapitation scenes with which Brontë tops and tails her text.
Chronologically, however, it is located at an unspecified point
outside the text's official time-frame. As he looks further yet
beyond the limits of his own initial future vision, Brontë's narrator
reveals the retribution which awaits the colonizer. This bleak
justice is not to be faced by Zamorna himself – now by implication dead – but by Julius, his 'eldest son ... and heir', and
Hermione, his wife. These unknowing figures are doomed to tread
a 'path of blood and mourning':

> Could Hermione have foreseen that hour when the gory head of
> her lord was flung into her lap by the stern, remorseless regicide,
> how would she have shuddered as it now rested on her shoulder
> with all its bright locks undimmed by sorrow or misfortune. Could
> Julius have prophesied the time when she, the dethroned and
> widowed empress, stole by night to the vault where his headless
> corpse was laid and moaned her last on his closed coffin, with what
> anguish would he have flung from him the fair hand which he now
> clasped so fondly in his own.   (p. 359)

Here the narrator fleshes out the 'coming desolation' his
'prophetic eye' had previously detected, only hazily, in chapter 1,
amid 'the fearful magnificence' of Zamorna's 'imperial city'
(p. 326). At the same time, the macabre vision he delineates is a
double one, in two senses. As well as dimming Julius's 'bright
locks' with the shadow of his future demise, the vision underlines
the ways in which Brontë's representation of colonial violence is
itself shadowed by the sexual anxieties colonialism instils in the
white male subject. The spectacle of Julius's 'gory head ... flung
into [Hermione's] lap by the stern, remorseless regicide' not only
marks a reversal of the violence done to Quamina by Zamorna. It
also transforms what is the most salient symbolic meaning of
Quamina's death, rewriting the sign of black castration into white.

Yet the passage which dramatizes the possibility of such sexual mutilation also works against it. This is suggested by the temporal and bodily dislocation of Julius's 'head', resting, for the present, on his wife's 'shoulder', but wrested, in the future, into her 'lap'. The narrator claims that Hermione 'would ... have shuddered' at the thought of this violent downfall, but the bizarre superposition in which it culminates – male 'head' upon female 'lap' – is not without its comforts. As it screens Hermione's 'lap', itself a euphemism concealing the female genitals, Julius's sundered 'head' simultaneously luxuriates in the role of the fetish. Like Quamina's, it becomes a sign whose meanings are in direct tension with one another, figuring and denying the prospective trauma of a racialized castration at the same time.

In contrast to Julius, for whom it is only the remotest future possibility, regicide constitutes for Zamorna a threat he must always negotiate in the present. The purveyors of this threat – Zorayda, Finic, Shungaron – are simultaneously variously linked with a more generalized menace, in the shape of the racial contamination resulting from sexual exchanges across the colour line. The most explicit warning against such exchanges is given in chapter 2. Here Zorayda refuses marriage to Adrian, who has become her suitor. The 'impossible barrier to [their] union' (p. 343) is in the first instance a political one: for Zorayda to marry Zamorna's son would constitute a stunning betrayal of the anticolonial cause she believes herself to embody and carry forward as Quamina's daughter. But, as the conversation with Adrian proceeds, Zorayda's political misgivings become compounded with other concerns. As the text's rhetorical emphasis suggests, the possibility of her marriage to Adrian is deadlocked less on political grounds than by an anxious sense of racial mixing as profane. As Zorayda exclaims: 'I will never consent. . . . Never, never shall the blood of my race mingle with that of yours, Lord Adrian! It would *not* mingle! Dissensions and hatred of the deepest dye ... would be the result of such an unhallowed union' (pp. 343–4; emphasis in original).

Miscegenation is a 'catastrophe' (p. 344) which Brontë's text wishes, as much as Zorayda herself, to avert. One of the ways in which it achieves this is by subjecting Zorayda to a process of racial death and rebirth, most strikingly staged in the scene, located towards the end of the text, of the botched assassination. The death Zamorna evades in this scene comes, ironically, to be suffered by Zorayda herself, in figurative form. The 'Black murder' she attempts turns into the murder of the blackness imputed to her throughout the text, as it is revealed that 'Quamina was not [her] father' and that 'a white man' is anticlimactically responsible for her 'existence' (p. 372) after all. This deathly racial passing from black to white is something which the text suggests in the descriptions of Zorayda located on either side of the assassination attempt, as she first assumes 'a corpse-like paleness' (p. 371) and then becomes 'dead-white in cheek and brow' (p. 372). Zorayda sets out to shed the white blood of Zamorna, but becomes the victim of a textual counter-plot, designed to purge her of the black blood she takes to be her own.

The double failure of the 'female debutante' (p. 371) at Zamorna's court – as 'murdress' (p. 372) and as hybrid – is to be expected, because it is already played out in the moment of Zorayda's debut in the narrative. This takes place at the troubled site of Quamina's execution:

> a female figure appeared in the square below, stealing cautiously forward from the gathering shades of twilight, towards the scaffold, which was now illuminated by the light of a newly risen moon. When she came in front of the ominous stake she suddenly threw herself on the pavement in an attitude of the deepest prostration and remained there perfectly motionless. (p. 331)

Zorayda's movement towards 'the scaffold' is also an indirect movement against Zamorna, whose 'commands', as Adrian remarks, are 'strict that none should approach it'. Yet such a trespass can be overlooked by Adrian because it is 'only a woman' (p. 331) who carries it out. Similarly, Zorayda's emergence from 'the gathering shades of twilight' would seem to function as a trope for a mixed-race inheritance, while the zone into which she moves is one 'illuminated by the light of a newly risen moon': Zorayda's shifting of her ground at this initial point anticipates the later displacement and reworking of her racial identity in the assassination scene.

Zorayda's fears that the likely progeny of miscegenation are 'Dissensions and hatred of the deepest dye' are confirmed in the relationship between Zamorna and Finic. Like Zorayda's, Finic's *raison d'être* is the destruction of Zamorna, while Zamorna seeks Finic's death in return, campaigning against the son he fails to recognize for some 'ten years' (p. 363). Yet the crucial difference between the two aspiring assassins – both of whom are 'stirred ... to vengeance' (p. 375) by Shungaron – is that Zorayda's hybridity is only an illusion or narrative hoax, while Finic's is genuine. As Brontë's text repeatedly makes clear, the status of the authentically hybrid subject is that also of the grotesque. The stigmatizing of the hybrid is powerfully evoked in the passage describing Finic's first clandestine appearance in the text, in chapter 3. Here he accompanies Shungaron into Zamorna's palace grounds, intent upon the murder of his colonial oppressor-father:

> two figures suddenly appeared on the lawn. One of them [Shungaron] wore the dress of a gardener, and his dark skin, peculiar physiognomy and woolly hair proclaimed that he was an aboriginal native of Africa. The other [Finic] had more the appearance of some hideous and unpropitious sprite than of a human being. It was not more than three feet high, broad set, and having a head which in itself, disproportionately large, derived a frightful increase of size from the matted coal-black elf-locks with which it was profusely covered. (pp. 350–1)

Such narratorial disgust is shared by Zamorna, who later describes the 'particular and constant aversion' (p. 364) which Finic – elsewhere arraigned as 'Misshapen abortion' (p. 375) and 'hideous monster' (p. 376) – incites in him. Zamorna's loathing of Finic is felt with an 'intensity ... unaccountable even to [him]self' (p. 364), because its true origins, in an act of miscegenation, have been repressed.

These origins are brought back to light in the text's final moments. Here Zamorna descends into the dungeons of his palace in order to extract from Finic and Shungaron, now both 'heavily laden with chains and fetter bolts' (p. 374), the precise motivation for his prisoners' earlier assassination attempt. Vowing to 'get to the bottom of this business or dislocate every joint in their bodies' (pp. 373–4), it is Zamorna himself, ironically, whose secrets are plumbed and who suffers dislocation, as his movement down 'a spiral staircase of nine hundred steps' becomes a descent into a psychic 'labyrinth'. While Zamorna is reluctant to 'unravel' the 'labyrinth''s 'mazes' (p. 374), his resistance is broken down by the defiant Shungaron. Speaking with a 'solemn and warning air', he enjoins Zamorna to 'remember Sofala; remember the shores of Neimad'. In so doing, Shungaron recalls the colonizer to the scene of interracial desire and sexual betrayal buried in his past, just as Sofala – dying for love of a 'treacherous white man' – has long lain 'buried in the desert' (p. 376). As he undergoes the rapid disclosure of his own 'secret history' (p. 377) and 'unlive[s] a quarter of a century' in 'five minutes' (p. 376), Zamorna comes curiously to resemble Zorayda, herself suddenly precipitated into a lost self-knowledge. Yet in the expeditious violence with which he responds to his situation, Zamorna resembles only himself. Erasing the traces of his past by eliminating those who embody and/or 'remember' it, Zamorna restores the 'Silence!' (p. 360) demanded, appropriately, by the first word he utters in the text.

As befits a text which begins with the displacement of one author by another, 'A Leaf from an Unopened Volume' is organized in terms of a double narrative: Zorayda's story yields to Finic's, as the bogus hybrid gives way to the bona fide. This narrative rhythm – dispelling the mixed-race subject only to reconstitute it in a different form, before once again negating it – is suggestive. One way it can be read is as a structural symptom or expression of Brontë's ambivalence towards the interracial desire with which her text deals thematically. Such an ambivalence is not confined to 'A Leaf from an Unopened Volume', however, but pervades the equally fraught 'Well, here I am at Roe Head', written two years later. While Finic may indeed be dead at the end of the earlier text, Brontë's simultaneous disgust and fascination with the kind of 'unhallowed union' from which he springs remains very much alive in the work that follows.

'Well, here I am at Roe Head'

With its 'Dark visions of the slain' (p. 349), the 'Twilight Song' (p. 348) performed by Zorayda in chapter 3 of 'A Leaf from an Unopened Volume' is described as a 'wild fragment' (p. 350). Such a description might equally be applied to Brontë's short but remarkable 'Well, here I am at Roe Head'. This is the first of six miscellaneous entries in the 'Roe Head Journal' (1836–7), kept by Brontë while teaching at the young ladies' school from which her text derives its title. In this piece, Brontë shifts the narrative focus from the figure of the racial hybrid (Zorayda, Finic) to the black man, as Quamina, miraculously recovered from the trials of the earlier narrative, comes to be positioned, amid the hyperventilations of the text's frenzied last paragraph, as the rapist of a white woman, Zamorna's wife, Mary. Quamina's rape of Mary does not occur in any literal sense in the text. It is, rather, an event imagined from what Meyer calls the 'safe removes of fantasy and metaphor'.[25] In his role as imaginary rapist, Quamina is predictably represented as an object of fear and disgust. As Peter Stallybrass and Allon White have argued, however, 'disgust always bears the imprint of desire'.[26] This dialectic of disgust and desire enables Brontë's sexual and racial fantasy to be read against its own official grain, making it a site of ambivalence, in which a different kind of coupling is legible. The overt repulsion towards the spectacle of interracial rape functions as a mechanism of defence, disavowing the attraction which black male sexuality covertly calls forth.

Such disturbing possibilities could hardly be further removed from the text's opening scene, as Brontë prosaically maps the coordinates of her immediate spatial and temporal location:

> Well, here I am at Roe Head. It is seven o'clock at night. The young ladies are all at their lessons; the schoolroom is quiet; the fire is low. A stormy day is at this moment passing off in a murmuring and bleak night.[27]

The sense of an embodiment within the 'here' of Roe Head is no sooner established than it is dissolved. Within a few lines of this opening, Brontë signals her isolation from 'the ongoings that surround [her]', confessing to a 'heart' strangely withdrawn from 'the task, the theme [and] the exercise' which define her lot as female pedagogue. Given these numbing routines, it is not surprising that their brief suspension should be exploited as an opportunity to escape back towards the secret spaces from which Brontë's 'duties' have made her an exile:

> I now assume my own thoughts. My mind relaxes from the stretch on which it has been for the last twelve hours and falls back onto the rest which nobody in this house knows of but myself. I now, after a day of weary wandering, return to the ark which for me floats alone on the face of this world's desolate and boundless deluge. (p. 410)

As she switches the perspective from external to internal worlds, Brontë engages in a kind of visionary truancy. She absconds from the English school where she drudges and ventures out to Africa, initially figured as 'a far and bright continent', upon whose 'distant river banks' her colonizers have long been building and settling their 'cities' (p. 410). In this way, the text gives geographic expression to the distance between public and private identities already marked out within the narrow compass of Roe Head itself.

In figuring the space of colonial vision as a biblical 'ark', Brontë underlines the extent to which her occupation of that space is, as much as anything, a strategy of survival, imaginative or otherwise. Yet the visionary space is not only imperilled by its potential submersion beneath the disaster of a mundane existence – 'this world's desolate and boundless deluge' – but also threatened from within. This becomes evident in the second paragraph, as the perspective switches once again, this time from present to past. The calm and ordered allure of the colonial vista with which the text begins is transformed into a site of colonial destruction, as the scene of writing becomes a terrifying scene of memory:

> Last night, I did indeed lean upon the thunder-wakening wings of such a stormy blast as I have seldom heard blow, and it whirled me away like heath in the wilderness for five seconds of ecstasy. And as I sat by myself in the dining-room while all the rest were at tea, the trance seemed to descend on a sudden, and verily this foot trod the war-shaken shores of the Calabar, and these eyes saw the defiled and violated Adrianopolis, shedding its lights on the river from lattices whence the invader looked out and was not darkened. I went through a trodden garden whose groves were crushed down. I ascended a great terrace, the marble surface of which shone wet with rain where it was not darkened by the crowds of dead leaves, which were now showered on and now swept off by the vast and broken boughs which swung in the wind above them. Up I went to the wall of the palace, to the line of latticed arches which shimmered in light. Passing along quick as thought, I glanced at what the internal glare revealed through the crystal.   (p. 411)

The language describing how Brontë is 'whirled ... away' into an 'ecstasy' by the 'trance' which 'descend[s] on a sudden' is quite precise. According to the *Oxford English Dictionary*, the state of 'ecstasy' entails being 'put out of place', 'beside oneself with anxiety, astonishment, fear, or passion'. It is reflected in this passage, as in the rest of the text, by the way in which Brontë takes on a divided role: she is not only passive spectator to the 'war-shaken' world she describes but also conscripted into it as active participant. It might even be argued that Brontë anticipates the twofold part she comes to play. Even before the onset of this vision, she seems to have fallen into a curiously disaggregated condition, sitting, as she does, 'by [her]self in the dining-room', alone and doubled at the same time.

With its 'rain' and 'crowds of dead leaves', alternately 'showered' and 'swept' by 'vast and broken boughs', Brontë's visionary 'ark' appears, ironically, to be capsizing under its own version of the 'boundless deluge' against which it is originally devised. One way of accounting for this crisis is in terms of the developments in Brontë's collaborative relationship with Branwell during the period of her employment at Roe Head. These are glossed in a note to the text:

> While Brontë was at school, her brother ... had initiated a series of wars that threatened the existence of their imaginary kingdom of Angria. Adrianopolis, the imperial capital, situated on the banks of the River Calabar, was invaded by neighboring Ashantee tribes under the leadership of Quashia Quamina.   (p. 411)

From this perspective, Brontë would seem to be something of a latecomer on the scene of Angria's apocalypse. This belatedness is suggested within the scene itself: Brontë can, after all, only follow, rather than shape, the path taken by 'the invader' – whether this phrase be understood to refer simply to the Ashanti or to Branwell in addition. On the other hand, Brontë makes the vision of colonial ruin she beholds entirely her own, by supplying it with an overtly gendered dimension. In the image of 'the defiled and violated Adrianopolis' especially, the Branwellian invasion of one collective body by another – white by black – is rewritten in the metaphorical form of an interracial rape.

Yet if it is the prerogative of the female writer to develop a difference of view from her male counterpart, Brontë remains unwilling fully to confront what this alternative perspective discloses. Even as she begins to conjure the spectre of interracial rape, her language subtly works to obscure it, particularly in the curiously mystifying description of the 'lattices whence the invader looked out and was not darkened'. The design of these windows might itself be read as an architectural trope for miscegenation. In 'look[ing] out' from them, however, the Ashanti not only return

Brontë's gaze, but at the same time, in the secondary sense of the phrase, appear to have been removed from the very spaces they have taken over. Similarly, as if in response to the activities of Zamorna's endangered capital, frantically 'shedding its lights on the river', the Ashanti seem to be divested of their blackness. To a man, in this strange photosphere, they are 'not darkened'.

As she reaches 'the wall of [Zamorna's] palace', Brontë narrows the textual focus from events taking place outside this edifice to a review of its sumptuous interior. The collective black presence of the Ashanti is replaced by reflections on the singular white presence of their oppressor, or rather the representation of that presence in the shape of a painting. This pictorial image dominates the 'room lined with mirrors' into which Brontë gazes and comes, in its turn, to dominate the text:

> There was ... one large picture in a frame of massive beauty representing a young man whose gorgeous and shining locks seemed as if they would wave on the breath and whose eyes were half hid by the hand, carved in ivory, that shaded them and supported the awful-looking raven head. A solitary picture, too great to admit of a companion. A likeness to be remembered, full of beauty not displayed, for it seemed as if the form had been copied so often in all imposing attitudes that at length the painter, satiated with its luxuriant perfection, had resolved to conceal half and make the imperial giant bend and hide, under his cloud-like tresses, the radiance he was grown tired of gazing on.   (p. 411)

The 'large picture' of Brontë's 'young man' offers an aestheticized version of the racial tempest by which his capital is convulsed, as Zamorna's 'hand, carved in ivory' is set against an 'awful-looking raven head'. What is perhaps more striking about the 'picture' is the way in which the representation of its subject tends towards non-representation, as the painting provides an image of 'the imperial giant' with 'eyes ... half hid' and is 'full of beauty not displayed'. Despite Brontë's syntactically isolated claim that it is 'too great to admit of a companion', Zamorna's 'picture' can usefully be viewed in relation to her own representation of the earlier invasion scene. In the one case, Zamorna's sexual charms are simultaneously revealed and concealed by the techniques of 'the painter' whom Brontë imagines to have depicted them. In the other, the sexual threats posed by the Ashanti are made present and absent at once, glimpsed through metaphor yet abstracted from the text by the same rhetorical means.

It is not only Zamorna who is absent from the mirror-lined 'room' on the 'evening' of Brontë's vision but also Mary. This absence is, as Brontë notes, an unusual one, it being Mary's custom to frequent the 'room' 'at [this] time'. On such occasions, she is to be found 'sitting on a low sofa' with 'her heart softly heaving under her dark satin bodice' (p. 411), chastely keeping a vigil for Zamorna (who, at this point in their marriage, has deserted her). In addition to being unusual, Mary's absence is felicitous, since the space she normally monopolizes – not just the 'room' but the 'sofa' itself – has been usurped by Quamina. As he penetrates the sanctum of Mary's 'bower' (p. 412), Quamina individualizes the Ashanti invasion previously represented in the text *en masse*. In so doing, he reintroduces the possibility of the interracial rape fleetingly figured in the text's second paragraph:

> this night [Mary] was not visible – no – but neither was her bower void. The red ray of the fire flashed upon a table covered with wine flasks, some drained and some brimming with the crimson juice. The cushions of a voluptuous ottoman, which had often supported her slight fine form, were crushed by a dark bulk flung upon them in drunken prostration. Aye, where she had lain imperially robed and decked with pearls, every waft of her garments as she moved diffusing perfume, her beauty slumbering and still glowing as dreams of him for whom she kept herself in such hallowed and shrine-like separation wandered over her soul, on her own silken couch, a swarth and sinewy moor intoxicated to ferocious insensibility had stretched his athletic limbs, weary with wassail and stupified [*sic*] with drunken sleep. I knew it to be Quashia himself, and well could I guess why he had chosen the Queen of Angria's sanctuary for the scene of his solitary revelling. While he was full before my eyes, lying in his black dress on the disordered couch, his sable hair dishevelled on his forehead, his tusk-like teeth glancing vindictively through his parted lips, his brown complexion flushed with wine, and his broad chest heaving wildly as the breath issued in snorts from his distended nostrils, while I watched the fluttering of his white shirt ruffles, starting through the more than half-unbuttoned waistcoat, and beheld the expression of his Arabian countenance savagely exulting even in sleep – Quamina, triumphant lord in the halls of Zamorna! in the bower of Zamorna's lady! – while this apparition was before me, the dining-room door opened and Miss W[ooler] came in with a plate of butter in her hand. 'A very stormy night, my dear!' said she.
> 'It is, ma'am,' said I.   (p. 412)[28]

Like the 'wine flasks' at its beginning, this monumental closing sequence is 'drained' of the very threat of interracial rape with which it is 'brimming' none the less. The most obvious way in which the passage empties itself of this threat is by transforming the potential rape scene into the site of a missed encounter. Since she is 'not visible' on 'this night', Mary is placed safely out of Quamina's reach. She is tantalizingly available to him only by proxy, in the metonymic traces of the erotic 'dreams' she leaves on the 'voluptuous' and later 'disordered couch'. Even were Mary to be *in situ* as normal, Quamina could not turn the presence of her 'slight fine form' to the advantage of his own 'dark bulk', because he has suffered the emasculation of a 'drunken prostration', which leads his 'sinewy' and 'athletic' body to become 'weary' and 'stupified'. But what is literally absent from Brontë's text is everywhere implied. The 'intoxicated' Quamina is revived into a nightmare-figure and his 'ferocious insensibility' anatomized into the components of a violent sexual arousal: he has 'hair' which is 'dishevelled'; 'tusk-like teeth'; a 'chest heaving wildly'; 'breath' turned to 'snorts' and a 'countenance savagely exulting even in sleep'.

Quamina's 'solitary revelling', like Brontë's solitary reverie, is finally interrupted by the Porlockian advent of Miss Wooler, headmistress of Brontë's school. With her 'plate of butter', homely and ludicrous at once, Miss Wooler puts Brontë back in her place, returning the errant teacher to the 'dining-room' in which her 'ecstasy' had first taken hold. Yet the overall drift of the text's final paragraph takes the reader one step further back than this, to Brontë's opening claim that her flights of vision enable her to 'assume [her] own thoughts'. This assertion turns out, in the end, to be untenable, as the autonomous and unified subjectivity it implies is decentred. The dehumanized figure of Quamina as rapist is not the simple protégé of a free-floating imagination. It is culled, rather, from that repertoire of 'terrifying stereotypes' analysed by Homi K. Bhabha, in which 'savagery, cannibalism, lust and anarchy' prevail as the principal traits of the racial other. As Bhabha explains, what is 'traumatic' about the 'return of the oppressed' in this vindictive guise is its ambivalence. The 'stereotypes' should not be read at face value, in other words, but form 'points of identification and alienation', appearing in 'colonial texts' as the signs of 'fear and desire'[29] alike. In so far as it 'opens the royal road to colonial fantasy',[30] such ambivalence makes

Brontë's parting vision of Quamina – 'triumphant lord in the halls of Zamorna!' – seem like an appropriate one.

With its fusion of autobiographical and fictional modes, the mundane and the extreme, 'Well, here I am at Roe Head' has a central place in any consideration of interracial desire in Brontë's Ashanti narratives, endowing the tensions intrinsic to the colonial encounter with a particularly raw sexual edge. But while the concerns of this text are broadly similar to those articulated in 'A Leaf from an Unopened Volume', the later fragment adds something new. What becomes apparent here is that miscegenation is an act which can involve not just two parties but three. As the provocative symbolism of Quamina lodged 'in the bower of Zamorna's lady!' would suggest, the white female body functions in this text as a kind of territory over which black and white men struggle for possession.

Brontë's insight into the potentially triangular nature of the relationships brought into play by miscegenation also informs the complicated racial and sexual intrigues of 'Caroline Vernon', Brontë's last Ashanti narrative. In this novella, however, the white female whom Quamina wishes to possess is not Mary but the text's eponymous 15-year-old heroine, Northangerland's illegitimate daughter by Louisa Vernon. Nor does Quamina simply face one opponent in the course of his struggles. Even as he directly vies with Northangerland for control of Caroline's destiny, she herself occupies the centre of a second power struggle conducted between Northangerland and Zamorna as part of their long-established mutual enmity. This second conflict mirrors the first, while at the same time indirectly setting Quamina and Zamorna against one another once more, with the latter winning out over the former, of course, as Caroline's eventual seducer. In so far as Zamorna thus emerges from this labyrinth of multiple homosocial conflicts as sexual victor, it would seem that Brontë's text safely avoids the spectre of miscegenation with which it so anxiously flirts. In what is a characteristically Brontëan irony, however, that which is excluded from the text in literal form repeatedly returns in other ways.

'Caroline Vernon'

The events of 'Caroline Vernon' take place during a period some three years after the defeat of the Ashanti invasion dramatized in

'Well, here I am at Roe Head'. At this terminal point in Angria's history, Zamorna has retired to Hawkscliffe, located in a remote part of his kingdom. Here he adopts the unlikely persona of a gentleman-farmer, cultivating rather than colonizing Africa's soil and ogling the 'smart active girls'[31] scattered among his workforce. Quamina is now exiled to Boulogne, separated both from his own people and those other 'bold nigger bands' (p. 278) which he had once enlisted into the anticolonial struggle. It is from Boulogne that Quamina sends Northangerland a 'mad letter' (p. 287), laced with 'biblical phrases and drunken slang',[32] demanding Caroline's hand in marriage. Northangerland derides Quamina's communiqué, even as the prospect of the mixed-race wedding it proposes galvanizes him into arranging an alternative match for the daughter he has entrusted to Zamorna's dubious guardianship.

If it is an animus towards miscegenation which marks the beginning of 'Caroline Vernon', there is a sense in which the text contradicts and compromises its own initial position, hinting at a residual appeal in the very possibilities it sets out to block. On the one hand, Northangerland refuses to comply with Quamina's coercive demand for Caroline as wife. Yet at the same time he plans to furnish her with precisely the things Quamina stipulates as prerequisites to their betrothal – 'a handsome house' and 'ten thousand a year' (p. 284). These ironies are compounded by the name of the 'separate establishment' Northangerland 'instantly' (p. 294) resolves to allocate to his daughter – Eden Cottage. The name directly recalls Quamina's poetic vision of the Orientalized marital habitat he pledges to create for his 'Lovely One', who will live 'Happy as houris fair – that braid their hair, / Glorious in Eden's bowers'. By the end of the narrative, none of Quamina's belligerent wishes has been met. He gets neither Caroline herself nor 'the Custody of [Northangerland's] Will', which he intends to rewrite 'according to [his] own directions' (p. 284). Yet the indeterminacies of the text contrive to suggest an illicit investment in the very scenes of interracial desire from which Northangerland strives to protect his daughter. To use Quamina's own word, Northangerland's matchmaking schemes for Caroline are so represented as to imbue them with a degree of 'cloudiness' (p. 283).

As well as proclaiming love for Caroline, Quamina's letter further scandalizes with its suggestion that such love is initiated by Caroline herself: 'this sweet blossom', Quamina writes, 'this little fluttering – fickle, felicitous fairy – this dear, delicious, delirious

mortal – comes into my arms & announces her intention of
marrying me straight away off-hand whether I will or no'.
Quamina's alliterative allegation is mere swagger, engendered by
the drunkenness he ennobles into 'Love's Intoxication' (p. 284).
None the less, the question of white female desire for the black
man which the allegation raises continues to haunt the text and is
addressed by means of allusion. In part 1, chapter 3, for example,
Northangerland learns that Caroline and Louisa are living in a
'House ... not above three miles' (p. 294) from Hawkscliffe. Just
before Northangerland visits his valetudinarian mistress and disre-
garded daughter in the next chapter, Louisa vents her feelings for
the 'man who has no heart'. Both infatuated and infuriated with
Northangerland, she takes revenge upon the 'barbarous usage'
(p. 300) she receives from him in the form of a violent sexual
fantasy driven by memories of her career as actress:

> 'O, I wish something would happen – that I could get a better hold
> of him. I wish he would fall desperately sick in this house – or
> shoot himself by accident so that he would be obliged to stay here
> & let me nurse him. . . . he'd love me, I'm sure he would – if he
> didn't & if he refused to let me wait on him – I'd come at night to
> his room & choke him while he was asleep – smother him with the
> pillow – as Mr Ambler used to smother me when he had the part of
> Othello & I had that of Desdemona – I wonder if I daren't do such
> a thing'.   (pp. 302–3)

The generically hybrid nature of Louisa's fantasy – a blend of
farce and tragedy – seems formally appropriate in the context of
the allusion to *Othello*, since Shakespeare's play is centrally concerned, like 'Caroline Vernon', with mixed-race marriage. What
makes *Othello* so disturbing a text for many critics of Brontë's
day is its willingness not only to explore but also stage the spectacle of the white female desire for the black male other which
Quamina celebrates. In Charles Lamb's view, for example, there is
'something extremely revolting in the courtship and wedded ca-
resses of Othello and Desdemona'.[33] For Samuel Taylor Coleridge,
Shakespeare's conception of a 'beautiful Venetian girl falling in
love with a veritable negro' is similarly quite 'monstrous'.[34] From
this perspective, it becomes clear that Louisa's fantasy exacts retribution upon her inconstant lover as much in terms of its form as
its murderous content. As he plays Desdemona's 'part' to Louisa
as Othello, Northangerland is not only feminized but also made to

suffer the desires Quamina deliriously imputes to Caroline. On the other hand, Louisa's imaginary re-enactment of *Othello* does not fully 'smother' the material realities underpinning early Victorian productions of Shakespeare's drama. In the reference to the anodyne 'Mr Ambler', Brontë's text implicitly reminds the reader that Othello's role would invariably be played, at this historical juncture, by a white actor.[35] The fantasy in which Northangerland is suffocated bears the traces of the transgressive white female desire inscribed in Quamina's letter, while counterbalancing them at the same time.

Brontë's text replays this double process as it extends its allusive reach beyond the English literary tradition towards the realms of contemporary popular culture in America. This movement occurs as the narrative focus shifts from the fantasies of the neurotic mother to the pastimes of the musical daughter:

> A distant sound of music in a room below was heard – a piano very well touched – 'Dear – Dear – ! there's Caroline strumming over that vile instrument again – I really *cannot* bear it ... that girl quite distracts me with the racket she keeps up –' Here her ladyship rose very nimbly & going to the top of the stairs which was just outside her room – called out with much power of lungs – 'Caroline! Caroline!' no answer except a brilliant bravura run down the keys of the Piano – 'Caroline!' was reiterated – 'give up playing this instant! you know how ill I have been all day & yet you will act in this way' – a remarkably merry jig responded to her ladyship's objurgations – & a voice was heard far off saying 'it will do you good, mamma!' 'You are very insolent!' cried the fair Invalid, leaning over the bannisters. . . . 'do as I bid you –' 'So I will, directly' replied the voice. 'I have only to play Jim Crow & then' & Jim Crow was played with due spirit & sprightliness.
>
> (pp. 303–4; emphasis in original)

The caricature figure of Jim Crow whom this passage invokes originally appears in an American song, written and choreographed by Thomas Dartmouth 'Daddy' Rice. As Sam Dennison puts it, this song became a 'superhit' in the late 1820s and 1830s and 'practically singlehandedly paved the way for the advent of blackface ... minstrelsy'.[36] A concise account of the song's genesis, development and significance is provided by Ted Olson:

> 'Jim Crow' dates back at least to 1828 when white blackface performer Rice witnessed the song-and-dance routine of a Louisville

slave owned by a Mr. Crow. Rice recast this slave's routine into a
blackface act called 'Jump Jim Crow.' Featuring dancing as well as
lyrics imitative of African American vernacular speech set to a well-
known British melody, 'Jump Jim Crow' was an immediate success
throughout the United States and Great Britain. . . . 'Jump Jim
Crow' was an early example of the exploitation of African
American culture by Anglo American popular entertainers.[37]

'Caroline Vernon' adds itself to this pattern of cultural 'exploitation', manipulating the figure of Jim Crow for its own
subtle purposes. In Brontë's text, he is present both musically
and visually. As well as 'jigging his round' on Caroline's piano,
Jim Crow is also to be seen in the lithographic form of the 'grin-
ning capering nigger' disported on the 'title-page' of the 'sheet
of music' (p. 304) from which Caroline reads. In bringing the
figures of colonizing white female and black male slave into
such proximity, Brontë fashions a scene which vibrates with an
implicit sexual frisson. Louisa's attempts to stifle her daughter's
'playing', the text suggests, are not merely aesthetically moti-
vated. They are cued, rather, by a distaste for the miscegenation
which the 'bravura' performance symbolizes. This distaste is
transferred, in its turn, onto Caroline's 'well touched' piano,
which, with its resonant juxtaposition of white and black 'keys',
is condemned as a 'vile instrument'. Yet Louisa's desire to
silence the duet between the 'contumaciously musical' (p. 284)
Caroline and Jim Crow only rehearses a strategy of censorship
already conducted by the text itself. Jim Crow functions as a
low transatlantic double for the more culturally elevated blackface figure of Shakespeare's Othello. The representation of
Caroline's musical activities partakes of the two-faced logic
structuring her mother's dramatic fantasies. The figure of the
black male other with whom Caroline consorts is tethered to a
white ground, as the threat of miscegenation is diluted, if not
entirely dissolved.

As a 'young lover of rebels & regicides', Caroline might seem
to be a perfect mate for Quamina. Yet the abiding object of her
adolescent fantasies is not the anticolonial insurgent but 'the
Majesty of Angria' (p. 312), Zamorna himself. Caroline remains
largely unaware both of Zamorna's lasciviousness and the
sexual nature of her own attraction to him until she goes to
Paris, in part 2, chapter 1, where her 'ideas' on both scores are
soon 'revolutionized'. Here it is disclosed to her, 'bluntly &

coarsely', 'that the Duke [is] a sad hand ... about women', a revelation which comes as 'an electrical stunning surprise' (p. 322)
and fills its recipient with 'feelings' which are 'strange, new &
startling' (p. 323). Prior to the Parisian excursus, the stories
Caroline tells herself about 'Love' are relatively innocent. At the
beginning of part 1, chapter 5, for example, she engages in 'a
reverie of romance', as 'undefined' as it is 'delicious'. Despite
the narratorial claim that the male figure at the centre of these
daydreams remains 'nameless', the reverse is in fact the case. He
is allotted a multitude of shifting 'designation[s] – being sometimes no more than simple Charles Seymour or Edward
Clifford, & at other times soaring to the titles of Harold,
Aurelius Rinaldo, Duke of Montmorency di Valdacella'. This
nominal contradiction is resolved by recognizing the 'mystic
being' and 'dread shadow' who is Caroline's mercurial 'Hero'
(p. 312) as a disavowed double for Zamorna:

> he was to drive all before him in the way of fighting – to conquer
> the world & build himself a city like Babylon – only it was to be in
> the moorish style – & there was to be a palace called the Alhambra
> – where Mr Harold Aurelius was to live, taking upon himself the
> title of Caliph, & she, Miss C. Vernon, the professor of Republican
> principles, was to be his chief Lady & to be called the Sultana
> Zara-Esmerelda – with at least a hundred slaves to do her bidding.
> (p. 313)

The initial details of this Oriental fantasy clearly establish
Caroline's 'Caliph' as Zamorna's surrogate. The global domination anticipated for the one parallels the colonial mastery already
established by the other, just as the 'city' the 'Caliph' builds is a
mirror for the nascent Adrianopolis, described, with its 'raw new
palaces', as a 'Great Baby [lon] Capital' (p. 277) in the story's first
paragraph. The most significant aspect of this vision of life in the
'Alhambra' is that it expunges the threat of miscegenation almost
entirely. As the 'Sultana Zara-Esmerelda – with at least a hundred
slaves to do her bidding', 'Miss C. Vernon' is remade in the image
of the Oriental other who is the manifest object of her desire. At
the same time, miscegenation lingers on in the vestigial and exotic
shape of the very name – compounded from Oriental and
European sources – which Caroline accords herself.

Caroline's sudden Parisian awakening to the truth about
Zamorna's sexual appetites, and indeed her own, transforms Eden

Cottage, on her return to Angria, into a 'Dungeon' (p. 349). The possibility of release from this confinement is provided by the letter she receives from Zamorna, which 'fire[s]' her with 'an unconquerable desire to reach & see the absent writer' (just as Quamina's original deranged billet-doux is driven by the desire to meet with Caroline). Caroline's longings are eventually fulfilled as she enters into the 'blind folly' (p. 341) of a solitary flight from Eden Cottage to Woodhouse-Cliffe, where, as the letter informs her, Zamorna is staying 'for a few days' on 'Business' (p. 339). It is here that the climactic encounter between the two figures takes place, as Caroline is shocked into the realization that 'her wild frantic attachment' for Zamorna is fully 'reciprocated' (p. 352):

> Miss Vernon sat speechless ... all was fever & delirium round her – The Duke spoke again – in a single blunt and almost coarse sentence compressing what yet remained to be said. 'If I were a bearded Turk, Caroline, I would take you to my Harem' – His deep voice, as he uttered this – his high-featured face, & dark large eye, beaming bright with a spark from the depths of Gehenna, struck Caroline Vernon with a thrill of nameless dread ... Her Guardian was gone – Something terrible sat in his place – The fire in the grate was sunk down without a blaze – this silent lonely library, so far away from the inhabited part of the house – was gathering a deeper shade in all its Gothic recesses. She grew faint with dread ... She attempted to rise – this movement produced the effect she had feared, [Zamorna's] arm closed round her – Miss Vernon could not resist its strength, a piteous upward look was her only appeal – He, Satan's eldest Son, smiled at the mute prayer – 'She trembles with terror' said he, speaking to himself.   (pp. 352–3)

Brontë's representation of this seduction scene is as bookish as the 'lonely library' in which the scene is set, breathlessly drawing, as it does, on the dreadful clichés of Gothic fiction. The Gothic elements of this passage do not work in isolation, however, but are cross-bred with an Orientalist rhetoric, furtively foreshadowed in the description of the 'library' as a space into which Caroline and Zamorna have 'levanted' (p. 350).

In its hybridizing of Gothic and Orientalist modes, Brontë's text seems to support H. L. Malchow's claim that Gothic fiction provides 'a language that [can] be appropriated, consciously or not' as a way of demonizing the racial other and articulating the 'terror, disgust, and alienation'[38] which it conventionally induces. It is, after all, in the precise moment of Zamorna's self-fashioning as 'bearded Turk' that Brontë's text is stimulated into the Gothic reflexes which transfigure him also into 'Satan's eldest Son'. Yet the representation of Zamorna is much less one-sided than Malchow might want it to be. The 'depths of Gehenna' Caroline beholds in Zamorna's 'dark large eye' contain an enticing 'spark' and the 'nameless dread' she feels is still a 'thrill'. These textual details, together with Caroline's inability to 'resist' what are literally the strong-arm tactics of her seducer, suggest an attraction towards as much as a repulsion from the figure of Zamorna as Gothicized Oriental. With its 'mixed wonder & fear' (p. 354), the denouement to 'Caroline Vernon' thus provides a succinct emblem for the ambivalence informing the treatment of miscegenation in Brontë's Ashanti narratives as a whole.

Despite their uncanonical status and sometimes vertiginous complexity, these irrefutably strange early works are a key element in the genealogy of Brontë's 'fiery imagination', opening up spaces of colonial encounter which the later novels seem determined to close down. Within those spaces, race and sexuality are melodramatically mixed in the typically double-edged shape of miscegenation. Yet Brontë's preliminary engagements with the question of colonialism are neither confined to the form of the prose narrative, nor reducible to the issue of interracial desire, important though this is. As the next chapter argues, she also calls upon the genres of poetry and the prose essay in order to further her colonial explorations. In so doing, she takes her work in a number of different directions.

2

'Climes Remote and Strange': Colonialism in the Poetry and Belgian Essays

> The language of poetry naturally falls in with the language of power.
>
> William Hazlitt, cited in Heather Glen, *Charlotte Brontë: The Imagination in History*, p. 20

> [T]he devoirs are rarely simple documents, even when they look brief and obvious. They refer to sources in French and English, some apparent, others little known or subtle. They link to other Brontë writings, earlier and later, again in ways both plain and less detectable. ...
>
> In sum, the devoirs are a network of resources for anyone concerned with the Brontës.
>
> Sue Lonoff, *The Belgian Essays: Charlotte Brontë and Emily Brontë*, pp. xiv–xv

> 'The trouble with the Engenglish is that their hiss hiss history happened overseas, so they dodo don't know what it means.'
>
> Salman Rushdie, *The Satanic Verses*, p. 343

In the Preface to *The Professor*, Brontë instructs the reader that the faults of her 'little book' should not be excused on the basis of a 'first attempt ... as the pen which wrote it had been previously worn a good deal in a practice of some years'.[1] Such a confession is something of an understatement. As well as gesturing back towards the large and convoluted body of materials examined in the previous chapter, Brontë's coy allusion to the 'many ... crude effort[s]'[2] of her literary apprenticeship encompasses two less extensive but none the less important fields of textual production – the poetry and the Belgian essays, or devoirs, as Lonoff calls them. It could not be claimed by any means that either of these fields is reducible to an exclusively colonial concern – their range is much wider and more varied than that. Even so, both have an indisputable place in any attempt to produce an inclusive postcolonial reading of Brontë's corpus. They also have the virtue of underscoring the extent to which, as in the Ashanti narratives, Brontë typically chooses to focus and refract the sinister English 'hiss hiss history' which 'happen[s] overseas' through the prism of the subject rather than the nation, locating her colonial imagination, in other words, at the interstices between the personal and the political, the private and the public.

In the first two of the four poetic texts to be considered in this chapter, the subjects concerned are both female, though they are to be found at opposite ends of the colonial and racial spectrum, one the dying but defiant Ashanti mother-queen who is the speaker of 'Last branch of murdered royalty' (1833), and the other the Englishwoman of 'The Letter' (1837). In the final two poems, 'Passion' (1841; rev. 1846) and 'The Missionary' (*c.* 1845), the subjects, by contrast, are colonizing men. This difference in gender results, in its turn, in a difference of fortune. While the female figures in the two earlier texts must suffer the consequences, to varying degrees, of the colonial struggles in which their spouses are implicated, the opposite is evidently the case for their male counterparts, both of whom exploit colonialism for their own particular ends. Concluding with 'Sacrifice of an Indian Widow' (1842), the chapter switches its attention to the Belgian essays and a text which itself returns the focus to the figure of the colonized and dying female subject. Yet the similarities which this might suggest between the essay and 'Last branch of murdered royalty' are outweighed by the differences. In the earlier poem, it is clear that the Ashanti queen is a rebellious figure, even in death. In the later essay, by contrast, the widow's act of self-sacrifice is more ambiguously represented, it remaining uncertain whether her death should be read as a heroic gesture of colonial resistance or the sign of a hapless submission to the patriarchal imperatives of native tradition.

'Last branch of murdered royalty'

This poem appears as the centre-piece to 'The African Queen's Lament' (1833), a short text which returns the reader to the Anglo-Ashanti conflicts examined in the previous chapter. The two elements of the text – poem and surrounding prose narrative – are not easily (or even desirably) separated from one another. Taken together, they tell the tale of the circumstances leading to Quamina's adoption by the Duke of Wellington, focusing, in particular, on how Wellington both kills Quamina's father-king at the battle of Coomassie and is implicitly responsible for the death of the child's grief-stricken mother-queen, which occurs soon afterwards.

The text opens with a moment of contretemps, which finds the youthful Quamina in retreat, 'stalk[ing] out of the room'[3] where he has just received 'a gentle remonstrance' from his ersatz father, relating to unnamed 'irregularities' allegedly 'committed … in the course of his wandering and vagrant mode of life'.[4] The 'offended and majestic manner' of this withdrawal gives its own offence, provoking Wellington into a series of anxious reflections, over-heard by Lord Charles Wellesley, one of his biological sons. In the disquieted 'words' to which Lord Charles becomes privy, Wellington assumes a double role. On the one hand, he is a paternal surrogate, concerned for the faults of an errant charge. On the other, he is a kind of colonial policeman, nervously scanning the conduct of an alien youth for signs of disaffection:

> 'I don't at all like that lad's demeanour, I fancy he will soon require rather a vigilant eye to observe his motions; he may give our nation trouble yet. His mother's last advice will not, I imagine, be entirely lost upon him, though at the time it was given he could not understand it, certainly.'   (p. 3)

Here it is evident that the 'vigilant eye' of colonial surveillance is already at work, since the recognition that it 'will soon [be] require[d]' is itself prompted by the dissatisfied review of Quamina's recent behaviour. Nor is it entirely surprising that Wellington should deem his volatile 'lad' capable of bringing 'trouble' to his fledgling 'nation'. After all, the rebuke 'administered' by Quamina's custodian is not just a trivial annoyance, leaving its recipient 'evidently nettled' (p. 3) in the present. It functions, rather, as a trace – however diluted and domesticated – of the violence which Wellington, in his own personalized brand of national trouble-making, has visited upon Quamina's true parents and the 'once mighty empire'[5] they represent.

Despite the racial differences between Lord Charles and his 'adopted brother', there are also some parallels. Just as the one finds himself baffled by 'the latter part' (p. 3) of his father's speech and requests that it be clarified, so the 'part' in question relates to the other's own failure immediately to understand the maternal 'advice' passed down to him. As Wellington responds to Lord Charles's puzzlement by elaborating upon his mysterious remarks, he himself comes to occupy a position analogous to that already shared by his real and adopted sons, eavesdropping on words at first not fully comprehended:

> 'Shortly after the destruction of Coomassie, I was, one sultry after-noon, walking by myself along the banks of the River Sahala and enjoying the cool faint wind which breathed from its surface when suddenly a distant sound of singing fell on my ear. The tune were exceedingly wild and plaintive, and as [it] rose and sunk at intervals on the breeze, I thought it sounded like a requiem for the dead, or a song which it is the custom in some African nations to chant over the dying. My curiosity being a little excited, I followed the sound till I reached a grove of palm trees, where I saw a very handsome black woman, richly dressed, reclining in their shade. She was evi-dently much exhausted, and famine, sickness or some other equally powerful cause had brought her to the very door of death. A little child of from 3 to 4 years old was stretched on the ground beside her in a deep sleep, and its mother was singing over it the wild strain which had attracted my attention.' (Then my father gave me the African song of which I have since attempted the following very inadequate translation into English verse.)   (p. 4)

In this extended flashback, Wellington deploys the 'vigilant eye' to which he had earlier referred, training it primarily upon Quamina's mother, the 'very handsome black woman, richly dressed', whom he discovers amid the 'grove of palm trees', soon to become the site of her grave. Yet the more dominant sense in this passage is not visual but aural, as Wellington's insouciant post-war stroll along the riverbank is both arrested and diverted by the 'distant sound of singing' which falls 'on [his] ear'.

Neither of the senses mobilized in this chance colonial en-counter proves, in the end, to be a reliable guide to the signs it must negotiate, though the visual has the power to correct the errors of the aural. Wellington is initially misled, for example, by the 'wild and plaintive' qualities of the 'tune' he overhears into thinking that it is 'a requiem for the dead, or a song which it is the custom in some African nations to chant over the dying'. This mistake is soon rectified by the gaze directed at the colonized female, which reveals that it is she who is at 'the very door of death', even as the reason for such a predicament remains hazy, veering uncertainly between 'famine, sickness or some other equally powerful cause'. In a further corrective to Wellington's original inference, the one to whom she sings – the 'little child', Quamina – is neither 'dead' nor 'dying': 'stretched on the ground' he may be, but his supine posture is the result of nothing more sinister than 'a deep sleep'.

While Quamina's somnolent condition helps to resolve the conundrum of the text's opening paragraph, it also means, of course, that he remains oblivious to his mother's singing voice and hence deaf to the act of cultural memory in which she is engaged. Yet the transmission of such a memory is not only blocked or thwarted here, but also ironically parodied. The 'African song' is first transmuted into a gift exchanged between a white father and his son and then subjected to a 'very inadequate translation into English verse', which is passed on, in its turn, from son to reader. This shift from oral to written forms is a particularly significant moment in the text because it makes quite clear the extent to which Wellington has misconstrued the meaning of the 'sound' he hears. The black woman's 'wild strain' is in part a song of loss, mourning the interlocking deaths of her husband and the Ashanti nation, desecrated by the colonizer. At the same time, though, her lament possesses a more insurgent resonance, being, in Firdous Azim's formulation, 'really a call to arms'.[6]

From its very beginning, the song of Quamina's mother-queen makes a case for colonial revenge which it is hard to gainsay. The equivocations by which Wellington retrospectively exonerates himself as 'cause' of the suffering he beholds are displaced by a language which is much more direct, not to say combative: 'Last branch of murdered royalty, / How calmly thou art sleeping / While the storm that bowed thy parent tree / Is still around thee sweeping' (lines 1–4). In this stanza, the figuration of the father-king as murder victim bluntly challenges colonialism's clichéd self-representation as civilizing mission, exposing the constitutive violence it would rather conceal. The perversity of such violence is underscored by the arboreal metaphors of 'branch' and 'tree' on which the stanza draws: in sundering father from son, the colonizer performs an action which is tantamount, it is implied, to a violation of nature.

The correspondence between the human and the natural established by metaphor is developed in the poem's next three stanzas. If the exercise of colonial power can be compared to an abuse of the natural order, nature itself seems, as it were, to register an anticolonial protest. For Wellington, the landscape over which he moves gives pleasure, bringing a degree of relief to the oppression of a 'sultry afternoon': as he recalls, he 'enjoy[s] the cool faint wind which breathe[s] from [the] surface' of the river whose course he follows. As represented by the Ashanti queen, however, the landscape is less a source of colonial gratification than a locus of threat, everywhere intent on retribution:

> Dost thou not hear in that wild moan
>   Mid the tall palm branches dying,
> A kindred, an ancestral tone,
>   For blood, for vengeance crying?
>
> Dost thou not hear faint mingled cries
>   In the murmur of the river
> Like those which death's last agonies
>   From flesh and spirit sever?
>
> Dost thou not hear in every sound
>   A sign, a warning token?
> Thou dost not, for thy soul is bound
>   In slumber most unbroken.   (lines 5–16)

The 'wild moan' is indeed akin. It not only echoes the cadence of the voice invoking it, but also vibrates with the same burden, 'crying', like the Ashanti queen herself, for 'blood' and 'vengeance'. In so agitated a climate, when even 'the murmur of the river' is doubly inflected with a syllabic hint of mur/der, it is little wonder that 'every sound' should seem to be 'A sign, a warning token'.

This pattern of call and response, in which the voices of Quamina's natural mother and an outraged Mother Nature are in harmony with one another, is manifest elsewhere. In the penultimate stanza, for example, it expands to embrace a new feature in the poem's imaginative geography. As she dies, Quamina's mother enjoins her young son, belatedly waking from his 'slumber', to 'Look' (line 49) towards the Lake of Hyle. It is around this watery source that the black female voice which sings the poem builds its last and most potent self-image. Earlier in the poem, the Ashanti queen envisages a gruesomely redemptive time when Quamina, fully grown, will 'take the holy sword of right / Through blood-stains redly gleaming' (lines 35–6) and 'Go piling heaps of dead' (line 38). Here, 'Hyle's waters' (line 49) would seem to resound to similar sentiments. As she listens to the 'voice' (line 51) which comes from them, Quamina's mother could almost be listening to herself, hearing, as she does, 'a sound of prophecy / Which speaks of bloody recompense' (lines 51–2).

In addition to the violent future cleansings to which they attest, 'Hyle's waters' provide more immediate consolations. In the stanza prior to this one, Quamina's mother begins to enter her last moments, describing how 'a tomb-like shade / Come[s] darkly creeping o'er [her]' (lines 45–6). While this formulation can be read as a signal for the imminence of an abstract death, it also arguably possesses a more chilling and concrete connotation, figuring, perhaps, the approach of the murderous colonizer himself. Whatever the precise bearing of the phrase, it could be said that the Ashanti queen gains a 'final victory' (line 56) over her encroaching enemies, abstract and concrete alike, by escaping their dominion. As the poem ends and the prose narrative briefly reopens for some few lines, Wellington periphrastically recounts how he arranges the queen's burial, 'caus[ing] her to be interred under the palm tree where she died' (p. 6). Yet there is a sense in which something comparable to this act of committal has long been under way. Throughout the poem, Quamina's dying mother works to disperse her voice amid the elements and, in so doing, ensure the survival of the 'death-swept' (line 22) history which the voice conveys: she becomes a kind of anticolonial *genius loci*. In this respect, Quamina ends the text not only with a surrogate father, who has taken him under a dubious 'protection' (p. 6), but a surrogate mother also, in the form of an historically awakened natural realm.

'Last branch of murdered royalty' occupies a unique position in Brontë's writings, poetic or otherwise, constituting, as it does, her only attempt at representing the voice of a colonized female subject. While this voice is nowhere else to be heard in Brontë, the critique of colonialism which it offers is audible, albeit less explicitly, in each of the three poems remaining for discussion in this chapter. At the same time, these three texts extend the scope of the critique by giving increased emphasis to the gendered nature of the colonial enterprise, focusing, in particular, on the different forms of masculinity which sustain and advance it.

'The Letter'

According to Isobel Armstrong, one of the characteristics of Victorian women's poetry is its 'doubleness'. This arises, she argues:

> from its ostensible adoption of an affective mode, often simple, often pious, often conventional. But those conventions are sub-jected to investigation, questioned, or used for unexpected pur-poses. The simpler the surface of the poem, the more likely it is that a second, and more difficult poem will exist beneath it.[7]

Armstrong's model of a Victorian female poetics in which 'con-ventions' are turned to 'unexpected purposes' provides a sugges-tive critical framework for 'The Letter'. This text was first written in 1837, but only published, in revised form, as part of *Poems*, nine years later, and could hardly stand in greater contrast to 'Last branch of murdered royalty'. Here the central figure is not a suf-fering black female but an upper-class Englishwoman enduring rather different trials, busily writing to a husband whose ill-defined colonial obligations have driven him to 'a strange and distant spot'.[8] At first glance, such a *mise-en-scène* would seem to promise a text indeed conventional, organized around the roman-tic conceit of the constant wife, longing for the return of her far-flung 'heart of hearts' (line 76). But the findings of a first glance are necessarily always open to amendment. This is especially so with regard to a poem whose opening line poses the question of textual inscription – 'What is she writing?' – as an enigma and which repeatedly invites the reader to engage in acts of scrutiny and revision: 'Watch her now' (line 1), 'look again' (lines 33 and 57) and 'watch her still more closely' (line 39). Though certainly relatively 'simple' on its 'surface', 'The Letter' becomes increas-ingly fraught with 'more difficult' meanings as it develops. These place its stereotypes and sureties in doubt. Does the poem fully endorse the colonial project in which the husband is involved and about which it seems to be so blasé? Is the young wife quite as keen to be reacquainted with him as she appears to be, or is such a prospect less warmly embraced? What exactly occurs at the geographical and textual margin to which her spouse is banished?

Following its initial question and the incitement to 'Watch her now', Brontë's text proceeds to give a more detailed account of the epistolary rituals in which the waiting wife is engrossed. These, it seems, are something of a marvel: 'How fast her fingers move!' (line 2), the narrator exclaims, 'How eagerly her youthful brow / Is bent in thought above!' (lines 3–4). The alacrity with which the wife 'Pursues her labour sweet' (line 12) is noted again in stanza three (lines 35–6) and functions, clearly enough, as a sign of affective intensity. Yet even as the poem begins by stressing the emotional closeness which the wife continues to feel towards her distant mate, it also introduces an element of tension. As she 'puts ... aside' (line 6) the 'long curls [which] shade the light' (line 5) she uses to compose her text, the wife inadvertently dislodges the 'band of crystals bright' (line 7) adorning her neck, so that 'It slips adown her silken dress' (line 9) and 'Falls glittering at her feet' (line 10). Given the status of glass within Brontë's imagination as a primal signifier of colonial power, this gesture is not quite as accidental or offhand as it seems. It implies a symbolic questioning of the colonial enterprise in which the husband in the poem is involved and might even perhaps foretell a colonial death.

The seemingly innocuous image with which 'The Letter' opens is taken up in stanzas two and three, as the loosened necklace is transformed into another bright but falling object, in the shape of 'the setting sun' (line 71). Like the slipping crystals before it, the sun's slow decline remains 'Unmarked' (line 11) by the writing woman, blotted out, as it is, by the 'absorbing task' (line 37) on which her 'eye' is 'fixed' (line 33). For the poem's narrator, by contrast, the descent of 'The golden sun' (line 15) is a captivating and delightful spectacle. It makes the time when it takes place seem like the 'very loveliest hour' (line 13), suffuses the sky with a 'deepening glow' (line 28) and can even be figured as a 'radiant dance' (line 31), performed during 'evening's rosy hours' (line 32). Such aesthetic raptures cannot wholly eclipse the more disturbing connotations which the trope of solar decline traditionally brings with it, however. In the context of 'The Letter', this trope is doubly ominous. On the one hand, it works symbolically like the falling necklace, figuring both the fading of colonial power and the deathly effacement of the husband himself, complete with the 'sunburnt cheek' (line 61) acquired in the course of his travels. On the other, it possesses more intimate implications, suggesting the demise of the marital love at the poem's core.

The evidence that this love is on the wane or has, at least, been compromised, is discernible, to recall Armstrong's formulation, beneath the conventionalities of the textual 'surface'. One of the points where the poem's submerged marital discords become most acute is in stanzas four to six. Here the prolonged focus of attention is the husband's portrait, hanging in 'The summer-parlour' (line 45) where the wife sits and writes. 'Sloped, as if leaning on the air' (line 51), this 'picture' (line 52) occupies a position curiously akin to that assumed by the writing woman in the poem's opening tableau, where she is 'bent in thought above' her manuscript. Yet as well as doubling the writer's posture, the painting suspends her compositional processes: 'her pen / Hangs o'er the unfinished line' (lines 41–2) and a 'tearful gleam' (line 43) steals from her eye, another in the poem's catalogue of bright but falling objects, to complement the 'band of crystals' and 'golden sun'. This tear would initially seem to be a bodily token of longing and desire, produced out of the ironic gap between the image of the husband – 'confine[d]' to a 'broad gold frame' (line 56) – and the husband himself, moving without check on an invisible colonial horizon. When his portrait receives a fuller narratorial appraisal in stanza six, however, the nature of the lachrymose response it elicits becomes less certain, as the poem's register changes from the sentimental to the more questioning:

> Black Spanish locks, a sunburnt cheek,
>   A brow high, broad, and white,
> Where every furrow seems to speak
>   Of mind and moral might.
> Is that her god? I cannot tell;
>   Her eye a moment met
> The impending picture, then it fell
>   Darkened and dimmed and wet.   (lines 61–8)

Here the 'determined face' (line 60) of the previous stanza is rendered indeterminate and may or may not be the faithful index of 'mind and moral might'. While the true nature of the husband's character remains suspended between these mutually exclusive alternatives, Brontë's language inclines the reader towards the more negative possibility that he is not entirely 'god'-like. Not just 'Sloped' but now 'impending', the husband's gold-framed 'picture' appears to be on the verge of toppling into the poem's seemingly catch-all reservoir of bright but falling things. Although, in the end, the painting does not fall, its precarious position functions as a neat visual metaphor for its subject's implied lack of rectitude. This is in turn reflected in the change which comes over the wife's 'eye', as it loses its earlier 'gleam' and, lowered in the 'picture''s place, becomes 'darkened and dimmed'.

The element of covert critique in 'The Letter' is twofold, directed towards the husband's colonial and sexual identities alike. These identities are hard, in the end, to disentangle, as the poem intimates in its closing lines. Here the letter the wife has been writing is finally 'sealed' (line 70) and sent on its perilous way:

> Three seas and many a league of land
>   That letter must pass o'er,
> Ere read by him to whose loved hand
>   'Tis sent from England's shore.
> Remote colonial wilds detain
>   Her husband, loved though stern;
> She, 'mid that smiling English scene,
>   Weeps for his wished return.   (lines 77–84)

Like the journey they chart, these lines are full of uncertainties, one of which arises from the word 'detain'. This word carries contradictory meanings themselves worth dwelling on. While it constructs the husband as passive victim, the word also suggests that the 'Remote colonial wilds' where he tarries are sources of fascination, possibly because they offer that 'easy range of sexual opportunities'[9] which, as Ronald Hyam has shown, is integral to the prosecution of empire. The insinuation that the husband's colonial detention is grounded in erotic indulgence finds support in the ambiguous allusion to his 'hand', 'loved' perhaps by the wife who writes from 'England's shore', or fetishized, equally, as the object of more exotic affections. Such ambiguities filter through into the poem's syntactically inconclusive final two lines, which find the wife at home but out of place, sorrowing amid a 'smiling English scene'. Is it she who 'wishe[s]' for her husband's homecoming at this juncture, 'Weep[ing]' in the knowledge that, for whatever reason, it has been delayed, perhaps permanently? Or is it the husband who is the actively desiring subject here? Does he crave 'return', moving his wife to tears, not on the basis of an indefinite absence but because of a presence whose arrival is threateningly imminent? These are questions which 'The Letter', characteristically, leaves unanswered, ultimately remaining, like the 'picture' it describes, a 'clouded mass of mystery' (line 55).

'Passion'

Like 'The Letter' before it, this text exists in an earlier version than the one which eventually surfaces in *Poems*. The later and original incarnations of the poem (separated by a gap of approximately five years) are substantially the same, though there is one key difference. This relates to the way in which Brontë reworks the military materials featured in her 1841 ur-text, producing, in Tom Winnifrith's concise but dismissive phrase, 'An interesting adaptation of the Peninsular War to Britain's Indian campaigns'.[10] As well as sounding somewhat patronizing, Winnifrith's comment is rather generalized. As it turns out, 'Passion' engages with one quite specific campaign, in the form of the First Sikh War, which took place between December 1845 and February 1846, in the valley of the Sutlej, situated in North West India.

There is something faintly opportunistic about the manner in which Brontë redraws her poem's historical and geographical boundaries for publication. The radical decamping to 'Indus' borders'[11] not only lends the later version of the text a topical edge but also increases its potential appeal, since the new region the poem annexes to itself was the site of a major colonial triumph. As a contemporary article in *Blackwood's Edinburgh Magazine* effuses, the Sutlej valley bore witness to 'the blaze of four mighty and decisive victories won in six weeks',[12] while in a similarly contemporary, if less elevated, ballad by John Sheehan, 'the fighting in India'[13] offers 'honour and plunder, galore' to the 'boys'[14] who sign up for it. At the same time, it offers such things – albeit in less generous measure – to the female poet herself, who, it could be said, raids the archive of British colonial history in the unmade name of her own poetic ambitions. Yet what is perhaps most striking about Brontë's foray into this archive is how it parallels the rhetorical strategies deployed by the soldier-lover who speaks the poem. He, too, turns colonial war to self-seeking purposes, honing his prospective conflict with the racial other into a weapon of persuasion in a private struggle for the love of the woman he addresses. The colonial field which flickers so suggestively into view between or beneath the closing lines of 'The Letter' provides a space in which the colonizer, freed from 'family ties and moral pressures',[15] is able to claim his sexual pleasure. In 'Passion', conversely, it acts as a kind of detour into which the colonizer enters in order to procure such pleasure within the ambit of home.

The opening three stanzas of 'Passion' entail a movement from the general to the particular, past to present. Noting how 'Some' (line 1) before him 'have won a wild delight, / By daring wilder sorrow' (lines 1–2), the speaker goes on to suggest that this is a courtship ruse he would be keen to emulate:

> Could I gain thy love to-night,
>   I'd hazard death to-morrow.
>
> Could the battle-struggle earn
>   One kind glance from thine eye,
> How this withering heart would burn,
>   The heady fight to try!
>
> Welcome nights of broken sleep,
>   And days of carnage cold,
> Could I deem that thou wouldst weep
>   To hear my perils told.   (lines 3–12)

If there is a mercenary recruitment of war to the service of male sexual desire in these lines, there is also a figuring of such desire in the lexicon of war: 'wild delight' is to be 'won', while 'love' is a 'gain'. Yet 'gain' is as much an economic as a military term and it is the word's economic connotation which is capitalized upon in stanzas two and three, as the speaker invokes 'the battle-struggle' as a speculative means of 'earn[ing]' the interest of his female listener. At this preliminary stage in the manoeuvrings, the erotic return from such risky investments seems fairly modest, merely a combination of 'One kind glance' and the tears shed in appreciation for the speaker's fictional reconstruction of his 'perils'. This is perhaps not quite yet the coveted 'wild delight' achieved by the elite corps of precursors whom the speaker admires, even as there is clear evidence of 'wilder sorrow', especially in the disturbed and chilling images of 'broken sleep' and everyday 'carnage'.

The 'heady fight' to which the poem gestures at its outset is non-specific. It has no obvious racial or colonial dimension and the 'lands' (line 15) to which the speaker imagines he will 'roam full far away' (line 14) are justly designated as 'distant' (line 15). These remote territories zoom into focus, however, in stanzas five to eight, as the 'carnage' of the poem's opening finds embodiment in a lurid colonial form:

> Wild, long, a trumpet sounds afar;
>   Bid me – bid me go
> Where Seik and Briton meet in war,
>   On Indian Sutlej's flow.
>
> Blood has dyed the Sutlej's waves
>   With scarlet stain, I know;
> Indus' borders yawn with graves,
>   Yet, command me go!
>
> Though rank and high the holocaust
>   Of nations steams to heaven,
> Glad I'd join the death-doomed host,
>   Were but the mandate given.
>
> Passion's strength should nerve my arm,
>   Its ardour stir my life,
> Till human force to that dread charm
> Should yield and sink in wild alarm,
>   Like trees to tempest-strife.   (lines 17–33)

As the *Blackwood's* account makes clear, the strategic significance of the river at the poem's core stems from its status as frontier. The Sutlej divides the territories held on either side of it by the Sikh and British armies, such that its crossing by the former, 'without a shadow of provocation',[16] represents an invasion of the lands defended by the latter and hence becomes the trigger to war. In Brontë's poetic vision of the encounter, however, it is not only geographical but also racial 'borders' which are overrun. 'Seik and Briton meet in war, / On Indian Sutlej's flow' in more senses than one. The 'Blood' of each party, with all its mid nineteenth-century connotations of racial purity and pollution, gets mixed, forming a single 'scarlet stain', just as national differences are first sacrificed to a collective 'holocaust' and then consumed by a 'death-doomed host', which incorporates friend and foe alike. The surrendering of demarcations between colonizer and colonized is complemented by a series of secondary dissolutions, in which human and natural orders become equally blurred. The intermingled 'Blood' flows into 'the Sutlej's waves', which it punningly 'dye[s]', while corpses blend with earth in open 'graves'. The pattern is extended and completed by the merging of the human and the divine, as the odour of the metaphorical conflagration described in these grisly lines 'steams' towards an indifferent 'heaven'.

In contrast to the undoing of racial difference articulated here, the identities of the poem's male speaker and his female listener remain distinct, even as they are organized according to a hierarchy of power not at all what it seems. As elsewhere in the poem, the amatory relationship between the two figures is represented in terms drawn from the realm of the military. The woman who 'bid[s]' and 'command[s]' her self-elected hero to answer war's 'Wild' call adopts a position of superiority towards him analogous to that which an officer might hold with respect to a subaltern. Yet the ironic truth of the situation is quite the opposite of this. It is the subaltern who orders his superior to order him, seeking to script her language, just as he had previously sought to write her body by making her 'glance' and tears into love-tokens. These two forms of female control, linguistic and bodily, are interrelated. For the beloved to incite the speaker to war, colonial or otherwise, is for her to connive in her own downfall, since, according to the logic of 'Passion' at least, demonstrations of military prowess perform a double duty as the violent foreplay to sexual conquest. The circuitous links between the two forms of domination are underlined by internal echoes, as the image of the enemy made to 'yield and sink in wild alarm' recalls the 'wild delight' of erotic mastery evoked in the poem's first line.

As the poem retreats from the colonial battleground carved out by its central stanzas and moves into its final phase, the speaker dispenses with his own rhetorical trickeries. In stanzas nine and ten, for example, there is no camouflaging the will to power over the woman who is the target of his affections. It may be possible for her to 'reprove' the 'fire' (line 36) aimed in her direction, but not to resist it. Defences of 'scorn, and maddening pride' (line 37) cannot hold out against the adamantine force of the speaker's ego: 'No – my will shall yet control / Thy will, so high and free, / And love shall tame that haughty soul – / Yes – tenderest love for me' (lines 38–41). The swift capitulation of 'No' into 'Yes' occurring in the course of these lines provides a neat prelude to the narcissistic fantasy of the next stanza. Here the speaker continues to train his gaze upon that feature of his beloved – her 'eyes' – which had first attracted his attention, now explicitly regarding them as a text in which he can 'read' his sexual 'triumph' (line 42). Yet no sooner do the speaker's military exertions grant him the 'noble prize' (line 44) he has been questing than the 'prize' is relinquished, as he resolves 'perchance … / Once more in arms to range' (lines 44–5). The 'arms' he initially embraces in order to reach his sexual goals are themselves taken up, in a final twist, as a new object of desire. As well as suggesting the cyclical nature of the speaker's logic, this shift in his priorities is accompanied by a fitting transformation in the poem's rhetorical mode. As 'Passion' closes, it is not the language of war which is used to figure male sexuality (as, for example, in the tropes of 'triumph' and 'prize'), but the language of male sexuality which is used to represent war: 'Then Love thus crowned with sweet reward, / Hope blessed with fulness large, / I'd mount the saddle, draw the sword, / And perish in the charge!' (lines 50–3). This rhetorically engorged moment brings to an end a poem whose colonial and sexual politics are troublingly cavalier in equal degree. As the speaker surges beyond the bounds of his text in a crude phallic 'charge', or discharge, the suspicion is that the woman whom he has been wooing would be glad to see him gone. Her silence throughout the poem is, at any rate, an eloquent comment on the kind of masculinity – aggrandizing itself at the expense of others – which the speaker personifies.

'The Missionary'

For the anonymous pundit writing in *Blackwood's*, 'the campaign of the Sutlej … form[s] the most extraordinary, the most brilliant, the most complete, and yet the briefest chapter' in 'the whole wonderful annals' of Britain's 'Indian Empire', its 'memorable deeds' adding 'lustre even to the dazzling renown'[17] of the nation. The construction of the 'campaign' in such glitteringly chauvinistic terms is at considerable variance with the way in which it features in 'Passion', where the war does not so much augment the nation's sense of its own greatness as become dragooned into a programme of private intentions. This subversive conscription of the colonial into the personal is also characteristic of 'The Missionary', an undated poem probably written in 1845 (as Juliet Barker speculates)[18] and turned, like 'Passion', towards an Indian vista. Here, however, the colonial space into which the poem's eponymous speaker projects himself possesses rather different functions to those it is accorded in the previous text. Far from being a diversion on the path to sexual mastery, India operates in 'The Missionary' as a place into which the speaker withdraws, taking flight both from his own desires and the shadowy Helen, the female figure who is their spur. But even as he strives to give up fleshly pleasures, the speaker succumbs to other temptations, representing his acts of romantic self-denial as a form of religious heroism. In so doing, he becomes caught up in the narcissistic logic of the martyr, exchanging earthly self-renunciation for spiritual self-magnification and identifying his own sufferings, in particular, with those of Christ.

As befits its title, 'The Missionary' begins with a moment of conversion, though one which is not so much spiritual as figurative. In the opening stages of his journey from domestic to colonial contexts, past to future, the speaker indulges himself in an apostrophe to the ship on which he voyages, urging it towards a broader horizon: 'Plough, vessel, plough the British main, / Seek the free ocean's wider plain',[19] he exclaims. In the redoubled efforts of this transitional couplet, water turns to earth, the change effected by a rhetorical device – the trope of cultivation – which furrows its way through the poem as a whole. The trope's next appearance is more or less immediate, occurring in the exacting vision of the new existence the speaker anticipates for himself amid the 'climes remote and strange' (line 5) to which he is bound:

> Hot action, never-ceasing toil,
> Shall stir, turn, dig, the spirit's soil;
> Fresh roots shall plant, fresh seed shall sow,
> Till a new garden there shall grow,
> Cleared of the weeds that fill it now, –
> Mere human love, mere selfish yearning,
> Which, cherished, would arrest me yet.   (lines 7–13)

This Brontëan passage to India not only takes the prospect of the speaker's 'altered life' (line 6) as its topic, but also renders its own meaning subject to change in the course of its unfolding. The first five lines of the passage would appear simply to offer a conventional description of the relationship between colonizer and colonized, missionary and heathen, in which the one directs his proselytizing energies towards the good of the other. Yet this meaning is overturned by the two lines which conclude the passage, when it transpires that the 'new garden' the speaker wishes to design is not external but internal. Before he can establish the 'gospel vine, / Where tyrants rule and slaves repine' (lines 109–10), the poem's speaker must, it seems, work over a ground closer to home, eradicating those 'weeds' which threaten, if 'cherished', to 'arrest' his own spiritual growth: 'human love' and 'selfish yearning'.

The problem for the speaker, though, is that his spiritual husbandry is not quite as efficient as he might like it to be. In figuring the soul as a 'soil' which he must 'stir, turn [and] dig' in order to 'plant' 'Fresh roots', he implicitly replays across his own interior terrains the more literal processes of colonial settlement,[20] effectively occupying the positions of colonizer and colonized at one and the same time. But the agricultural language on which the speaker calls does not only carry a colonial resonance. As he 'grasp[s] the plough' (line 14) and inseminates the spiritual landscape which it breaks open with 'fresh seed', he undergoes another doubling and splitting. Casting himself into the roles of male and female, ploughman and earth, tiller and tilled alike, the speaker becomes a kind of spiritual hermaphrodite, performing an act of self-salvation which sounds much like a 'love' not just 'human', but peculiarly sexual. The implication is that the attempt to 'Unbind' and 'dissever English ties' (line 4) is far from straightforward, whether the links in question be to the feminized nation to which the speaker claims he was once 'Wedded' (line 22) or the rejected bride for whom his 'heart' once 'burned' (line 50). If there is 'a conflict wild' (line 27) for the speaker to face, it is not only between 'Nature and hostile Destiny' (line 26) but also between the poem's sexualized metaphors and the aura of spiritual self-discipline they are supposed to uphold. Despite his best intentions, the traces of the desire the speaker claims to have relinquished are embedded in the key rhetorical field which 'The Missionary' initially opens up for itself and within which it remains throughout.

From the sexually encoded language at the poem's outset, it is evident that the renunciation of pleasure leaves something to be desired in this text. Yet it is equally clear that Brontë's poem is animated by a certain pleasure of renunciation, its speaker at once fetishizing and aggrandizing the original moment of spiritual crisis which precipitates his flight into the colonial future as missionary.

No sooner, for example, does he confidently assert that 'there's no returning' (line 14) to the country he has left than his gaze is drawn back to 'England's shores', which 'are yet in view' (line 16). More particularly, the speaker does not only look back even as he embarks upon his voyage, but also lingeringly recalls the 'task of anguish' (line 21) preceding it. The act of recollection is figured as if it were a compulsion: 'I cannot yet Remembrance flee' (line 19), he laments, additionally insisting that the scene in which he gives up his 'selfish yearning' is something he 'must again ... firmly face' (line 20). At the same time, he is eager that the reader fully appreciate the extremity of the suffering he has experienced, crafting himself into the hero of his own spiritual narrative. The speaker's self-heroizing techniques are typified in the following lines:

> Smouldering, on my heart's altar lies
> The fire of some great sacrifice,
> Not yet half quenched. The sacred steel
> But lately struck my carnal will,
> My life-long hope, first joy and last,
> What I loved well, and clung to fast;
> What I wished wildly to retain,
> What I renounced with soul-felt pain;
> What – when I saw it, axe-struck, perish –
> Left me no joy on earth to cherish;
> A man bereft – yet sternly now
> I do confirm that Jephtha vow:
> Shall I retract, or fear, or flee?
> Did Christ, when rose the fatal tree
> Before Him, on Mount Calvary?   (lines 32–46)

Here the most brutally obvious means the speaker uses to impress his 'soul-felt pain' upon the reader is, paradoxically, a language of the body, wielding the castrating trope of 'sacred steel' against his 'carnal will' and rendering himself 'A man bereft' as a result. In addition to this, the speaker represents and indeed inflates the personal agony entailed in the renunciation of desire by identifying it with examples of heroic self-denial taken from the two religious traditions, Hindu and Christian, which clash so unevenly across the text. The first of these traditions is implicitly aglow in the allusion to the speaker's desire cremated upon the 'heart's altar', an image which evokes the practice of *sati*, the immolation of the Hindu widow upon the funeral pyre of her deceased husband. Yet even as this image unites the two figures, speaker and widow, in

'The fire of ... sacrifice', it also holds them apart: the speaker's loss of his 'life-long hope' is a far cry, after all, from the more material sufferings sustained by the burning woman selected as colonial double. The parallels between the speaker and the two figures whom he nominates as sacrificial twins from the Christian tradition – Jephtha and 'the Nazarene' (line 98) – are equally dubious. Despite his hyperbole, the burnt offering of male sexual longing is hardly comparable to the only daughter whose life the biblical Jephtha must cede to God,[21] and even less so to the crucified body which Christ yields up to his Father 'on Mount Calvary'.

Such is the speaker's fixation upon the gesture of romantic self-sacrifice he has made that his movement beyond the time of its occurrence is also a return to it. This is suggested by the parallels the poem creates between the spells respectively cast by his beloved and the 'pagan-priests' (line 67) who dominate the deathly zones into which the speaker ventures. As he recalls the epochal moment of separation from the woman with whom he 'dare[s] not stay' (line 54), the speaker notes how his 'eyes' become 'dim' (line 60) 'with the bitterest tear / [He] ever shed' (lines 59–60). But even as 'passion's agony' (line 58) clouds bodily sight, 'the spirit's vision' (line 61) remains unimpaired, drawing this 'soldier of the Cross' (line 104) towards an Oriental scene in which the Hindu religion is figured as a ubiquitous and demonic presence: 'Hell's empire, vast and grim, / Spread on each Indian river's shore, / Each realm of Asia covering o'er' (lines 62–4). As this 'vision' continues, it becomes clear that the 'empire' it discloses is even more corrupting in its effects than the female 'love' from which the speaker has 'turned' (line 49): it actualizes the condition of spiritual blindness which Helen's charms certainly threaten but ultimately cannot bring about. Perhaps this is why the speaker sounds so authoritative with regard to the benighting influence the Hindu ministers are able to exert over their disciples, with their 'creed' (line 67) of 'Wrong, / Extortion, Lust, and Cruelty' (lines 67–8)? He well enough knows 'how hell the veil will spread / Over their brows and filmy eyes' (lines 99–100) because this is a fate he has potentially endured at the tempting hands of the woman he has so resolutely renounced and whose name is itself, appropriately, half-infernal.

As he sets out to confront and dismantle this 'empire', the speaker acknowledges the danger he courts, invoking monitory tales of 'missionary blood, / Shed in wild wilderness and wood' (lines 114–15) before him. Ironically, though, the possibility of meeting the same murderous fate does not so much discourage as entice and incite. As well as imagining 'the martyr's prayer' (line 117) which his predecessors might have uttered to 'the unblest air' (line 116) at the moment of death, the speaker delivers an equally melodramatic appeal of his own:

> Though such blood-drops should fall from me
> As fell in old Gethsemane,
> Welcome the anguish, so it gave
> More strength to work – more skill to save.
> And, oh! if brief must be my time,
> If hostile hand or fatal clime
> Cut short my course – still o'er my grave,
> Lord, may Thy harvest whitening wave.
> So I the culture may begin,
> Let others thrust the sickle in;
> If but the seed will faster grow,
> May my blood water what I sow!   (lines 126–37)

In this peroration, the speaker goes one better than his forerunners. It is not simply that he wants to be posthumously numbered among 'those Pioneers' (line 143) who have given up their lives for the Christian good of all. His higher ambition, rather, is to be identified with Christ himself, mixing his own 'blood-drops' with those which 'fell in old Gethsemane'.[22] This audacious *imitatio Christi* is combined with a revival of the cultivational rhetoric with which the poem begins. The speaker represents himself not just as one 'who steps on foreign soil' (line 108), but a figure prepared, if necessary, to go under it in order to reach his missionary goals. His future corpse he imagines as a source of spiritual nourishment, capable of turning its 'grave' into a fertile site from which the 'Lord' can glean a metaphorical 'harvest' of Christian converts, just as his 'blood' miraculously accelerates the growth of the 'seed' from which the crop will 'grow'. Yet it is not only God or those unnamed 'sickle'-thrusting 'others' who reap the benefits of such radical selflessness, but the speaker also. Death by 'hostile hand or fatal clime' is to be welcomed because it quickens his spiritual climb and 'bestows the Martyr's crown' (line 154). The speaker's 'ultimate reward' (line 156) for propagating Christ's doctrine with such zeal is, it seems, to have his praises unanimously proclaimed by the highest of authorities: 'Then for the world-rejoicing word – / The voice from Father – Spirit – Son:

/ "Servant of God, well hast thou done!"' (lines 157–9). The divine congratulations here are double-edged, involving an ironic reversal of hierarchies. On the one hand, they undercut the identification with Christ with which the speaker repeatedly flirts in the course of the poem, by designating him as 'Servant' not just to the 'Father' but to the 'Son' as well. On the other, they position the Holy Trinity itself in the role of collective megaphone, broadcasting the speaker's missionary feats across the globe: the final word of 'The Missionary' may stem from a divine origin, but it is one subordinated to the glorification of the human.

'Sacrifice of an Indian Widow'

'The fire of … sacrifice' invoked at line 33 is not the only allusion in 'The Missionary' to the practice of widow-burning. The tradition is also euphemistically implied in the speaker's reference to the 'fiendish rite' (line 113) which it is his Christian duty to extinguish and is perhaps even to be glimpsed in his closing and transcendent self-figuration as one who 'stand[s] 'mid testing fires unhurt' (line 151).[23] In this respect, Brontë's poem looks forward to *Jane Eyre*, which regularly kindles its own ghostly echoes of *sati*, particularly in its latter stages. At the same time, though, the poem is retrospective, linked to three earlier moments in Brontë's *oeuvre* at which the subject of *sati* is broached. The first two of these are relatively incidental, occurring *en passant*, as it were, in 'The Spell, An Extravaganza' and 'The Scrap Book',[24] Ashanti narratives composed in 1834 and 1835, respectively. The third moment, by contrast, is much more fully elaborated and exists in the shape of 'Sacrifice of an Indian Widow', the Belgian essay of 1842 to which, by way of conclusion, this chapter now turns.

'Sacrifice of an Indian Widow' is a text marked by curious doublings and double standards. These first emerge amid the Christian pieties of its opening paragraph, in which the rhetorically questioning narrator expatiates upon the attractions and the flaws of the colonial space in which he finds himself:

> Hindustan is rich, she is powerful, but despite her wealth and power she is enslaved. What good are her diamonds and her gold, while she remains subject to the despotism of an arrogant and cruel Hierarchy?, Are all the mines of Golconda worth a single ray from that star of Bethlehem which the Magi saw of old in the East?[25]

Feminized and bejewelled, Brontë's Hindustan parallels and prefigures the doomed but resplendent widow at the essay's heart, 'diamonds glitter[ing] in her hair, and pearl ornaments adorn[ing] her arms and her brown neck' (p. 4). Yet if both the nation and its female subjects are 'enslaved' to a male-driven religious 'despotism', the narrator himself is not beyond establishing a colonial 'Hierarchy' arguably just as 'arrogant and cruel' as the indigenous order he berates. In privileging the spiritual lustre emanating from the 'star of Bethlehem' above the earthly treasures lodged in 'the mines of Golconda', the narrator simultaneously articulates a preference for Christian rather than Hindu tradition. In so doing, however, he necessarily embraces a mode of belief predicated upon an act of self-sacrifice whose Oriental manifestation as *sati* he so confidently condemns. Some institutionalized forms of self-immolation are more valid than others, it seems: the Christ who suffers so flamboyantly on Calvary's 'fatal tree', to recall 'The Missionary', is clearly a superior figure to Brontë's distasteful widow, her death dismissed as just another 'of those horrible sacrifices that have stained every page of the history of Hindustan with blood'.

Throughout the course of his account, the narrator situates himself as 'spectator', figuring the widow's fiery death by turns as a 'tragedy' and 'heartrending spectacle' to which he innocently bears 'witness' (p. 2). The common-sense neutrality of this stance is not wholly convincing, however, placed, as it is, in direct tension with the more complex ways in which the colonizer actively shapes the very scenes he appears merely to observe. As Ania Loomba argues, one of the unintended effects of early nineteenth-century British legal interventions against *sati* was paradoxically to increase its incidence 'as a form of anti-colonial disobedience'.[26] This irony gives rise to a second doubling and casts a strange light on 'the ordinance of Lord Bentinck' (p. 2), to which Brontë's essay at one point makes an explicit intertextual allusion. Denouncing it as 'revolting to the feelings of human nature',[27] Bentinck's decree finally criminalized *sati* on 4 December 1829, deeming 'all persons convicted of aiding and abetting' the practice as 'guilty of culpable homicide'.[28] Those nefarious 'persons' who are the subject of Bentinck's oddly pleonastic ire do not just include the native population, however, but to some degree the colonizers also, since it is they, as Margery Sabin puts it, 'who somehow incite the very horrors they deplore'.[29] The distance between self and other, the makers and the breakers of colonial law, comes to be unsettled.

As much as he is a 'spectator', Brontë's narrator is also a listener, peculiarly attuned to sounds and their absence as signifiers of cultural difference. As he notes, for example, the funeral cortège which departs from 'the house of the deceased' (p. 2) is quite other – with its 'dreadful cries' and cacophonous 'orchestra' (p. 4) – to 'the sad and silent train, which, in European countries, accompanies the dead man to his burial' (pp. 2–4). Despite such dissonances in the acoustics of mourning, however, there are also striking harmonies between the Oriental and Occidental worlds the narrator straddles. Just as he is himself obliquely mirrored and multiplied in the 'turbulent troupe of pagan savages' (p. 4) who attend the widow to her death, so she in turn offers a troubling reflection of her own, uncannily doubling the plight of the middle-class Englishwoman who is her textually invisible counterpart. The difference between these two female figures is that death for the one is literal, while for the other it is metaphorical, a death-in-life. As Sandra M. Gilbert and Susan Gubar write:

> Whether she becomes an *objet d'art* or a saint ... it is the surrender of her self – of her personal comfort, her personal desires, or both – that is the beautiful angel-woman's key act, while it is precisely this sacrifice which dooms her both to death and to heaven. For to be selfless is not only to be noble, it is to be dead. . . . the spiritualized Victorian woman ... having died to her own desires, her own self, her own life, leads a posthumous existence in her own lifetime.[30]

The strange sisterhood between Oriental widow and Occidental 'angel-woman' exposes another double standard in the text, as colonial and patriarchal ideologies collide with one another. As enlightened colonizer, the narrator is obliged to abhor the events he beholds, 'hop[ing]', accordingly, that the widow will 'renounce the sacrifice' (p. 4). At the same time, though, he is the envoy of a culture grounded in its own routine barbarism, accepting and extolling female self-sacrifice as the unquestioned and unedifying norm.

The narrator's construction of the widow as hapless 'victim' (pp. 4, 6) of Hindu religious ritual is firmly in accord with nineteenth-century representations of *sati* in general and serves two interrelated purposes. On the one hand, as Suvendrini Perera notes, using a strikingly sexualized phrase, it provides 'justification both for empire and for increased missionary penetration'.[31] On the other, it allows the male colonizer to cast himself in a particularly self-flattering light: he is the chivalric hero, capable of liberating the Oriental woman as much from her deluded self as from custom and setting her on the path to true Christian righteousness. In the end, however, Brontë's text is not fully reducible to the protocols of its contemporary discursive milieu, as the widow moves uncertainly between opposed identities. There is little doubt that the main narrative stress falls on her status as 'victim', a figure passively subjugated to a religio-patriarchal regime whose inflexibility is aptly signalled in the image of the husband's corpse, borne to its pyre by 'Four Brahmins'. As the narrator remarks, abruptly switching to a cold-bloodedly third-person idiom: 'One did not see the body; it was covered with a kind of mortuary cloth, whose folds outlined the rigid contours of the man who was laid out beneath them' (p. 4). Against this, however, there are indications that the widow is not without a degree of agency and volition, choosing her role in the 'tragedy' rather than having it foisted upon her. As the narrator recollects, using the reflexive pronoun for emphasis, neither Bentinck's edict 'nor the efforts of the authorities had sufficed to hinder the sacrifice. The widow herself resisted all the entreaties of those who wished to save her life' (p. 2).

This conflict between female victimhood and female agency is important because it endows Brontë's widow with that 'complex subject status' which, as Sabin notes, is so often denied to 'Indian women'[32] by the discourse of *sati*. Such complexity reaches its zenith in the essay's closing moments, as the widow makes her valediction:

> She sat down close to the corpse, which had already been laid on the pyre. Then she turned her head to bid the world an eternal farewell.
>
> Never in my life will I forget that moment; her eyes sought the sun, the azure sky – I thought I saw in their gaze an agonizing struggle between bodily weakness and spiritual power.   (pp. 4–6)

The manner in which the widow's 'agonizing struggle' is resolved remains unclear: does she yield herself up to 'flame' and 'fire' under duress or is her surrender an act of free will? For the narrator, at least, the former interpretation is the one to which he most strongly adheres, even as his concluding statement is so qualified and equivocal as to undermine its own credibility: 'in the feeble lamentations of the wind I seemed to hear a voice deploring the fate of that unhappy woman' (p. 6). In that crucial 'seemed', the narrator allows for the possibility that the 'lamentations' he hears do not say what he says they say and, by extension, that the 'woman' whose death he has witnessed is not necessarily 'unhappy'. Brontë's essay thus ends on a radically uncertain note, unravelling what should be an authoritative last word into an open question. Is the narrator's translation of the native 'voice' detected in the 'wind' to be relied upon, or is it merely a convenient colonial projection which is itself to be 'deplor[ed]'?

In 'Sacrifice of an Indian Widow', Brontë not only writes of a foreign land, but also in a foreign land, Belgium. As Lonoff argues, there are some suggestive parallels between the narrative scenario developed in Brontë's essay and the cultural conditions in which it is produced:

> the consciousness of living among foreigners was strong in her. She wrote, as does her narrator, in alien territory, gazing from her window at the garden of the pensionnat, one of two Protestants surrounded by Catholics who struck her as benighted, if not heathen.[33]

In Lonoff's reading, Anglo-Indian conflicts mask religious and implicitly national tensions closer to home. This veiling of the continental by the colonial is a process reversed in *The Professor*, the subject of the next chapter. In this novel, Brontë's imaginative horizon appears to contract dramatically. In contrast to those other parts of her corpus considered so far – the Ashanti narratives, the poetry and the Belgian essays – she no longer takes her reader on exotic voyages into Africa or India. She seems largely content, instead, to remain within a European provenance, reworking the experiences of the Belgian sojourn into fictional form (just as she would rewrite *The Professor*, in its turn, in *Villette*). This is not to say, however, that *The Professor* should be read in isolation from the Afro-Oriental concerns of the writings which precede it. While Brontë's colonial imagination may well display itself less visibly in the later text, it remains active none the less, shaping the materials of the earlier work into new forms.

3

'Mixed up in Foreign Hodge-Podge': Slavery and Sexuality in *The Professor*

> As we look back at the cultural archive, we begin to reread it not univocally but *contrapuntally*, with a simultaneous awareness both of the metropolitan history that is narrated and of those other histories against which (and together with which) the dominating discourse acts.
>
> Edward W. Said, *Culture and Imperialism*, p. 59

> How could one tolerate a foreigner if one did not know one was a stranger to oneself?
>
> Julia Kristeva, *Strangers to Ourselves*, p. 182

The opening chapter of *The Professor* features a 'copy of a letter, sent ... a year since' by William Crimsworth, the novel's first-person narrator and central protagonist, to Charles, 'an old school-acquaintance',[1] whom Crimsworth had known at Eton. While the letter is designed to furnish Charles with an account of its writer's activities after leaving Eton, such a purpose remains unrealized. As Crimsworth explains at the end of the chapter, his missive meets with no reply because its desired recipient is no longer at home to read it:

> To this letter I never got an answer – before my old friend received it, he had accepted a government appointment in one of the colonies, and was already on his way to the scene of his official labours. What has become of him since I know not.   (p. 14)

Charles's silent withdrawal to an unspecified colonial margin provides Crimsworth with the opportunity to take up where the letter leaves off, regaling 'the public at large' with the autobiography, in the shape of the novel itself, originally begun for the 'private benefit' (p. 14) of his mysteriously estranged correspondent.

The story of his professional and personal fortunes which Crimsworth goes on to narrate has three distinct phases. The first sees him moving from the south of England to the north, where he is employed as 'second clerk' in the Yorkshire textile mill owned by the entrepreneurial Edward, his elder brother, and 'manage[s] the foreign correspondence of the House' (p. 18). Dissatisfied with the task of 'copying and translating business-letters' and feeling victimized, in particular, by the 'Antipathy' (p. 30) his employer-brother demonstrates towards him, Crimsworth invokes the translator's prerogative, converts his linguistic mobility into geographic form and travels to Belgium. Here he teaches English as a foreign language, first to male and then to female students in boarding-schools run by Monsieur Pelet and Zoraïde Reuter, respectively. It is here, also, through a combination of endeavour and chance, that he eventually secures his financial independence. In the novel's brief final stage, Crimsworth returns to England, accompanied by his Anglo-Swiss wife and former pupil, Frances Evans Henri, and their refractory young son, Victor.

For many critics, the epistolary manoeuvre with which Brontë begins The Professor is both artificial and clumsy. It is, they argue, the sign of an early gaucherie on the part of a would-be novelist perilously aspiring, like Charles and Crimsworth in their own spheres, to secure a professional status within the male-dominated literary establishment of mid nineteenth-century England. Yet if The Professor is indeed Brontë's first novel proper, the scene of her formation as writer stretches back, of course, to the Ashanti narratives which she began to produce in the late 1820s and is interwoven with a colonial history evident also in the poetry and Belgian essays. It is thus apparent that the divergence of career between Charles and Crimsworth with which The Professor begins both allegorizes and enacts a certain shift in Brontë's own literary trajectory: like Crimsworth, her work will remain, from The Professor onwards, securely located within English and/or continental territories.

But if colonialism is excluded as a literal presence in Brontë's novels, no longer setting the 'scene' for her own 'official labours', as it were, it continues to return in a variety of significant unofficial forms. In the case of *The Professor*, Crimsworth's practice as 'English Master' (p. 67) in Belgium 'can easily be viewed', as Firdous Azim has suggested, 'against the class-bound and colonial tradition that accompanies the teaching of English'.[2] In this respect, the severed epistolary exchange with which the novel opens is ironically inverted, as a correspondence with colonial margins is implicitly kept up: Crimsworth's supremacist assumptions about his own language and culture take their place alongside those informing the kind of colonial pedagogy beginning to emerge in the context of British expansion in India, as advocated, for example, in Thomas Babington Macaulay's infamous 'Minute on Indian Education' of 2 February 1835.[3]

Azim's reading of *The Professor* is an important one, not least because it represents the first sustained attempt to situate Brontë's novel within a colonial frame of reference. At the same time, however, there are two respects in which *The Professor* invites a development of Azim's approach. The first of these relates to the re-emergence of colonialism as a textual resource. The unequal power relations which the novel charts in the contexts of class and gender are repeatedly figured in terms of a slavery only recently abolished in Britain's colonies, and still firmly institutionalized in the American South, when *The Professor* was first composed.[4] In this way, it becomes evident that *The Professor*'s rhetorical operations are involved in a politics of identification which is highly problematic.

The second concerns the way in which, more broadly, questions of nation and race come to be played out in the register of sexuality. Throughout the narrative, Crimsworth associates sexuality with forms of foreignness, whether these be continental or Oriental, thus constituting it as something which threatens to infect and undo his sense of himself as Englishman. Although he claims not to know 'What has become' of his friend in the wake of Charles's colonial posting, Crimsworth's own traveller's tale dramatizes fears and fantasies of contamination analogous to those entailed in the colonial venture itself. *The Professor*'s use of slavery as figure implies an identification with the other whose impetus reverses, in the context of sexuality, into flight and defence.

The rhetoric of slavery

In the Preface to *The Professor*, Brontë records her 'surprise' (p. 3) at the unfavourable response which her novel has elicited (it was rejected for publication nine times in total during her lifetime).[5] Having deliberately eschewed 'the ornamented and redundant in composition' in preference for the 'plain and homely', and 'adopted a set of principles on the subject of incident &c.' (p. 3) which is stringently realist, she discovers that the novel's prospective 'Publishers, in general – scarcely approved this system' and, it transpires, 'would have liked something more imaginative and poetical' (p. 4) than the worldly tale of self-advancement which she tells. This unexpected state of affairs leads to a reflection on the deceptiveness of appearances in which gender stereotypes are overturned. Herself concealed behind the masculine mask of 'Currer Bell' (p. 5), Brontë comments:

> until an author has tried to dispose of a M.S. of this kind he can never know what stores of romance and sensibility lie hidden in breasts he would not have suspected of casketing such treasures. Men in business are usually thought to prefer the real – on trial this idea will be found fallacious: a passionate preference for the wild wonderful and thrilling – the strange, startling and harrowing agitates divers souls that shew a calm and sober surface.   (p. 4)

For Brontë's text to be judged by 'Men' who are the (feminized) opposites of what they seem is oddly appropriate for, as Penny Boumelha has argued, '*The Professor*'s is a world of doubleness' in which 'Virtually every major character is radically divided'.[6]

In changing the original title of her novel from *The Master* to *The Professor*, Brontë appears to signal this sense of 'doubleness' and radical self-division. In one respect, the new title might be considered to be something of a misnomer. As Crimsworth soon comes to learn from Mr. Brown, his contact on arriving in Belgium, the appellation bestowed on him does not possess quite the same meaning, or cachet, as in England. It translates differently: 'The word professor struck me. "I am not a professor," said I. "Oh," returned Mr. Brown – "Professor, here in Belgium, means a teacher – that is all" ' (p. 60). Yet if 'The word professor' distorts and inflates Crimsworth's standing within the pedagogical hierarchies of the establishments run by Pelet and Zoraïde alike, it is, at the same time, an accurate designation. Like several of the other key figures in the text, Crimsworth is precisely a 'professor' in the alternative, or non-professional sense defined by Boumelha, repeatedly 'manifesting one motive, feeling or state of mind but also privately harbouring another'.[7]

Crimsworth's tendency, in that lightly pleonastic phrase, to make 'false professions' (p. 181) is evident not just in the context of the personal images he shapes for others (as for himself) in the course of the narrative. It is also to be discerned in terms of his textual practices as an autobiographer and, in particular, his habitual use of metaphor, a trope itself traditionally linked to notions of deception and duplicity. Especially in *The Professor*'s first six chapters, metaphor functions as the figurative vehicle for the return of the colonialism seemingly so pointedly renounced at the novel's outset, as Crimsworth draws on a historically burdened language of mastery and enslavement in order to represent the fraternal and class conflicts in which he is initially implicated. As his unread introductory letter attests, Crimsworth is the product of a marriage that crosses class boundaries: his mother is of aristocratic descent, with a 'rare ... class of face' (p. 14), while his father is a '—shire Manufacturer' who becomes 'bankrupt a short time previous to his death'. On the demise of his mother, 'some six months' (p. 7) after these events, Crimsworth is entrusted to the care of the affluent 'maternal uncles' (p. 6) who will later fund his education. By subsequently rejecting their patronage, he is forced to enter the realm of mercantile capitalism in which Edward is 'fast making a fortune' (p. 8). At the end of chapter 4, Crimsworth returns to his 'lodgings' to prepare for the next day's labours, flooded with 'regrets' (p. 39) as to the unpromising position to which he has been reduced. He is further agitated by the repeated 'goading' (p. 37) of Hunsden Yorke Hunsden. As his palindromically shaped name suggests, Hunsden's unpredictable appearances in the text are typically marked by an enigmatic poise that contrasts sharply with the uncertainty of Crimsworth's own prospects:

> Why did I make myself a tradesman? Why did I enter Hunsden's house this evening? Why, at dawn to-morrow, must I repair to Crimsworth's Mill? All that night did I ask myself these questions and all that night fiercely demanded of my soul an answer. I got no sleep, my head burned, my feet froze; at last the factory-bells rang and I sprung from my bed with other slaves. (p. 39)

The 'bells' which ring here are literal and metaphorical at once. Crimsworth's participation in the routines of the factory worker is evidently for him the cue for other echoes and resonances, prompting a cross-racial identification with the disciplined body of the slave.

In summoning the enslaved worker to his duties, those 'bells' would seem to reverberate with the promise that the capitalist order of things will be renewed and soundly maintained. Yet equally, if obliquely, they constitute a call to insurrection which finds its response, in personal if not collective terms, in the next chapter. Crimsworth's literal dawn rising, in the passage above, prefigures what he refers to as '"The Climax"' (p. 40), the moment of his rebellion against the oppressor-brother. Violently accused of spreading slanders about Edward which are subsequently traced back to Hunsden, Crimsworth is finally moved to liberate himself from the 'yoke' (p. 59) of his brother's employ:

> 'Come, Edward Crimsworth, enough of this. It is time you and I wound up accounts. I have now given your service three months' trial and I find it the most nauseous slavery under the sun. Seek another clerk – I stay no longer.'
> 'What! Do you dare to give me notice? Stop at least for your wages.' He took down the heavy gig-whip hanging beside his Mackintosh.   (pp. 42–3)

Crimsworth's rebellious turning against Edward is also a linguistic one, again performing, as it does, a troping of class in terms of race, the domestic in terms of the colonial.

The presence of slavery as metaphor in *The Professor* has some curious effects, the first of which relates to Crimsworth's role as 'tradesman'. While his decisive altercation with Edward clearly confirms Hunsden's taunting prophecy that '[he]'ll never be a tradesman' (p. 38; emphasis in original), there is a sense in which Crimsworth's vocation as metaphorist at the same time both reinterprets and challenges Hunsden's assertion: his trade is in language, regulated by the exchange of the literal meanings of words for figurative ones. The second effect is to qualify the stylistic assertions Brontë makes in her Preface, as the novel turns out to be much less 'plain and homely' than she claims it to be. Not only is Crimsworth's narrative recurrently 'ornamented', quite plainly, by a particular figure of speech, but the figure in question is one which entails a kind of departure from the 'homely' also. For metaphor, as Eric Cheyfitz points out, is a rhetorical operation in which words are transferred from literal to figurative usages, travelling from familiar to foreign destinations.[8] If Crimsworth will, for the bulk of the novel, be an Englishman abroad, there is a sense in which such a spatial relocation only recapitulates the itinerary laid down in advance by his own language.

Even as they question Brontë's reading of her own text, Crimsworth's rhetorical strategies cast a different kind of doubt on themselves. The essential problem with his rituals of metaphorical self-representation is that, ultimately, they can only seem like hyperbolic gestures, variously ironized by the unstated historical truths which *The Professor* encrypts within itself. To compare class relations in the north of England to slavery would seem, on the one hand, to be an effective means of underscoring the oppression and injustice to which the worker is subjected by early to mid nineteenth-century industrial capitalism. On the other, however, Crimsworth's self-figuration carries out its own injustice. The 'other slaves' whom he blithely fashions out of metaphor have their counterparts in the shape of black subjects literally enslaved either in the context of the British West Indies or the American South. As several critics, from Marx to Fanon and beyond, have argued, it is the regulated bodies of these other 'other slaves', so to speak, which drive the capitalist economy from which Crimsworth freely withdraws his labour.[9] In identifying himself with the figure of the slave, Crimsworth in effect performs a metaphorical colonization, or colonization through metaphor, expropriating the racial other for his own self-serving ends.

The discrepancies between Crimsworth and the slave in terms of whom he sees himself are most visible, of course, with regard to the privileges which accrue to him by virtue of what Macaulay calls the 'aristocracy of skin'[10] – the fact of Crimsworth's whiteness. Although he has not followed the obscure colonial career of the correspondent alluded to in the novel's first chapter, Crimsworth none the less shares the assumed racial superiority on which such a career is predicated. Both figures are in turn racially elevated above the white Creole pupil, the 15-year-old Juanna Trista, whom Crimsworth encounters in Zoraïde's school. As a 'girl ... of mixed Belgian and Spanish origin' who is born 'in the —Isles' (p. 100), Juanna is not quite to be included in the same racial echelon as her 'English Master'. Even so, as she leaves Europe to return to her father's unnamed West Indian estate, she does so 'exulting in the thought that she should there have slaves whom, as she said, she could kick and strike at will.' With 'the legible graving of ... Mutiny and Hate' on her 'brow' (p. 101), Juanna's celebration of her future role as colonial mistress underscores the dubious politics of Crimsworth's figurative tendencies. Its effect is to expose the realities of colonial and racial conflict which the logic of metaphor, stressing sameness over difference, threatens to efface.[11]

Crimsworth's metaphorical identifications open up *The Professor* to the kind of contrapuntal reading proposed by Said in the first epigraph to this chapter, inviting themselves to be placed and considered, for example, alongside Frederick Douglass's *Narrative of the Life of Frederick Douglass, An American Slave, Written by Himself* (1845). Douglass's text is exactly contemporary with Brontë's composition of her novel and, as one of the formative works in the African American autobiographical tradition, centrally concerned, like *The Professor*, with processes of self-making. These processes are encapsulated in the famous liberatory chiasmus of Douglass's 'You have seen how a man was made a slave; you shall see how a slave was made a man.'[12] They are subsequently initiated by the pivotal physical fight between Douglass and the '"nigger-breaker"',[13] Edward Covey. From this conflict, lasting 'nearly two hours', Douglass emerges triumphant, his 'sense of ... manhood' both 'revived' and transfigured in a 'glorious resurrection, from the tomb of slavery, to the heaven of freedom'.[14] Douglass's account of his experiences provides a powerful counterpoint to the terms in which Crimsworth likes to frame his own, driving his metaphors back towards their literal ground. If Crimsworth's 'brazen face' fails to 'blush black' (p. 44) during the course of his brother's verbal assault, his narrative is characterized, it would seem, by rhetorical displays which are their own impertinence.

Douglass goes on to offer an explicit corrective to the dangerous affront of slavery as trope in another context. In the course of a lecture given to a meeting in Newcastle upon Tyne on 3 August 1846, he defines it as his 'duty to direct ... attention to the character of slavery, as it is in the United States'. He proceeds to inform his audience of the urgency of his task:

> I am the more anxious to do this, since I find the subject of slavery identified with many other systems, in such a manner, as in my opinion, to detract to some extent from the horror with which

> slavery in the United States is so justly contemplated. I have been
> frequently asked, since coming into this country, 'why agitate the
> question of American slavery in this land; we have slavery here, we
> are slaves here.' I have heard intemperance called slavery, I have
> heard your military system, and a number of other things called
> slavery, which were very well calculated to detract from the dread-
> ful horror with which you at a distance contemplate the institution
> of American slavery.[15]

Here Douglass spells out the potential ironies that attend the slave
trope. The language of a domestic politics needs to be properly
disciplined if it is not simultaneously to collude with, diminish and
perpetuate a 'horror' which, even 'at a distance', seems 'dreadful'.

Whether the effects are 'calculated' or not, *The Professor* deploys
slavery as trope in the context not only of class but also gender relations. At several junctures, white female figures are associated, either
by Crimsworth or themselves, with rebel slaves and/or a violent
blackness. This is the way in which, in chapter 10, for example,
Caroline de Blémont, one of the three self-crowned 'queens' in
Zoraïde's school, forces herself upon her teacher's attention:

> Caroline shook her loose ringlets of abundant but somewhat coarse
> hair over her rolling black eyes, parting her lips, as full as those of a
> hot-blooded Maroon, she showed her well-set teeth sparkling
> between them and treated me at the same time to a smile 'de sa
> façon'. (p. 86)

In this passage (whose syntax is almost as 'loose' as Caroline's
'ringlets'), Crimsworth's vision is a double one. The danger embodied in white female sexuality is represented as a colonial rebellion signalled in the allusion to the 'hot-blooded Maroon'.[16] If the
allusion is defensively misogynist in its figuring of white female
sexuality in terms of slave revolt, it is at the same time racist, as
the stereotypical traits of blackness slide between Caroline and
'Maroon' alike. Both have 'lips' described as 'full', while the
former has 'rolling black eyes' and a characteristic 'smile' which
discloses, in those 'well-set teeth', a cannibalistic appetite.

It is not only the sexually excessive female who comes to be
identified with a rebellious blackness but the conventionally feminine Frances also. In the novel's final chapter, after Crimsworth
and Frances have been married for some ten years, he speculates
on what might have become of his 'good and dear wife' had she
married 'a profligate, a prodigal, a drunkard or a tyrant'. To

Crimsworth's insistent pursuit of these curious possibilities, Frances responds, with an equally 'strange kind of spirit in her eye': 'if a wife's nature loathes that of the man she is wedded to', she asserts, 'marriage must be slavery. Against slavery all right thinkers revolt' (p. 255). The potential for (un)wifely revolt which Frances hints at here is still more emphatically associated with blackness in the previous chapter. During an exchange concerning the merits and demerits of her native land, Frances tells Hunsden that if he were to 'take a wife out of Switzerland' and subsequently impugn her nation – as he has indeed just done by unwisely 'mention[ing] the word *ass* in the same breath with the name Tell' – his insolence would meet with lethal consequences: his 'Mountain Maid' would 'some night smother' him, 'even as ... Shakspeare's Othello smothered Desdemona'. As if immediately to partake in the reprisal imagined against Hunsden, the future 'plan' which Frances 'sketche[s]' involves an attack on a figure central to Hunsden's sense of his own cultural supremacy. Frances's revisionary drama is, as he himself recognizes, 'a travesty of the Moor and his gentle lady in which the parts [are] reversed' (p. 242; emphasis in original), as white female revenge becomes shockingly wedded to a monstrous black male violence.[17]

In its invocations of slavery as a trope for other conditions of disempowerment, *The Professor* reveals itself to be a rhetorically exorbitant text. At the same time, such figurative gestures stand in marked contrast to the principles of self-control in terms of which Crimsworth's sexuality is organized. This clash between linguistic excess and libidinal restraint gives rise, in its turn, to another conflict. Since Crimsworth's sexual self-restraint is a cardinal sign of his Englishness, it follows that he must set himself against those foreign bodies whom he perceives to be more freely sexualized, lest the closely tailored sense of his own national identity come to be unravelled. This imperative results in a violent alienation of self from other, native from foreign, which is antithetical to the equally violent fusions of white and black identities precipitated by the slave trope.

Sexuality, nation, race

At the beginning of chapter 3, Crimsworth recalls his time as a subject under surveillance in his brother's mill:

> I served Edward as his second clerk faithfully, punctually, dili-
> gently. What was given to me to do, I had the power and the de-
> termination to do well. Mr. Crimsworth watched sharply for
> defects but found none; he set Timothy Steighton, his favourite
> and head-man, to watch also, Tim was baffled; I was as exact as
> himself, and quicker: Mr. Crimsworth made enquiries as to how I
> lived, whether I got into debt – no – my accounts with my land-
> lady were always straight; I had hired small lodgings which I con-
> trived to pay for out of a slender fund – the accumulated savings
> of my Eton pocket-money; for as it had ever been abhorrent to my
> nature to ask pecuniary assistance, I had early acquired habits of
> self-denying economy; husbanding my monthly allowance with
> anxious care.   (p. 22)

All the values which define a bourgeois masculinity are operating
here, 'faithfully, punctually, diligently' present and correct – from
'industry and perseverance', in Heather Glen's taxonomy, to 'self-
reliance and independence, self-respect and self-control'.[18] By inter-
nalizing these values, Crimsworth necessarily leaves Edward and his
'head-man' 'baffled': in true Foucauldian fashion, he subjects
himself to the very strategies of surveillance deployed against him.[19]

The 'accumulated savings', 'habits of self-denying economy' and
'husbanding' of his 'monthly allowance' to which Crimsworth
alludes literally refer to his talents of financial self-management. At
the same time, though, the terms he uses have a vital currency in
contemporary medical discourses, where they circulate as figures
for the ways in which male sexuality is ideally to be ordered. The
Victorian *locus classicus* for such discourses is William Acton's
*The Functions and Disorders of the Reproductive Organs in
Childhood, Youth, Adult Age and Advanced Life Considered in
their Physiological, Social and Moral Relations*, published in 1857,
the same year as Brontë's novel. Despite the apparent comprehen-
siveness of its title, Acton's inquiry is, as Steven Marcus points out,
almost exclusively concerned with the sexual economy of the
male.[20] Within this economy, Acton defines semen as a kind of
inner resource which, to adopt Crimsworth's term, requires careful
'husbanding' both prior to and during marriage. Sexual expendi-
ture occurring outside marital intercourse, especially in the baleful
shape of masturbation, is simply a waste. Summarizing Acton's
linkage of the sexual and the financial, Marcus writes:

> The fantasies that are at work here have to do with economics;
> the body is regarded as a productive system with only a limited

amount of material at its disposal. And the model on which the notion of semen is formed is clearly that of money. Science, in the shape of Acton, is thus still expressing what had for long been a popular fantasy: up until the end of the nineteenth century the chief English colloquial expression for the orgasm was 'to spend.'[21]

Given this discursive construction of male sexuality, the 'anxious care' with which Crimsworth disposes of his 'Eton pocket-money' takes on a new significance. The latter phrase is a covertly sexual coinage: both metonymically and metaphorically, it unites the genital and the financial.

Crimsworth's investment in the kind of sexual self-discipline obliquely figured in his restrained monetary 'habits' is not surprising. To lose such mastery, as Acton and other medical commentators repeatedly insist, is for the male subject to become increasingly implicated in a range of moral, psychic and bodily disorders, resulting, ultimately, in madness and/or death. For Crimsworth, though, such a loss also entails something else. If Pelet's description of Crimsworth, in chapter 11, as a 'cold frigid Islander!' (p. 96) makes the connection between sexual repression and English masculinity explicit, Crimsworth, for his part, establishes an equally emphatic and complementary link between sexual licence and Pelet's identity as Frenchman:

> He was not married and I soon perceived he had all a Frenchman's, all a Parisian's notions about matrimony and women; I suspected a degree of laxity in his code of morals, there was something so cold and blasé in his tone whenever he alluded to, what he called, 'le beau sexe'; but he was too gentleman-like to intrude topics I did not invite, and as he was really intelligent and really fond of intellectual subjects of discourse, he and I always found enough to talk about, without seeking themes in the mire – I hated his fashion of mentioning Love, I abhorred, from my soul, mere Licentiousness, he felt the difference of our notions and, by mutual consent, we kept off ground debateable. (p. 70)

The 'difference of ... notions' between these mutually consenting interlocutors resolves itself into a difference of nations, as Crimsworth scrupulously retreats from the lavish expenditures of a continental sexuality. Yet while Crimsworth is 'willing', at this point in their acquaintance at least, 'to take Pelet for what he seemed' (p. 70), he himself less easily earns the same favours from the reader. As one whose monetary and sexual customs are marked alike by 'habits of self-denying economy', Crimsworth is necessarily a subject self-divided. The self-control he arrogates to himself throughout the novel is simultaneously a mask for and symptom of an inner split. As Sally Shuttleworth argues:

> The picture [Brontë] draws is not of an innate, assured masculinity, but rather of a social and gender identity created and sustained only through violence: the violence of self-repression and of repudiation of all who might threaten the carefully nurtured illusion of self-control.[22]

Difference between is difference within. The oppositions by which Crimsworth recognizes and defines himself – between English and continental masculinities, sexual probity and 'mere Licentiousness', self and other – are the objectification of internal conflicts. These conflicts make of Crimsworth's own subjectivity a peculiarly vexed site, itself a 'ground debateable'. What he claims to have 'perceived' in the other is, more properly, the projection, or exportation, of what he represses in himself.

For Crimsworth, a deregulated sexuality is a national scandal, as the border, or '"l'allée défendue"' (p. 108), between English and continental masculinities is crossed and violated. Yet the self-protective stance he adopts towards Pelet is ultimately the sign of anxieties concerning racial as well as national contamination. These are manifested in the context of *The Professor*'s treatment of miscegenation, no doubt one of the 'themes' Crimsworth would want to consign firmly to his 'mire', and previously broached, of course, in the Ashanti narratives. Contemplating the physical charms of Caroline, Pelet treats himself to a fleeting fantasy of interracial desire in which she is Orientalized: 'Ah there is beauty! beauty in perfection – what a cloud of sable curls about the face of a houri! What fascinating lips! What glorious black eyes!' (pp. 95–6). Despite his own previous figuration of Caroline in terms of a furious blackness, Crimsworth predictably recoils from these imaginings, debunking them merely as the product of an artificial 'enthusiasm' and hearing 'something in [Pelet's] tone which indicated got-up raptures' (p. 96).

This recoil parallels a gesture made originally in chapter 1, when the fantasy of miscegenation first articulates itself. In this version of the fantasy, gender identities are transposed across the lines of race. Introduced to his brother's 'handsome young wife',

Crimsworth 'peruse[s] the fair page of [her] face' and finds it wanting:

> I sought her eye, desirous to read there the intelligence which I could not discern in her face or hear in her conversation; it was merry, rather small; by turns I saw vivacity, vanity – coquetry, look out through its irid, but I watched in vain for a glimpse of soul. I am no Oriental, white necks – carmine lips and cheeks, clusters of bright curls do not suffice for me without that Promethean spark which will live after the roses and lilies are faded, the burnished hair grown grey. (p. 13)

Crimsworth's discriminatory assertion that '[he is] no Oriental' is one instance of what Glen calls the 'marked negativism'[23] of the novel's prose. The negation operating here, however, is not only stylistic but also psychic. It is suggestive of the kind of defensive strategy elaborated by Freud:

> To negate something in a judgement is, at bottom, to say: 'This is something which I should prefer to repress.' A negative judgement is the intellectual substitute for repression; its 'no' is the hall-mark of repression, a certificate of origin – like, let us say, 'Made in Germany'.[24]

Crimsworth's revealingly fleshly claim that he has no desire for female bodies which withhold 'a glimpse of soul' and are not supplemented by a classically enduring 'Promethean spark', is thus an admission of just such a desire, albeit in disguised or antithetical form. What is particularly important about the self-cancelling logic in which Crimsworth is enmeshed is not so much the desires it discloses as where those desires are located. The sexuality he renounces is not of European origin, something '"Made in Germany"', Belgium or France, for example, but of more exotic provenance. Sexual desire thus poses a double problem for Crimsworth. On the one hand, it threatens to make him a male counterpart to those girls whom he teaches and dismisses as 'continental English'. These are 'the daughters chiefly of broken adventurers' (p. 102), whose exilic exposure to European culture has imbued them with 'an imbecile indifference to every sentiment that can elevate humanity' (p. 103). On the other, it confronts him with the more alienating possibility of his own Orientalization.

Crimsworth's projection/exportation of his own desires onto the figures of Pelet and the phantom 'Oriental' is a process repeated in

the context of his relations to the female other. The desires for the
female body which Crimsworth represses return to him in the distorted form of a persecutory female sexuality. The central scene for
this drama of repression and return is Zoraïde's '"Pensionnat de
demoiselles"' (p. 61), where the erotic seems thoroughly to saturate
the pedagogical. Its presence is immediately registered, in chapter
10, in the prurient comedy of the preparations Crimsworth makes
before introducing himself to his class for their first lesson.
Entering Zoraïde's 'sanctum sanctorum' (p. 83) and noting 'a large
tableau of wood painted black and varnished', 'a thick crayon of
white chalk' and 'a wet spunge', Crimsworth comments:

> having handled the crayon, looked back at the tableau, fingered the
> spunge in order to ascertain that it was in a right state of moisture –
> I found myself cool enough to admit of looking calmly up and
> gazing deliberately round me.   (p. 84)

What Crimsworth sees, on raising his eyes, is an array of girls and
young women, aged between 'fourteen' and 'twenty', whose
'forms [are] full even to solidity' (p. 84). These superabundant
figures are neither the prelapsarian 'angels' (p. 76), nor even 'half-
angels' (p. 85), to whom he typically dedicates his 'sentimental
reflections' (p. 66). Quickly 'relieved' of such a 'fond and oppres-
sive fancy' (p. 85), Crimsworth comes to view his female pupils,
by chapter 12, as 'a swinish tumult' (p. 101). With the 'isolated'
exception of the 'British English', with their 'grave and modest
countenances' and 'general air of native propriety and decency'
(p. 103), his class becomes the object of a violent disgust:

> They were each and all supposed to have been reared in utter un-
> consciousness of vice – the precautions used to keep them ignorant,
> if not innocent, were innumerable; how was it then that scarcely
> one of those girls having attained the age of fourteen could look a
> man in the face with modesty and propriety? An air of bold, impu-
> dent flirtation or a loose, silly leer was sure to answer the most or-
> dinary glance from a masculine eye. I know nothing of the arcana
> of the Roman-Catholic religion and I am not a bigot in matters of
> theology, but I suspect the root of this precocious impurity, so
> obvious, so general in popish Countries, is to be found in the disci-
> pline, if not the doctrines of the Church of Rome. I record what I
> have seen – these girls belonged to, what are called, the respectable
> ranks of society, they had all been carefully brought up, yet was the
> mass of them mentally depraved.   (p. 98)

Here Crimsworth claims for himself a scientific or empirical objectivity: 'I record what I have seen'. This enables him, with seeming authority, to trace the genealogy of the hypersexualized continental female back to its twisted 'root' in 'Romish wizard-craft' (p. 102). But Crimsworth's narrative perspective is no more reliable at this point in the novel than elsewhere. On closer inspection, the 'ordinary glance' cast by the 'masculine eye' seems to bear witness less to the sexual truth of women who inhabit 'popish Countries', than to the 'sexual paranoia'[25] of the Protestant subject from whom that glance first emanates. Despite his contempt for 'the discipline ... of the Church of Rome', Crimsworth, in this passage, is not unlike the confessor to Sylvie, 'at once the ugliest and the most attentive' (p. 87) of his students. Crimsworth hesitates to reward Sylvie's attentiveness by even the slightest physical gesture for fear that such a 'token of approbation' will be subsequently 'misinterpreted and poisoned' (p. 121) by her confessor as a sign of sexual impropriety. Yet he himself engages in just such an erroneous and overcharged hermeneutics. The depravity Crimsworth claims to behold in the collective visage of the schoolgirls 'under [his] eye' (p. 97) is a reflex of the sexuality he refuses to confront in himself.

In relation to Zoraïde's schoolgirls, Crimsworth is, paradoxically, the very source of the contamination by which he feels himself to be endangered. Such a paradoxical position is similarly evident in the context of his relation to Zoraïde herself. Despite her imminent marriage to Pelet, and Crimsworth's own growing love for Frances, Zoraïde continues in her efforts to seduce the 'English Master'. Just before the marriage is 'solemnized' (p. 198), Crimsworth outlines the 'singular effect' which Zoraïde produces upon him:

> her presence and manner ... sealed up all that was good, elicited all that was noxious in my nature; sometimes they enervated my senses, but they always hardened my heart. I was aware of the detriment done, and quarrelled with myself for the change. I had ever hated a tyrant; and behold the possession of a slave, self-given, went near to transform me into what I abhorred! There was at once a sort of low gratification in receiving this luscious incense from an attractive and still young worshipper and an irritating sense of degradation in the very experience of the pleasure. When she stole about me with the soft step of a slave – I felt at once barbarous and sensual as a pasha – I endured her homage sometimes, sometimes I

rebuked it – my indifference or harshness served equally to increase
the evil I desired to check.   (p. 184)

This complex passage looks back to an earlier point in the text,
where Pelet speculates that Zoraïde will 'leave the print of her
stealing steps on [Crimsworth's] heart' (p. 94). It also reintroduces
the slave trope, while rerouting it from British colonial/American
contexts into the realms of the Oriental. Zoraïde is figured here as
'slave' because she readily submits herself to her own desires, to
which – as much as to Crimsworth – she is 'self-given'. Far from
being the paragon of 'abstract reason' she appears to be at first,
Zoraïde is ultimately subject to the euphemistic rule of 'strong
propensities' (p. 90). Yet her self-Orientalization is a means to
gain mastery over Crimsworth, precisely by subjugating him to the
role of 'tyrant' over her. What is so 'singular' about Zoraïde's
'effect' is that it brings to light Crimsworth's own doubleness, as
he struggles between the repression of and the yielding to desire.
By the same token, it underlines the ways in which the contradictory elements of Crimsworth's 'nature' are organized in terms of
racial categories. If Crimsworth is 'transform[ed]' 'into what [he]
abhor[s]', the reversal in question involves not only the dissolution
into 'gratification' and 'pleasure' of his customary 'Scipio-like self-
control' (p. 119). It is also figured as the assumption of a 'noxious'
Oriental identity, as he becomes 'at once barbarous and sensual as
a pasha'.

   Against the sexual toxin of Zoraïde, her 'body depraved by the
infectious influence of the vice-polluted soul', Frances functions,
for Crimsworth, as antitype or perhaps even 'antidote' (p. 187).
At the same time, she elicits from her teacher-lover and eventual
spouse a desire which is distinctly narcissistic. In this way, she
confirms Crimsworth's worldly suspicion that nothing 'pleases
egotistical human beings so much as a softened and refined likeness of themselves' (p. 24). In the first of a series of doublings,
Frances, like Crimsworth, subscribes openly to the bourgeois ideology of self-improvement, initially attending his lessons 'in order
to perfect her knowledge of English' and so 'qualify herself for a
higher department of education' than that of the 'lace-mending'
and 'ornamental needle-work' (p. 116) by which she earns her
living. In the course of her 'instruction in English' (which is
rapidly co-opted by Crimsworth as 'a channel for instruction
in literature' [p. 146]), Frances proves herself to possess

'Perseverance and a Sense of duty' to 'a somewhat remarkable degree' (p. 131). In this respect, indeed, she succeeds where her teacher, during his apprenticeship as 'tradesman', had failed: Frances's approach to her studies is genuinely resolute, while Crimsworth soon recognizes he is unable to 'set up' even the simulacra of resolution – 'the image of Duty [and] the fetish of Perseverance' – as his 'household gods' (p. 30). Her ambitions are finally rewarded when, like Crimsworth again, she becomes a successful teacher. The most significant of the doublings between the two figures occurs, finally, in terms of sexual taste. What makes Frances seem 'for a sensualist – charmless', is what defines her, for Crimsworth, as 'a treasure' (p. 168). As the 'personification ... of self-denial and self-control' (p. 169), Crimsworth's 'best object' (p. 168) reflects back to him the qualities which are the 'guardians' and 'trusty keepers' of his own sexuality and integral, for a middle-class Victorian ideology, to 'the sanctuary of home' (p. 169).

As Crimsworth's double, however, Frances necessarily also reproduces, rather than resolves, the sexual contradictions by which he is beset. In her culturally hybrid status as the daughter of an English mother and a French-speaking Swiss father, she is a living embodiment of the conflict between the sexual restraint and sexual excess associated, in this text, with English and French/continental identities, respectively. Crimsworth's insistence at the beginning of the first of their 'conferences' (p. 138), that Frances 'keep to English' (p. 139), instead of lapsing into the French which is her penchant, is thus not simply the sign of a certain linguistic colonization. At the same time, it connotes a drive not only to quarantine Frances from the rabidly libidinized bodies of her classmates but also to rid 'that Genevese girl' (p. 176), as she is at one point called, of the sexuality Crimsworth strives to exile from himself. The prosecution of such sexually repressive policies under the guise of linguistic instruction is at its clearest in the moment of Crimsworth's marriage proposal. Even as he acknowledges that French is 'the language of [Frances's] own heart' (p. 216), he none the less demands, once again, that she 'Speak English' when replying to the offer of his hand. By the same token, in agreeing to 'pass her life' (p. 224) with Crimsworth, Frances, in the same breath, also consents to a different kind of passing: as wife and mother, she will continue to play the role of the 'well-educated lady in Essex or Middlesex' (p. 126) for whom Crimsworth, on first hearing her voice, had mistaken her. This masquerade extends even to the point, it seems, of learning 'how to make a cup of tea in rational English style' (p. 246).

By means of the disciplinary techniques of a pedagogy and courtship often indistinguishable from one another, Crimsworth would appear to have refined his 'young Genevese' (p. 252) into an ideally desexualized partner. Yet the prospect of marriage to the 'serviceable' (p. 217) Frances works, paradoxically, only to uncover the sexual degradation he both fears in himself and projects onto others. Following their betrothal, Crimsworth uncharacteristically confesses that he appreciates Frances not only because of her 'mental points', her intellectual and moral virtues, but also for 'the graces of her person', even endowing her with the 'well-set teeth' previously seen, in the 'Maroon'-like Caroline, to be the mark of a racialized sexuality. Recognizing that he derives 'a pleasure purely material' from Frances's 'delicate form', he is forced into belated acknowledgement of the similarities between himself and those he otherwise detests – Pelet, his schoolgirls, Zoraïde: 'It appeared then, that I too was a sensualist, in my temperate and fastidious way.'

The signs of Crimsworth's sensuality are subsequently manifested in the erotic fantasies precipitated by thoughts of carnal union with Frances in marriage. Although these fantasies are textually censored, they are deducible from the nocturnal restlessness which takes hold of Crimsworth as the immediate result of securing Frances as wife. As he returns to his rooms and tries to sleep, Crimsworth discovers that the 'sweet delirium' of 'the last few hours' (p. 227) will not 'subside' and continues, indeed, 'till long after midnight' to break his 'rest' with 'troubled ecstacy'. What he also discovers, however, is that sleep itself is the means by which his troubles only ramify:

> At last I dozed, but not for long; it was yet quite dark when I awoke and my waking was like that of Job when a spirit passed before his face, and like him, 'The hair of my flesh stood up.' I might continue the parallel, for in truth, though I saw nothing yet 'A thing was secretly brought unto me, and mine ear received a little thereof; there was silence and I heard a voice,' saying:
> 'In the midst of Life, we are in Death.'   (p. 228)

While Crimsworth's sudden 'waking' propels him into identification with the biblical Job, the terms in which he couches his return to consciousness bring it into 'parallel' with a different kind of arousal. The implication, crude but coded, is that it is not just '"The hair of [his] flesh"' but the 'flesh' itself that 'st[ands] up' here. The language spoken by the hallucinatory 'voice' is similarly risqué in its combination of climactic pleasure with extinction. Its death-in-life ejaculation is a *double entendre*, hinting at the discharge in the 'midst' of whose occurrence Crimsworth, on stirring, is alarmed to find himself located.

Crimsworth's elided dream of Frances is thus adulterated by the vagaries of the masturbatory body. This is a reading confirmed by the manner in which his nocturnal ordeals develop, as the sexual intimacies he both anticipates and prematurely enjoys effect a disruptive return of the past upon the present. In one of *The Professor*'s strangest and most haunting sequences, Crimsworth describes how, in the aftermath to his solitary blisses, he feels his 'chamber invaded by one [he] had known formerly, but had thought for ever departed'. Identifying this revenant as the feminized figure of 'Hypochondria', he goes on to detail their first encounters:

> She had been my acquaintance, nay my guest, once before in boyhood; I had entertained her at bed and board for a year; for that space of time I had her to myself in secret; she lay with me, she eat with me, she walked out with me, shewing me nooks in woods, hollows in hills, where we could sit together, and where she could drop her drear veil over me, and so hide sky and sun, grass and green tree; taking me entirely to her death-cold bosom, and holding me with arms of bone. What tales she would tell me, at such hours! What songs she would recite in my ears! How she would discourse to me of her own Country – The Grave – and again and again promise to conduct me there erelong; and drawing me to the very brink of a black, sullen river, shew me on the other side, shores unequal with mound, monument and tablet, standing up in a glimmer more hoary than moonlight. 'Necropolis!' she would whisper, pointing to the pale piles, and add 'It contains a mansion, prepared for you.' (p. 228)

As both Azim and Shuttleworth suggest, the 'Hypochondria' which 'accost[s]' Crimsworth '*now*' and '*then*' (p. 229; emphases in original) is a symptom whose aetiology, in contemporary medical discourse, is frequently linked, precisely, to the practice of masturbation.[26] Just as it is in the nature of the symptom both to disguise and disclose its cause, so Crimsworth's prose might be said to operate in terms of a symptomatic logic. This is evidenced by the way that the specifically sexual nature of the hidden origin from which his condition first arises and then recurs is flagrantly exhibited by the language in which the condition itself is articulated. In both its past and present incarnations, 'Hypochondria' figures as mistress. As the 'acquaintance, nay ... guest' of Crimsworth's pubescence, she is pursued and possessed in 'secret' across a range of erogenous zones. These stretch from domestic locations ('bed and board') to the wilder scenes of 'nooks in woods' and 'hollows in hills' which themselves map out, in Shuttleworth's phrase, 'the symbolic terrain of the female body'.[27] Similarly, on her subsequent advent, 'Hypochondria' takes the form of 'a dreaded and ghastly concubine coming to embitter a husband's heart towards his young bride'. As if to underwrite the continuity between past and present, her second coming is stimulated by the anonymous 'caress of a soft hand' (p. 229). Is this the 'hand' of marriage or masturbation, belonging to Frances or to Crimsworth?

The Professor's own 'discourse' on 'Hypochondria' is consistent with contemporary medical assumptions about the deleterious effects of masturbation upon the male subject.[28] Even as Crimsworth remembers himself as initially enjoying his symptom, 'Hypochondria' is soon revealed to be an agent of destruction rather than *jouissance*, or rather destruction through *jouissance*. She is less mistress than femme fatale and, ultimately, grave-tender. The 'Necropolis' to which she threatens finally to 'conduct' her young charge is a concrete symbol for the terrifying dead end for which, according to Victorian sexual ideology, the self-abusive male is destined. At the same time, it functions as another site in which the novel's association of sexuality with forms of foreignness is dramatized. By describing 'The Grave' over which 'Hypochondria' presides as 'her own Country', Crimsworth implies that the prospective burial-ground of a misspent youth is located in an alien space or *terra incognita*. His psychic geography is further exoticized by 'Hypochondria''s second visit, in which she takes the form of 'concubine'. In this latter guise, she seems much like one of the 'oriental odalisques' (p. 26) with whom Hunsden associates aristocratic women in chapter 3. More disturbingly, she seems, also, to resemble the Zoraïde whom Crimsworth has renounced for Frances and whose 'soft step' leads out towards an Oriental space.

After some nine days of struggle against his 'evil spirit', Crimsworth begins slowly to regain his equilibrium and, within a 'fortnight', declares himself fit to 'seek Frances and sit at her side' once more. Yet even as he resists the 'sway' of his foreign cum Oriental 'demon' (p. 229), Crimsworth's married life with Frances is not quite patterned according to the symmetry of mutual restraint for which he might have hoped. Much to his chagrin, it bears a somewhat closer resemblance to the adulterous geometry of the 'Modern French novel' (p. 187) in which he suspects Zoraïde will entangle him after her marriage to Pelet. For in Frances, Crimsworth seems, as he puts it, 'to possess two wives' (p. 250). Moving from English to French, Frances simultaneously translates herself across the fragile border between sexual self-control and sexual excess. Her mimicry of Crimsworth, that 'man of regular life and rational mind' (p. 159), is also a mockery:

> Talk French to me she would, and many a punishment she has had for her wilfulness – I fear the choice of chastisement must have been injudicious, for instead of correcting the fault, it seemed to encourage its renewal. . . . In those moments ... she would shew me what she had of vivacity, of mirth, of originality in her well-dowered nature. She would shew too some stores of raillery, of 'malice', and would vex, tease, pique me sometimes about what she called my 'bizarreries anglaises', my 'caprices insulaires', with a wild and witty wickedness that made a perfect white demon of her while it lasted. This was rare, however, and the elfish freak was always short: sometimes when driven a little hard in the war of words, for her tongue did ample justice to the pith, the point, the delicacy of her native French, in which language she always attacked me – I used to turn upon her with my old decision, and arrest bodily the sprite that teased me. Vain idea! no sooner had I grasped hand or arm, than the elf was gone; the provocative smile quenched in the expressive brown eyes, and a ray of gentle homage shone under the lids in its place: I had seized a mere vexing fairy and found a submissive and supplicating little mortal woman in my arms. Then I made her get a book, and read English to me for an hour by way of penance. I frequently dosed her with Wordsworth in this way and Wordsworth steadied her soon.   (pp. 252–3)

In this long passage, language is the sado-masochistic medium in which questions of sexuality, nation and race are fused. When Frances 'Talk[s] French' to her husband, she disrupts the 'illusion' Crimsworth has carefully built around her. On these occasions, she behaves less like the 'fair-complexioned, English-looking girl' (p. 174) of his repressive fantasies than the 'arrant coquettes' (p. 95) of the daymares suffered at Zoraïde's school. Such linguistic lapses are also implicitly sexual ones, as Frances unnervingly changes from angel in the house to 'perfect white demon'.

In the 'war of words' between husband and wife, Crimsworth will always be the loser, not least because the language in which he recounts their struggle is, as much as Frances and her aggressively capable 'tongue', beyond his control. This loss of linguistic mastery is marked in two ways, the first of which relates to the glaring contradiction underpinning Crimsworth's marital pedagogy. By being compelled to 'read English ... for an hour' and 'frequently dosed ... with Wordsworth', Frances, Crimsworth claims, is 'steadied ... soon'. But this itself is surely an unsound assertion, since it has already been conceded that 'the choice of chastisement' is 'injudicious' and 'correcting the fault' of Frances's linguistic and sexual orientations merely 'encourage[s] its renewal'. The authority of Frances's embattled 'English professor' (p. 252) is challenged, secondly, by the silent misdemeanours of allusion. While Frances earlier consciously rewrites *Othello* with 'parts ... reversed', Crimsworth here rehearses Shakespeare's play with the main roles more conventionally, if unconsciously, distributed, as the striking disciplinary failures of his marriage parallel those of Othello's relation to Desdemona (whose own character, race and name are respectively echoed in the figuring of Frances as 'perfect white demon'). According to Stephen J. Greenblatt, 'rather than confirming male authority, [Desdemona's] submission eroticizes everything to which it responds', including even the 'mistreatment'[29] she receives from her husband. As she herself muses, confiding to Emilia: 'My love doth so approve [Othello] / That even his stubbornness, his checks, his frowns – / Prithee, unpin me – have grace and favour in them'.[30] In the same way, the 'punishment', in the shape of Wordsworth, to which Crimsworth resorts simply results in further wrongdoing, making him the victim of an irony that is, in fact, Shakespearean.

In the novel's closing scenes, Crimsworth, now permanently resident with his family in England, turns his attentions, and the reader's, towards the question of his son. Victor, 'soon [to] go to Eton' (p. 265), like his father before him, is a figure stranger even than that child of 'strange hybrid race' who, as Hunsden speculates, is the potential 'progeny' (p. 203) of Zoraïde's marriage to Pelet. There is, his father complains:

> a something in Victor's temper, a kind of electrical ardour and power, which emits, now and then, ominous sparks – Hunsden calls it his spirit and says it should not be curbed – I call it the leaven of the offending Adam and consider that it should be if not *whipped* out of him, at least soundly disciplined, and that he will be cheap of any amount of either bodily or mental suffering which will ground him radically in the art of self-control.   (p. 266; emphasis in original)

In figuring the 'something in Victor's temper' as 'the leaven of the offending Adam', Crimsworth diagnoses in his son a condition that covers a multitude of sins, ranging from the vices of a generalized carnality to the more personal falls of his own 'boyhood'. From this perspective, the 'sparks' periodically emitted by Victor are 'ominous' indeed: they are the first signs of an implicit sexual impurity that is the mark, in turn, of national and racial infections. Victor must be 'soundly disciplined', body and mind, in order that his Englishness, already compromised by the line of a double-speaking mother, be duly insulated against further violations.

With its closing vision of a supererogatory paternal violence, *The Professor* draws slavery and sexuality together, as Crimsworth condones extreme 'bodily [and] mental suffering' as the means necessary to schooling his son in the dubious 'art of self-control'. At the same time, this fearful vision brings Brontë's novel back to its narrative point of departure, since Victor is to be exposed to these forbidding disciplinary regimes at Eton, his father's alma mater, and thus cloned or customized, in effect, in Crimsworth's image. The novel's circularity is not just a matter of narrative structure, though, but also figurative. As if in a somewhat unconvincing linguistic exhibition of his own proficient self-mastery, Crimsworth magnanimously stops short of casting the ill-named Victor as literal whipping-boy. Even so, the generally sadistic terms in which the son's future is set forth by the father work to recall the language of slavery on which *The Professor* relies elsewhere, particularly in its earlier stages. They also look forward to *Jane Eyre,* Brontë's next novel, where such a language is more fully, and indeed more self-consciously, elaborated.

4

'Incongruous Unions': Slavery and the Politics of Metaphor in *Jane Eyre*

> Oh the horrors of slavery! – How the thought of it pains my heart! But the truth ought to be told of it; and what my eyes have seen I think it is my duty to relate; for few people in England know what slavery is. I have been a slave – I have felt what a slave feels, and I know what a slave knows; and I would have all the good people in England to know it too, that they may break our chains, and set us free.
>
> Mary Prince, *The History of Mary Prince*, p. 21

> Metaphor, in fact, is never an innocent figure of speech.
>
> Alain Robbe Grillet, *Snapshots and Towards a New Novel*, p. 78

In what remains the classic feminist reading of *Jane Eyre*, Sandra M. Gilbert and Susan Gubar argue that Charlotte Brontë's novel is in large measure an expression of a 'rebellious feminism'.[1] For these critics, as for many other Anglo-American feminists, Jane Eyre's story provides 'a pattern for countless others'.[2] It is a tale, they say:

> of enclosure and escape, a distinctively female *Bildungsroman* in which the problems of the protagonist as she struggles from the imprisonment of her childhood toward an almost unthinkable goal of mature freedom are symptomatic of difficulties Everywoman in a patriarchal society must meet and overcome ... . Most important, her confrontation, not with Rochester but with Rochester's mad wife Bertha, is the book's central confrontation, an encounter ...

79

not with her own sexuality but with her own imprisoned 'hunger, rebellion, and rage,' a secret dialogue of self and soul on whose outcome ... the novel's plot, Rochester's fate, and Jane's coming-of-age all depend.[3]

These comments are themselves symptomatic, ironically, of one of the difficulties underlying the analysis in which they occur. The casual troping of Brontë's protagonist as 'Everywoman' performs a kind of racial legerdemain, by which a female narrative of oppression and resistance which is distinctively English (and for the most part lower middle class) becomes silently representative of women's experience as a whole. To view the eponymous narrator-heroine of Brontë's novel as somehow universally normative is at the same time for criticism to suggest a certain blindness with regard to female histories which are racially and culturally other.[4]

In *Jane Eyre*, such histories are most obviously, if ambiguously, woven around the figure of Bertha Mason, the Creole heiress whom Rochester marries, for financial gain, in Jamaica and subsequently transports (following the onset of her supposed madness) to England, imprisoning her in the third-storey attic of Thornfield Hall for some ten years. Precisely as a Creole, Bertha's presence in the text is intriguingly equivocal. In its nineteenth-century context, the term can refer equally to persons born and naturalized in the West Indies of either European or African descent, having, as the *OED* emphatically declares, 'no connotation of colour'.[5] Whatever the exact nature of Bertha's racial identity, her inclusion in *Jane Eyre* is something which Gilbert and Gubar seem to want to resist. This resistance takes the form of an interpretative strategy which resolutely denies Bertha's status as an autonomous subject in Brontë's novel, favouring, instead, a psycho-feminist emphasis on her role as the metaphorical expression of Jane's own unconscious desires and discontents. Bertha thus becomes 'Jane's truest and darkest double: she is the angry aspect of the orphan child, the ferocious secret self Jane has been trying to repress ever since her days at Gateshead'.[6] While Jane is constructed as 'Everywoman', Bertha figures, or is figured, here, as her 'double' or alter ego. In this way, the racial and cultural differences she embodies are effectively erased, together with their ambiguities.[7]

Gilbert and Gubar's reading of the 'central confrontation' in *Jane Eyre* along these lines is, it is true, one which Brontë's text appears openly to encourage through its fabrication of numerous parallels and correspondences between Jane and Bertha from first to last. As Laura E. Donaldson has argued, however, the consequences of such a reading, both methodologically and politically, are highly disconcerting and themselves to be read as the effects of what she calls a critical 'Miranda Complex'. Donaldson develops this notion from an early exchange in William Shakespeare's *The Tempest* in which Miranda declines Prospero's invitation to visit the enslaved Caliban by saying, ''Tis a villain, sir, / I do not love to look on'.[8] For Donaldson, Miranda's aversion of her gaze from Caliban is replicated in the exemplary failure of Gilbert and Gubar to address issues of slavery, colonialism and race in *Jane Eyre*, as in nineteenth-century women's texts in general. Worse still, the very critics who see Bertha as Jane's 'secret self' find themselves simultaneously locked into an ironic repetition of the workings of patriarchal oppression within the text they read. Just as Rochester literally and figuratively shuts up his first wife at Thornfield so, as Donaldson puts it, 'Gilbert and Gubar's interpretation of Bertha ... not only imprisons her within the privatistic cell of Jane's psyche, but also deprives her of any independent textual significance'.[9]

In maintaining a certain silence with regard to *Jane Eyre*'s submerged colonial dimensions, Gilbert and Gubar might be said to collude with the text itself and its own historical evasions. For, despite the pivotal and determinant role of the West Indies in *Jane Eyre* in terms of the narrative and economic fortunes of its major characters, Brontë's text nowhere explicitly refers to the institution of British slavery or the colonial project with which, for the early Victorian reader, the West Indies would be strongly associated. But if the subject of British colonial slavery is elided by *Jane Eyre*, it is none the less visible discursively, in terms, that is, of the language through which Brontë's heroine characteristically organizes and represents her experience. While the novel's autobiographical conventions presuppose an emphasis on the personal, Brontë's text also offers a powerful analysis of larger socio-economic structures in England during the first half of the nineteenth century, focusing upon the aspirations of lower middle-class women, such as Jane, in particular. This concern with forms of domestic oppression created by gender and class is, paradoxically, the vehicle for the return of the colonial, as Brontë's novel formulates its critique of gender and class relations by means of an habitual recourse to a metaphorical language of enslavement and mastery.

The play of absence and presence surrounding slavery in *Jane Eyre* is reminiscent, of course, of *The Professor*. As with the earlier novel, what needs to be borne in mind here is the double-ness or reversibility of the rhetorical tendencies which *Jane Eyre* displays. On the one hand, the novel's articulation of domestic oppression in terms of slavery is a kind of shock-tactic, designed to move the reader into a dramatic awareness of the severity of particular conditions of disempowerment existing at home. On the other, the simultaneous counter-effect is to lessen and disguise the realities of slavery. For this latter reason, *Jane Eyre* emerges as a text in which, to modify the terms of this chapter's second epigraph, the guilt of metaphor is liable to be particularly acute. This proves, indeed, to be the case, as evidenced by the novel's unfolding as a double inscription. *Jane Eyre* does not only exploit the slave trope for its own purposes but also simultaneously comments upon and critiques its rhetorical procedures and the political problems they entail. In this sense, Brontë's text significantly differs from even as it repeats *The Professor*, subjecting the language of slavery to a much greater degree of questioning.

Metaphors of slaves and masters

The first sign of such questioning comes in the shape of an allusion to William Makepeace Thackeray offered in the Preface to the second edition of Brontë's novel. Thackeray, according to the enthusiastic Preface-writer, is 'the very master of that working corps who would restore to rectitude the warped system of things', the immediate stimulus for such a complimentary judgement being Thackeray's *Vanity Fair* (serialized 1847–8). No sooner is Thackeray figured as 'master', however, than he is implicitly disfigured: it turns out, in the end, that 'no commentator on his writings has yet found the comparison that suits him, the terms which rightly characterize his talent',[10] a claim which, strictly speaking, must embrace the one who makes it, Brontë herself.

Such a prefatory play of figuration and disfiguration is, in terms of *Jane Eyre* as a whole, a telling one. Positing and then revoking the representation of Thackeray as 'master', Brontë's Preface marks out for itself a subtle distance from the rhetorical idiom which dominates the novel. This linguistic self-questioning is underscored in more general terms by the problematic status of the address to Thackeray itself. Having dedicated *Jane Eyre*'s second edition to her fellow-author, Brontë comes soon to discover the existence of a certain 'coincidence ... equally unfortunate and extraordinary'[11] between Thackeray's own marital circumstances and Rochester's. The two figures, the real and the fictional, become weirdly compounded. Thus, by a rueful and bizarre intersection of fiction and biography, the disfiguring of Thackeray's mastery itself implies a questioning of the figurative status comparably accorded throughout the novel to Rochester (he is invariably Jane's 'master') and hence an unsettling also of that position as slave adopted by Jane herself.

The Thackeray/Rochester relationship leads on to the narrative itself. Having 'drawn parallels in silence', the 10-year-old Jane is subsequently provoked into hyperbolic utterance of them, at the end of the novel's first chapter, by the physical violence of John Reed: '"Wicked and cruel boy!" I said. "You are like a murderer – you are like a slave-driver – you are like the Roman emperors!"' (p. 11). The significance of this incident lies not only in the fleeting parallels it advances between domestic oppression and slavery but also in its linkage of the very creation of such parallels (even in the lesser mode of simile, as opposed to metaphor) with transgression – Jane's outburst being, as it is, part of that 'moment's mutiny' (p. 12) directly leading to her incarceration in the red-room in the next chapter. At a narrative or thematic level, the red-room functions as punishment for female defiance of patriarchy: Mrs Reed offers to 'liberate' Jane from its terrors 'only on condition of perfect submission and stillness' (p. 18). At the same time, Jane's punishment works to dramatize the text's recognition of the transgressiveness of its own linguistic actions. It is almost as if the speaking 10-year-old were a kind of preliminary 'scape-goat' (p. 16) for her later writing self.

During her sojourn in the red-room, the young Jane is represented by her older narrating self as a 'rebel slave' (p. 12) and, again, as a 'slave' who has 'revolted' (p. 15). The effect of such self-figurations is to mystify, through language, those hierarchies of racial difference on which slavery is predicated. Perhaps this is why the 'looking-glass' (p. 14) scene in the red-room is also a scene of failed self-recognition? For the young Jane to grasp 'the strange little figure there gazing at [her], with a white face and arms specking the gloom' (p. 15) as her own reflection would also be for the narrative to expose the ways in which its rhetoric works to slight the differences of race.

While such an exposure is symbolically avoided by Jane's failed self-recognition in the mirror, it is effected in another way, since the divisions between oppressor and oppressed, the Reeds and Jane, are indeed mapped in terms of racial difference: 'I was a discord in Gateshead Hall: I was like nobody there: I had nothing in harmony with Mrs. Reed or her children', Jane comments. She is 'a heterogeneous thing ... a useless thing' (p. 16) and forced, consequently, to concede the improbability of gaining affection from Mrs Reed, who could not, Jane comes to realize, 'really like an interloper not of her race' or 'an uncongenial alien permanently intruded on her own family group' (p. 17).[12]

By means of the identification of slavery with racial otherness, these reflections reinscribe the differences which *Jane Eyre*'s use of slavery as metaphor implicitly works to obscure. They function, that is, to bring to light, and into question, the political implications of the novel's central rhetorical devices and are thus part of the critique to which the text subjects itself. This is evidenced also in Jane's self-description as a 'thing', a linguistic turn giving rise to a striking paradox. On the one hand, the reified status Jane ascribes to herself is one experienced by the enslaved black subject through the fact of his or her body being legally defined as the property of another, the white master. Yet the very condition which is synonymous with the negation of black subjectivity precisely affords the figurative materials out of which the novel's narrator comes into possession of her own identity. As female autobiography, *Jane Eyre* constitutes a form of fictional self-empowerment, enabling Jane to assume that position as subject traditionally denied to women by the codes of Victorian patriarchy. The text's empowerments remain problematic, however, because of the rhetorical strategies in which they are implicated.

This is a point also borne out in terms of the structure of metaphor. For Eric Cheyfitz, the Aristotelian definition is 'still basic'.[13] According to this definition: 'Metaphor consists in giving the thing a name that belongs to something else; the transference being either from genus to species, or from species to genus, or from species to species, or on grounds of analogy.'[14] Metaphor becomes a scene of redistribution wherein a word which is by convention the property of one thing is assigned to 'something else'. From this perspective, the very form of metaphor recapitulates the material relations of colonial history as they are articulated in the transference of the enslaved body from Africa to the New World and from its rightful owner to the white master. The historically specific referent from which *Jane Eyre* holds back in literal terms is thus not only alluded to by the text's figurative language but also appears to inhabit its structures.

The transferences of metaphor (translated by the classical rhetorician, Quintilian, as *translatio* or 'carrying over'),[15] constitute a re-enactment of history in another way, which is illuminated by means of Paul Ricœur's observation (extending Aristotle), that metaphor is 'doubly alien'.[16] It is, in Patricia Parker's glossing of Ricœur, 'a name that belongs elsewhere and one which takes the place of the word which "belongs"'.[17] In *Jane Eyre* the transferences are from the colonial to the domestic, West Indian slavery to oppression within the metropolis – a movement scrupulously figured, or logged, by the text in Rochester's account of his return to Thornfield from Jamaica with the 'mad' Bertha: 'To England, then, I conveyed her: a fearful voyage I had with such a monster in the vessel' (p. 326). None the less, the above description of metaphor (a word whose origins are 'elsewhere' which 'takes the place' of one which 'belongs') suggests once again how linguistic structure can rehearse colonial history, with its own usurpations of the native by the foreign.

The notion of metaphor as place-taking provides an apposite perspective from which to view *Jane Eyre* because the events occurring in the novel seem themselves to be largely ordered in terms of a logic of substitution. Mrs Reed 'must stand in the stead of a parent' (p. 17) to the orphaned Jane at Gateshead who, given her status as heterogeneous 'interloper' or intrusive 'alien', herself begins to seem like a strangely metaphorical figure. This impression is one confirmed in the novel's second phase at Lowood school. At the end of volume 1, chapter 5, Jane's companion at the school, Helen Burns, is unfairly 'dismissed in disgrace ... from a history class, and sent to stand in the middle of the large schoolroom' (p. 54). Two chapters later, her place has been taken by Jane, publicly punished by Mr Brocklehurst, equally arbitrarily, it seems, for her alleged compulsion to lie by being made to stand upon a stool 'in the middle of the room ... exposed to general view on a pedestal of infamy'. Though the narrator claims that 'no language can describe' the 'sensations' this incident instils in her, it is not long before the text resumes its familiar idiom, sliding from simile to metaphor:

> just as they all rose, stifling my breath and constricting my throat, a girl came up and passed me: in passing, she lifted her eyes. What a strange light inspired them! What an extraordinary sensation that ray sent through me! How the new feeling bore me up! It was as if a martyr, a hero, had passed a slave or victim, and imparted strength in the transit. I mastered the rising hysteria, lifted my head, and took a firm stand on the stool. (p. 70)

While Helen's otherworldly gaze eventually stabilizes Jane, it is not before it has also revealed, 'in passing', how something as apparently personal and localized as the self's relationship to its own body is typically to be rendered, throughout *Jane Eyre*, in terms of a shifting rhetoric of colonial struggle: the body threatens to make the self the 'slave' to a 'rising hysteria' and must be 'mastered' accordingly.

The hystericized body can either enslave the self through rage, or be enslaved by it, through spiritual repression. Though it is not only the female but also the male body which is prone to the latter effect,[18] the suggestion of the text – in figuring control over the body as 'mastery' – is that to lose such control, becoming enslaved to the somatic, is also to be 'feminized', occupying what patriarchal ideology defines as the place of a woman. Similarly, the extended burden of *Jane Eyre* is that to be a woman under patriarchy, whether governess, lover, mistress or wife, is to have the place of a slave. Of the numerous passages illustrating this point, one which is particularly relevant to the concerns of this reading occurs during the period of the lovers' engagement. Here Jane's evasions of Rochester's sexuality cause him to remind her of its imminent marital assertion:

> 'it is your time now, little tyrant, but it will be mine presently; and when once I have fairly seized you, to have and to hold, I'll just – figuratively speaking – attach you to a chain like this' (touching his watch-guard). (pp. 283–4)

Like Rochester, the text speaks 'figuratively', using the slave idiom as a polemical means by which to mark out the limits of possibility for nineteenth-century women. Rochester's linguistic self-consciousness is momentary and bland, however, while that of

Brontë's text is sustained and critical, a constant underlining of limits and problems.

The way in which relationships between the figures at the narrative level of Brontë's novel enact the metaphorical play within it becomes particularly noticeable during the long central section at Thornfield. Here, for example, Grace Poole recurrently figures, in Jane's bewildered view, as a stand-in for Bertha as the agent of domestic violence.[19] Correlatively, the role adopted by Blanche Ingram, especially with regard to the charade sequence where she acts out 'the pantomime of a marriage' (p. 192) with Rochester as pretend groom, has the effect of making her a double stand-in with respect to Bertha and Jane alike. For both of the latter figures, in their different ways, are drawn into weddings with Rochester which are themselves mere mockeries (Bertha in Spanish Town, Jamaica and Jane at Thornfield, 15 years later). By the same token, Blanche stands in for herself because her position as mock-bride in the charades is a duplication of her status in what passes for the reality beyond them.

The most important example of the workings of the characterological relationships in the text as a figuring of metaphor is that between Jane and Bertha. This relationship can be defined as a play of reversible substitution. For Gilbert and Gubar, Bertha's function is to assume the tasks of a kind of psychic and ultimately suicidal stunt-woman:

> Jane's profound desire to destroy Thornfield, the symbol of Rochester's mastery and of her own servitude, will be acted out by Bertha, who burns down the house and destroys *herself* in the process as if she were an agent of Jane's desire as well as her own.[20]

Equally, however, Brontë's novel can be viewed as the drive, finally achieved in the last chapter, to put Jane in Bertha's place as wife to Rochester. Yet the plot resolution is anti-climactic, a 'quiet wedding' indeed, which not even the narratorial nudge of 'Reader, I married him' (p. 473) can much enliven. The eventual marital place-taking comes to be displaced, ironically marginalized by the earlier scene of its not taking place, at the end of volume 2.

As the substitution of one woman for another, Rochester's attempted marriage to Jane at this point is evidently arranged on the basis of her differences from Bertha. These, in Rochester's estimation, are considerable. Jane, he declares, is 'something at least human', while Bertha constitutes a 'bad, mad, and embruted partner!' (p. 306). He drives the point home a little later:

> 'That is *my wife*,' said he. ... 'And *this* is what I wished to have ... this young girl, who stands so grave and quiet at the mouth of hell, looking collectedly at the gambols of a demon. I wanted her just as a change after that fierce ragout. ... look at the difference! Compare these clear eyes with the red balls yonder – this face with that mask – this form with that bulk.'   (p. 308; emphases in original)

In so far as metaphor, the figure of speech which centrally enables *Jane Eyre* to articulate its domestic critique, is self-consciously re-enacted at the level of narrative, the status of Brontë's heroine as absolutely other to Bertha ('the antipodes of the Creole', p. 328) might seem to create a contradiction. How can the projected marriage be viewed as a staging of metaphor when, on the one hand, the substitutions it involves are marked by radical difference while, on the other, those of the Aristotelian transference demand an analogical ground? Such an apparent difficulty is, however, exactly why the suspended union between Jane and Rochester can be seen in the way suggested. The 'impediment' (p. 303) placed against the marriage functions as the sign of the text's own unspoken but none the less 'pronounced objection' (p. 309) to the figurative policies which it seeks to implement – the representation of modes of domestic oppression in terms of slavery. The charade of marriage at the end of volume 2 is indeed a pantomime of metaphor but in a way which discloses *Jane Eyre*'s anxieties about the dubiety of its own tropological compulsions.

That the text's revelation of its narrative mysteries is also a metaphor for the exposure of rhetorical secrets is underscored by the language describing Jane's, and the reader's, first formal introduction to Bertha. This occurs in the recesses of what is, in a felicitous pun, both Thornfield's and the novel's 'third story' (p. 191): 'In the deep shade, at the further end of the room, a figure ran backwards and forwards' (p. 307). Narrative and rhetorical modes come together here as Bertha's movements suggest, by inversion, the oscillations of the slave trope itself. The figure of slavery moves forward from colonial to domestic worlds, in *Jane Eyre*, as a means of highlighting forms of oppression at home even as, once again, such a movement can only culminate in its own undoing, shifting the reader's attention back from the domestic to the colonial context from which the figure emanates. This pattern gives rise to a vantage from which a subsequent return to the realm of the domestic can occur, whose own effect is to bring the political dangers of the slave trope into focus: while it is integral to *Jane Eyre*'s ideological critique, the language of slavery purchases its effects at the expense of a veiling of the history of colonial oppression which is its literal ground.

Rebellions

For Gilbert and Gubar, Bertha's destructive impulses – directed as they are against men (Rochester and Richard Mason, her brother) as against marriage and Thornfield itself – enact Jane's own 'secret fantasies',[21] the 'fire and violence' (p. 251) of her rage against patriarchal oppression. Yet the third of Bertha's actions (there being five in all)[22] suggests not only the limits of such a reading but also provides a particularly spectacular illustration of the ways in which *Jane Eyre* sets its own rhetorical operations in question.

This action involves the tearing of Jane's wedding-veil two nights before the scheduled marriage to Rochester and is recounted in detail in volume 2, chapter 10. While the veil is, as Adrienne Rich notes, a 'symbol of matrimony',[23] it is also the sign of Rochester's economic power. Purchased in London with 'princely extravagance' (p. 294) for a reluctant bride, it consequently functions as an oblique token for slavery, the source from which Rochester's 'English gold' (p. 146), like Jane's own inheritance, is derived. Thus to read its destruction in solely patriarchal terms is, in a metaphorical sense, critically to mend the veil, covering over the question of colonialism which *Jane Eyre* itself chooses to put aside.

In terms of the evasiveness of Brontë's novel towards the truth of British colonial slavery in the West Indies, the moment of Bertha's veil-tearing can be viewed as a model of what the text consistently fails to do, preferring to manipulate colonialism-as-figure rather than represent it directly. Indeed, in those moments when the language of enslavement is made culturally specific (as in volume 2, chapter 9, for example), it is in a way that lures the reader beyond British frames of reference, safely transporting the material realities of slave-oppression and rebellion into Oriental contexts (pp. 281–2).

However, it is not only that colonialism (literally absent at one level) is transformed by *Jane Eyre* into a consequential presence at another, that of figuration, but that it is also figured by Brontë's text. At one point, Jane deems herself to be 'purposely excluded' from the 'mystery at Thornfield' (p. 174). Yet the irony is that in one sense Rochester's eventual revelation of his secret only compounds it: as already noted, Bertha's status as a Creole makes the question of her race significantly uncertain. Even so, the suggestively indeterminate nature of Bertha's racial identity (as specified in volume 2, chapter 11 and volume 3, chapter 1) seems, at other junctures, equally suggestively, to be less vague. As Susan Meyer puts it:

> [Bertha] is clearly imagined as white – or as passing for white – in the novel's retrospective narrative. ... But when she actually emerges as a character in the action of the novel, the narrative associates Bertha with blacks, particularly with the black Jamaican anti-slavery rebels, the Maroons. In the form in which she becomes visible in the novel, Bertha has *become* black.[24]

In these terms it can be seen that the targets of Bertha's violence are not exclusively patriarchal: a 'crime' breaking out, 'now in fire and now in blood, at the deadest hours of night' (p. 221) with a 'black and scarlet visage' (p. 327), Bertha is also a figure for colonial rebellion, 'symbolically enacting precisely the sort of revolt feared by the British colonists in Jamaica'[25] in the years of their dominion prior to the writing of *Jane Eyre*.

The subtext of colonial rebellion not only supplements and disrupts feminist constructions of Bertha as patriarchal rebel, but in so doing also helps to reveal the continuing preoccupation of Brontë's novel with the propriety, or otherwise, of its own figurative designs. As one confined to and subversive of what is literally a domestic space (Thornfield), Bertha metaphorizes Jane's own predicament as Englishwoman. Conversely, Bertha is a figure for the very literality (colonialism) Jane exploits as a figurative system through which self-representation is facilitated: Bertha stands in, in other words, for the 'rebel' or 'revolted slave' to whom Jane systematically likens herself (and those like her) throughout the novel. However, the moment of their meeting in volume 2, chapter 10 is implicitly marked by Jane's failure to see the resemblances between Bertha's two roles – as her own patriarchally oppressed double, on the one hand, and as a surrogate for the

victims of colonialism, on the other. Jane's statement of her nocturnal encounter with Bertha is given in a series of exchanges with
Rochester on the next night. Inquiring whether Jane saw the face
of her bedroom-intruder, Rochester prompts the following
dialogue:

> 'Not at first. But presently she took my veil from its place; she held
> it up, gazed at it long, and then she threw it over her own head, and
> turned to the mirror. At that moment I saw the reflection of the
> visage and features quite distinctly in the dark oblong glass.'
> 'And how were they?'
> 'Fearful and ghastly to me – oh, sir, I never saw a face like it! It
> was a discoloured face – it was a savage face. I wish I could forget
> the roll of the red eyes and the fearful blackened inflation of the
> lineaments!'
> 'Ghosts are usually pale, Jane.'
> 'This, sir, was purple: the lips were swelled and dark; the brow
> furrowed; the black eye-brows wildly raised over the bloodshot
> eyes. Shall I tell you of what it reminded me?'
> 'You may.'
> 'Of the foul German spectre – the Vampyre.'
> 'Ah! – What did it do?'
> 'Sir, it removed my veil from its gaunt head, rent it in two parts,
> and flinging both on the floor, trampled on them.'   (p. 297)

As noted above, the division of the veil combines patriarchal with
colonial aggressions. Despite both this, however, and the physiog-
nomic stereotyping of Bertha as black, her 'savage face' is not revealed, in Jane's account, as what it is for Donaldson, the
'rem(a)inder of slavery'.[26] Instead it is reveiled or masked through
a Eurocentric association with 'the foul German spectre – the
Vampyre': in what amounts to a moment of repressive bathos,
Jane precisely fails to see the likeness between Bertha and the
'rebel slave' for which she is the hyperbolic or literally inflated
figure. But since Bertha is also Jane's double, the failure of recognition is itself twofold, a failure to see the very correspondences
between patriarchal and colonial oppression on which, ironically,
Jane's text both insists and relies so fully.

Jane's non-apprehension of Bertha as a figure or counter-double
for the colonial oppression and rebellion in terms of which she ap-
prehends herself provides another instance of her text's scepticism
towards its own rhetorical operations. One of the ironic consequences of this is to suggest the resemblances between Jane and

Bertha. Being the signifier of 'matrimony' on the one hand and slavery on the other, the veil concomitantly signifies precisely the kind of conjunctions which Brontë's text seeks to establish through metaphor. In rending the veil 'from top to bottom in two halves!' (p. 298), Bertha thus aligns herself with the impulses of *Jane Eyre*'s rhetorical self-critique, grounded as it is in a subversive counter-emphasis on the discrepancies rather than similarities between the 'two parts' – domestic and colonial oppression – of the novel's central figure, the master trope of slavery.

With its bafflements and loss of consciousness, the encounter with Bertha recalls the events in the red-room of volume 1, chapter 2, though this time it is a 'savage' rather than a 'white face' – 'a lurid visage' (p. 298) – from which Jane is alienated. The encounter leads briefly back, equally, to the charade-sequence of volume 2, chapter 3, introduced in the following passage:

> Mrs. Fairfax was summoned to give information respecting the resources of the house in shawls, dresses, draperies of any kind; and certain wardrobes of the third story were ransacked, and their contents, in the shape of brocaded and hooped petticoats, satin sacques, black modes [and] lace lappets, &c., were brought down in armfuls by the Abigails: then a selection was made, and such things as were chosen were carried to the boudoir within the drawing-room.   (p. 191)

Notwithstanding the improbable transvestism of Rochester's subsequent appearance as a gipsy-woman, 'almost as black as a crock' (p. 202), these garments are Bertha's – their removal and appropriation to other uses itself a glancing reminder of the relocation of meaning from literal to figurative in *Jane Eyre* as a whole. In volume 2, chapter 10, however, Bertha begins her own charade with a counter-raid on the 'suit of wedding raiment' (p. 288) in Jane's wardrobe, sorting out the veil (manifold symbol of marriage and slavery and marriage-as-slavery) from the rest.

In the act of Bertha's veil-tearing, as in the larger scene in which it occurs, Brontë's text dramatizes a rejection of the very rhetorical operations it brings into play, giving them what Jane calls 'the distinct lie' (p. 298). It is in the context of this kind of textual self-critique that the charade sequence can be situated. What most obviously links these two moments in the text is their common concern with marriage. The first element of the word acted out by

Rochester and his company is 'Bride!' (p. 192), while the 'divining party' is asked to infer the second from a rendering of the biblical scene at the well in which Eliezer recognizes Rebekah as the future wife to Isaac, his master's son.[27] Themselves married together in the '"tableau of the Whole"', the two verbal units spell out Rochester's private meaning, yet in a way which reveals his figurative mode, at this point at least, to be inconsistent with that of the text at large:

> Amidst this sordid scene, sat a man with his clenched hands resting on his knees, and his eyes bent on the ground. I knew Mr. Rochester; though the begrimed face, the disordered dress (his coat hanging loose from one arm, as if it had been almost torn from his back in a scuffle), the desperate and scowling countenance, the rough, bristling hair might well have disguised him. As he moved, a chain clanked: to his wrists were attached fetters.
> 'Bridewell!' exclaimed Colonel Dent, and the charade was solved. (p. 193)

Through the metaphorical pun that turns marriage into a prison (for which 'Bridewell' in the nineteenth century is a synonym), Brontë's text appears indeed momentarily to have liberated itself from the confines of its own rhetorical system. Such an impression is, however, misleading. At some level Rochester is no doubt the victim of the 'steps' (p. 133) taken by his own and Bertha's father in order to procure his fortune. Yet the terms in which he figures this plight could hardly be more questionable: even as Rochester theatricalizes himself as marital prisoner, he stands as Bertha's literal warder, creating for her the material conditions in terms of which he sees himself. The fact subverts the figure.

Structurally, then, the metaphor with which Rochester entertains both himself and the reader (who, apart from the remembering Jane, is its sole audience) only extends the figurative closure which it seems, in terms of content, to transcend. His charade rehearses, in other words, the problems built into the emancipatory strategies of the novel as a whole. As if to confirm this point, the ostensible prisoner seems, from 'begrimed face' to clanking 'chain' and 'fetters', much like a slave in poor disguise. In this way, he illustrates the wrong-headedness of Jane's assumption that the charade is 'solved' with 'Bridewell!' and hence the manner in which meaning escapes the Rochesterean attempt to fix it.[28]

Translations

The discovery of Bertha's place as prisoner at Thornfield causes Jane to lose her own. Leaving Rochester, she embarks upon the desperate moorland journey which leads to the eventual exhausted arrival at Moor House. In the course of her recuperation, Moor House becomes 'more' house, in two senses. Not only does Jane gain the Riverses – St John, Diana and Mary – as her cousins but, through the mutual avuncular link of John Eyre, her fortune also (pp. 396–409). This in turn – through John Eyre's Madeiran connection with Richard Mason, a Jamaican wine-maker – indicates, as Meyer notes, that Jane's wealth, like Rochester's, has colonial origins. As throughout, the colonial realities at the text's 'ravished margin' (p. 401) have, in this phase of the narrative, a centrally figurative function, continuing to dictate Jane's constructions of female possibility. Nowhere is the clash of referential margin against figurative centre sharper than in Jane's struggle to persuade St John that he and his sisters should share her windfall, rather than remain dispersed into hardship. As 'governesses in a large, fashionable, south-of-England city' (p. 371), Diana and Mary are envisaged, for example, as 'slaving amongst strangers' while Jane is 'gorged with gold [she] never earned and [does] not merit!' (p. 408). Similarly, imagining a life as Rochester's mistress in Marseilles turns Jane, at an earlier point, into a 'slave in a fool's paradise' (p. 379), just as, later, she can only contemplate working as a missionary with St John in India if her 'natural ... feelings' remain 'unenslaved' by marriage (p. 429).[29]

St John's missionary ambitions in India indicate *Jane Eyre*'s expansion of its own frame of colonial reference.[30] This broadening of narrative range is accompanied by the incursion into the novel of what Suvendrini Perera calls a 'vocabulary of oriental misogyny'.[31] Such a vocabulary manifests itself in the form, particularly, of a series of figurative allusions to *sati*, a subject with which Brontë had most fully engaged, some five years earlier, in 'Sacrifice of an Indian Widow'. Despite the obvious differences between *Jane Eyre*'s colonial contexts – the West Indies and India – the two none the less become firmly interlocked by the ideological purposes to which Brontë's novel puts them.

The first and most direct of the allusions to *sati* occurs, in fact, prior to St John's emergence in the narrative, in volume 2, chapter 9, while Jane is still at Thornfield. In this chapter, Rochester, 'his face all kindled', serenades her with a song in which he declares, with coercive lyricism: 'My Love has sworn, with sealing kiss, / With me to live – to die!' and, as Jane puts it, talks of 'his future wife dying with him'. The sexual connotations of 'dying' in these erotic exchanges are traditional and obvious, though they are resisted both by Jane's stubborn assertion of the 'right to die' when she rather than Rochester pleases and her dilatory statement that she will 'not be hurried away in a suttee' (p. 286). Here the text uses *sati*, paradoxically, as a metaphor with which to describe marriage, when it literally refers, of course, to the act of suicide the Hindu woman must undertake when she is bereaved by her husband. The implication is clear and startling: marriage is being seen or represented as a kind of living death.

This pattern of allusion is intensified during Jane's sojourn at Moor House. Urged by St John, in volume 3, chapter 8, to 'give up German, and learn Hindostanee' (p. 418), Jane soon enough finds herself 'poring over the crabbed characters and flourishing tropes of an Indian scribe' (p. 421). Yet the figures she reads thrive equally well in the foreign soil of her own writing, as the trope of *sati*, like that of slavery, generates the inscription of the patriarchal and religious oppression of women. In the eyes of St John, Jane's is 'a soul that revel[s] in the flame and excitement of sacrifice'. Such spiritual refinement prompts his proposal (or ultimatum) that she not only support his aims in the role of 'helper amongst Indian women' (p. 425) but do so, moreover, by becoming his wife. Even before she comes to consider the hollow blisses of domestic relations with St John, the prospect of giving assistance to 'Indian women' is figured as *sati*, precisely one of the practices which the nineteenth-century missionary sought to outlaw: 'If I *do* go with him – if I *do* make the sacrifice he urges, I will make it absolutely: I will throw all on the altar – heart, vitals, the entire victim' (p. 426; emphases in original). Marriage to St John, as previously to Rochester, is represented, similarly, as a kind of *sati* from within:

> but as his wife – at his side always, and always restrained, and always checked – forced to keep the fire of my nature continually low, to compel it to burn inwardly and never utter a cry, though the imprisoned flame consumed vital after vital – *this* would be unendurable.   (p. 429; emphasis in original)

At Moor House Brontë's novel mixes its metaphors, *sati* with slavery, in terms of marriage as in other respects.[32] The differences between the colonial spaces from which the metaphors are drawn, as also between the forms of oppression, the histories and cultures with which those spaces are associated, should not be overlooked. On the other hand, it is evident that in this section of the novel, the Orientalist language of *sati* effectively restates (like Rochester's figuring of marriage-as-prison) the problems inherent to the slave trope. *Jane Eyre*, that is, co-opts *sati*, like slavery, as metaphor and channels it into a process of ideological critique at home whose liberative aims are compromised by the discursive re-enactment of the very oppressions which form their enabling ground. It is almost as if the text were translating the dilemma at its tropological heart into another idiom whose limits, risks and delusions are already implied by the original.

Such an effect is not surprising because Moor House is itself a place where translation from and into other languages – German, Hindustani – occurs continually. Translation is indeed the occupation of Diana and Mary during Jane's first uncanny sight of them:

> I had nowhere seen such faces as theirs: and yet, as I gazed on them, I seemed intimate with every lineament. I cannot call them handsome – they were too pale and grave for the word: as they each bent over a book, they looked thoughtful almost to severity. A stand between them supported a ... candle and two great volumes, to which they frequently referred; comparing them seemingly with the smaller books they held in their hands, like people consulting a dictionary to aid them in the task of translation. (p. 350)

Nor is the passage here from the strange to the familiar – 'I had nowhere seen such faces as theirs: and yet ... I seemed intimate with every lineament' – entirely unexpected. Diana and Mary not only relate to Jane as her cousins but also because their 'task of translation' is one upon which she, as a manipulator of metaphor, has been engaged throughout the life of her writing. For Quintilian, metaphor is *translatio*, like translation a form of 'carrying over'. The translator strives to transport meaning intact from one language to another, while in metaphor it is transferred from one level to another, within the same language – the literal to the figurative. Such a metaphorical movement is also, as Cheyfitz points out, a translation from the 'familiar' to the 'foreign',[33] (even as the translation in this particular instance is from foreign to familiar, the German of Schiller's *Die Rauber* to English).[34]

Translation, in this light, can be a figure for metaphor in the same way that metaphor can stand in for translation.

A significant example of the former possibility comes in volume 1, chapter 10, during the transition from Lowood to Thornfield. Having suddenly 'tired of the routine of eight years in one afternoon' (p. 89), Jane resolves to 'get a new place' by advertising her services as a governess in the '—shire Herald' (p. 90). Advertisement is concealment, however, the would-be governess styling herself as 'J. E.', rather than 'Jane Eyre', and citing Lowton post office, rather than Lowood, for an address. The act of acronymic substitution is a kind of translation at one remove: 'Jane Eyre' is an alias for the 'I' which names the self even as the letters which replace it, 'J. E.', spell out that 'I''s foreign counterpart, the French 'Je'. In so far as Jane Eyre's 'I' literally emerges at this point in translation, it enacts a process which in turn provides a figure for *Jane Eyre*'s own self-constitution through metaphor, and its translations of the language of slavery from literal to figurative, colonial to domestic settings. Appropriately, the kind of surveillance under which Brontë's novel places itself also marks the transactions carried out by the anxious post-seeker, 'J. E.': in the course of receiving the reply from Mrs Fairfax which leads Jane on to Thornfield as a governess, she is also twice given an 'inquisitive and mistrustful glance' (p. 92) by the 'old dame' who both runs the post office and hands over the 'document' (p. 91) in question.

Jane Eyre's metaphorical translations are complemented by narrative structure, the series of crossings which take the heroine from place to place: Gateshead to Lowood; Lowood to Thornfield; Thornfield to Moor House; Moor House to Ferndean, as if Jane's life were itself a protracted play, or charade, of metaphor. The final removal, from Moor House to Ferndean, also sees Jane carried across another threshold by dint of the marriage to Rochester originally blocked at the end of the second volume. The earlier débâcle constitutes a narrative inscription of *Jane Eyre*'s misgivings with regard to its own textual strategies. In this light, as one of the 'incongruous unions' (p. 328) to which he refers during his confession to Jane at the beginning of volume 3, Rochester's marriage to Bertha suggests the interesting possibility that a bad match is itself an apposite figure for a suspect metaphor: both involve the joining together of two terms whose similarities cannot offset their differences.

Conversely, Brontë's novel constructs Rochester's relationship to Jane (at least in its ideal form) in terms of what Carolyn Williams calls a 'rhetoric of romantic congruence'.[35] As Williams notes, it is in the proposal scene of volume 2, chapter 8 that such rhetoric is 'most graphic'.[36] Consider, for example, the fraught cries of the following:

> 'Do you think, because I am poor, obscure, plain, and little, I am soulless and heartless? – You think wrong! – I have as much soul as you, – and full as much heart! And if God had gifted me with some beauty, and much wealth, I should have made it as hard for you to leave me, as it is now for me to leave you. I am not talking to you now through the medium of custom, conventionalities, nor even of mortal flesh: – it is my spirit that addresses your spirit; just as if both had passed through the grave, and we stood at God's feet, equal, – as we are!' (pp. 265–6)

As if to authenticate Jane's closing claim, Rochester mirrors its terms: '"My bride is here," he said ... "because my equal is here, and my likeness. Jane, will you marry me?"' (p. 267). Just as the 'rhetoric of romantic congruence' is here a question of the congruence of rhetoric, so the good match is by implication a kind of figuring, displaced into the register of marriage, of the adequation which the text lacks at the level of metaphor. The eventual marriage of Jane and Rochester is similarly displaced into the form of a 'double retirement' (p. 8) to Ferndean. On the one hand, such a conclusion can be seen as a realization of the 'feminist manifesto'[37] outlined in volume 1, chapter 12 where 'women feel just as men feel' (p. 115). Yet, as several critics have observed, such egalitarianism is distinctly asocial.[38] *Jane Eyre* thus ends with the tacit admission that equality between men and women constitutes a sexual utopia which indeed has no place in the realms of the socially real. At the same time, Brontë's novel reaches a conclusion with regard to its own practices at which, from the outset, it seems already to have arrived, suggesting that the kind of rhetorical harmony metaphorized in its lovers' 'perfect concord' is a textual possibility which has always lain out of reach.

However it is construed, the idyllic rapport with which *Jane Eyre* ends appears to preclude any potential imbalance in the power relations between Rochester and Jane, man and wife. The differences between them, it seems, have all but been dissolved: 'No woman was ever nearer to her mate than I am', Jane confidently declares, 'ever more absolutely bone of his bone, and flesh of his flesh'. Equally, though, the text is unable, even in its final pages, quite to shake off its old rhetorical habits. After two years of marriage, Rochester's sight begins slowly to return to one of his eyes, the first object he sees being 'a glittering ornament' (p. 475) around Jane's neck, which, as she informs him, is 'a gold watch-chain' (p. 476). The image of Jane thus bedecked is not entirely reassuring. As well as working to remind the reader of the playful threat Rochester had made during the courtship of his prospective wife – to 'attach [her] to a chain' – the image serves, more broadly, as a kind of signature for the novel's rhetorical strategies as a whole, forging a questionable metaphorical bond, as it were, between white woman and slave.

Such strategies, in their turn, are the sign of *Jane Eyre*'s continuity with *The Professor*. They also partially anticipate Brontë's next novel, *Shirley*, whose conclusion is similarly marked by the figuring of the marriage of its eponymous heroine as a form of slavery. *Shirley*, however, does much more than simply recirculate the rhetorical patterns so self-critically manipulated in *Jane Eyre*, attaching itself to a chain of metaphors already quite substantial. The novel's most salient difference from its predecessor takes the form of a certain shift in the kind of colonial history it comes to negotiate. In the later novel, the concern is not with 'the horrors of slavery' in the West Indies, but with sufferings much closer to home.

5

'Shamrocks and Potatoes': Embodying the Irish Famine in *Shirley*

> Without a doubt, the presentation of Charlotte Brontë's ... work as being related to her Irish heritage is both complicated and complicating. It requires, at a minimum, a spirit of interpretive openness; at most, the subordination of the conventional hermeneutic to a new set of methodological principles entirely.
>
> Kathleen Constable, *A Stranger within the Gates*, p. 135

> In fact, Ireland, during the season, or rather the year, we are describing, might be compared to one vast lazar-house filled with famine, disease, and death. The very skies of heaven were hung with the black drapery of the grave; for never since, nor within the memory of man before it, did the clouds present shapes of such gloomy and funereal import. Hearses, coffins, long funeral processions, and all the dark emblems of mortality, were reflected, as it were, on the sky, from the terrible works of pestilence and famine, which were going forward on the earth beneath it.
>
> William Carleton, *The Black Prophet*, p. 211

> The speech of the book comes from a certain silence.
>
> Pierre Macherey, *A Theory of Literary Production*, p. 85

Towards the end of *Jane Eyre*'s second volume, Rochester teases Jane with the prospect that he is about to marry Blanche Ingram and that she, consequently, 'must get a new situation'. As he pursues this playful fiction, Rochester informs Jane that the arrangements for such a placement are, in fact, already well in hand:

> 'I have ... through my future mother-in-law, heard of a place that I think will suit: it is to undertake the education of the five daughters of Mrs. Dionysius O'Gall of Bitternutt Lodge, Connaught, Ireland. You'll like Ireland, I think: they're such warm-hearted people there, they say.'[1]

The terms in which Jane's projected exile is framed are obviously designed to be comic, but the contemporary condition of the country to which she is seemingly bound would suggest that Brontë's humour here is perhaps not in the best of tastes. At the time when *Jane Eyre* was first published, Ireland was in the grip of a catastrophe, in the shape of the Famine or Great Hunger, which had begun in 1845 and was to last until 1851. The result, in the first instance, of a fungus which attacked and decimated the Irish potato crop, the Famine claimed the lives of approximately one million Irish people, either through starvation or disease. In the light of such devastation, it is not surprising that these events have come to be generally regarded as constituting 'the most important episode of modern Irish history and the greatest social disaster of nineteenth-century Europe'.[2]

Jane's residency as governess to Mrs O'Gall's interchangeable bevy of 'five daughters' is, of course, merely fanciful and, considered from an historical perspective, this is clearly just as well: Brontë's novel seems, that is, briefly to open up a narrative connection to Ireland only to close it down again, just as quickly. Such a broken link is restored, however, in *Shirley*, a novel engaging with the very circumstances of the Famine with which Jane herself is momentarily threatened by Rochester's snugly English whimsy. The 'Irish cataclysm'[3] is not in any sense the explicit subject of Brontë's text. Nor would it be, given the historical displacement which sets the narrative against the international backdrop of the Napoleonic Wars, in 'eighteen-hundred-eleven-twelve',[4] almost four decades prior to the novel's composition and publication in 1848–9. Yet even as *Shirley*'s third-person and implicitly female narrator begins the text with a sleepy celebration of her capacity to 'evade' and 'forget' 'present years' and 'dream of dawn' (p. 5) instead, the tale she tells is intimately shaped by the colonial trauma framing the novel's production, albeit in ways which are oblique, covert and coded. The principal means by

which the Famine's unspoken presence is ventriloquized in *Shirley*
is in terms of the alimentary and corporeal economies structuring
the power relations at work within the novel in three interlocking
contexts – racial, capitalist and patriarchal. The simmering tensions with which *Shirley* opens are generated, amongst other
things, by questions of food – its quantity and quality alike – as
the Irish curate, Peter Augustus Malone, clashes over dinner with
the Yorkshire landlady, Mrs Gale. Similarly, the conflicts between
the novel's working-class men and their master, the Anglo-Belgian
mill-owner, Robert Moore, are dramatized as something felt most
acutely, for both parties, at the level of the gut. The two middle-
class heroines in the text, Caroline Helstone and Shirley Keeldar,
both suffer, in their turn, from illnesses whose major symptom
takes the form of self-starvation. *Shirley*'s veritable obsession with
food and the body, eating and hunger, is not arbitrary but, rather,
the fictional reflex of the colonial history out of which the novel is
born.[5]

The Famine was not only a local catastrophe, turning Ireland
into a 'vast lazar-house', as Carleton puts it, but also a global phenomenon, prompting the perilous exodus of over a million Irish
subjects to a range of geographically and culturally diverse places
– England, Australia and, especially, America.[6] As one contemporary newspaper account records, the scale of the transatlantic
passage alone was 'so great as to suggest the idea, and almost
justify the belief, of a gradual depopulation of Ireland'.[7] These
mass movements are writ small in the narratives of migration pep-
pering Brontë's text. Together with its initial focus on the displaced and disruptive presence of Malone, the novel both
transports the ringleaders who organize resistance against Moore
to Australia and sketches some curious visions of new life in
America's 'wild West' (p. 613). What is particularly striking about
these American sketches is that even as they echo and extend the
Famine's main diasporic trajectory, they also reverse it, recalling
the very land from which, historically, the migrant set out.

Viewed in terms of the historical materials with which it surrep-
titiously engages, *Shirley* is a very different text from *Jane Eyre*,
with the Irish Famine taking the place of slavery in the West Indies
as the novel's submerged colonial ground. This difference is coun-
terbalanced, however, by the similar manner in which the two
novels reinscribe the respective colonial histories with which they
deal. In *Jane Eyre*, colonial history resurfaces in the form of a

politically suspect metaphorics of slavery. In *Shirley*'s case, it is to be sought amid the novel's representation of the varied bodies it includes within itself, and the patterns of consumption, starvation and movement which develop around them.

Anglo-Irish animosities

If food in a literal sense is a ubiquitous presence in *Shirley*, it is also a capacious source for the novel's metaphors. The earliest example of this is to be found in the second paragraph of the first chapter. Here the narrator interrupts herself, at some length, in order to figure the story she has just begun as a spartan 'meal' which may not be entirely to the liking of her readership:

> If you think, from this prelude, that anything like a romance is preparing for you, reader, you never were more mistaken. Do you anticipate sentiment, and poetry, and reverie? Do you expect passion, and stimulus, and melodrama? Calm your expectations; reduce them to a lowly standard. Something real, cool, and solid, lies before you; something unromantic as Monday morning, when all who have work wake with the consciousness that they must rise and betake themselves thereto. It is not positively affirmed that you shall not have a taste of the exciting, perhaps towards the middle and close of the meal, but it is resolved that the first dish set upon the table shall be one that a Catholic – ay, even an Anglo-Catholic – might eat on Good Friday in Passion Week: it shall be cold lentiles and vinegar without oil; it shall be unleavened bread with bitter herbs and no roast lamb. (p. 5)

This would appear to be a fairly accurate description of what is on the fictional menu for the romance-hungry 'reader' of Brontë's third novel. Recently surfeited on *Jane Eyre*, published two years before *Shirley*, such a reader might be forgiven for 'expect[ing]' more of the 'passion, and stimulus, and melodrama' confected from the preceding novel's three-sided imbroglio of Jane, Rochester and Bertha Mason, herself described in culinary terms at one point in *Jane Eyre*, it should be recalled, as a 'fierce ragout'.[8] These elements are indeed part of *Shirley*'s narrative recipe, appearing in the overlapping contexts of the two central love-stories which unfold between Caroline and Robert, on the one hand, and Shirley and Louis Moore (Robert's brother and Shirley's ex-tutor) on the other. Before s/he can indulge the 'taste' for romance, however, the reader must force down 'the first dish set upon the table', whose primary ingredients range from industrialization and class struggle to matters of political economy and military conflict. These are already being discreetly doled out in the reference to 'all who have work', with its concomitant suggestion that some do not. For the reader who has savoured the romantic piquancies of *Jane Eyre*, such a repast is no doubt as unpalatable as it sounds: 'it shall be cold lentiles and vinegar without oil … unleavened bread with bitter herbs and no roast lamb'.

The entrée to Brontë's novel establishes a relationship between narrator and reader marked by a certain strain, as the one withholds what the other demands, or at best rations it out. The structure of this somewhat punitive relationship has its analogue in the fractious dinner-table scene which takes place shortly afterwards, as the novel moves from initial apostrophe to narrative proper. In this scene, the omnivorous and unholy trinity of curates – Mr Donne, Mr Sweeting and the 'isolated Hibernian' (p. 11), Malone – descend like 'locusts' (p. 9) upon Donne's lodgings, where they are fed and served by the grudging Mrs Gale:

> 'More bread!' cries Mr. Malone, in a tone which, though prolonged but to utter two syllables, proclaims him at once a native of the land of shamrocks and potatoes. Mrs. Gale hates Mr. Malone more than either of the other two, but she fears him also, for he is a tall, strongly-built personage, with real Irish legs and arms, and a face as genuinely national; not the Milesian face – not Daniel O'Connell's style, but the high-featured, North-American-Indian sort of visage, which belongs to a certain class of the Irish gentry, and has a petrified and proud look, better suited to the owner of an estate of slaves, than to the landlord of a free peasantry. Mr. Malone's father termed himself a gentleman: he was poor and in debt, and besottedly arrogant; and his son was like him.
>
> Mrs. Gale offered the loaf.
>
> 'Cut it, woman,' said her guest; and the 'woman' cut it accordingly. Had she followed her inclinations, she would have cut the parson also; her Yorkshire soul revolted absolutely from his manner of command. (p. 8)

In Elsie Michie's reading, this complex passage exemplifies a process of textual screening whose effect is to make 'direct references to the Irish … difficult to identify'.[9] As Michie notes, Malone has the distinction of being one of Brontë's 'few identifiably Irish characters'[10] and is subjected, accordingly, to stereotypes both ignominious and mocking: he is 'the native of a conquered land' and 'the priestly Paddy, from whose anatomy the bowels of natural affection' have 'somehow been omitted'. Here, however, the identity of this '"Irish Peter"' (p. 10) is no sooner announced than it is occulted, as if *Shirley* were retreating from Malone's Irishness, just as it has already distanced itself from the immediacies of its own blasted historical present: like the voice whose 'tone' is the inimitable sign of his '"counthry"' (p. 10) and his bona fide limbs, Malone's 'face' is 'genuinely national', yet quickly veiled by the wholly unpredictable narratorial imposition of a 'North-American-Indian sort of visage'. This transformation is accompanied by the equally surprising reversal of Malone as colonized other, 'menac[ing] rebellion' and 'vent[ing] bitter hatred against English rule' (p. 10), into an oppressor-figure, 'the owner of an estate of slaves'.

Malone's first appearance in *Shirley* is, in this sense, just as much a disappearance, as his physiognomy undergoes a sudden racial makeover. Equally, though, the novel's exoticizing flight from the truth of Malone's Irishness is offset by a movement of return to the blighted 'land' from which he hails, as the circumstances of the Famine are at once evoked and rewritten in the shifting emphases of the text. If it is merely by chance that Malone's name is an anagram of 'no meal', it is surely no coincidence, by contrast, that the first words to be spoken in Brontë's novel should issue from an Irish mouth and constitute a raucous demand for additional food – 'More bread!' – which is directed towards a hostile English source reluctant to provide it. On the other hand, Malone's status as a 'strongly-built personage' suggests that he is hardly convincing as a victim of malnourishment.[11] Indeed, as Malone completes his meal, it becomes evident that 'his great Irish frame' (p. 119) to some extent feeds off the hunger it helps to engender in an English stomach. With the aid of his dinner companions, Malone swiftly consumes, 'by way of dessert', a 'spice-cake', which 'vanishe[s] like a vision' and is 'no more found'. In so doing, he deprives 'Abraham, Mrs. Gale's son and heir', of the leftovers 'he had reckoned upon'. The disinherited 'youth of six summers' makes his protest clear: 'he lifted up his voice and wept sore' (p. 9).

In his subsequent cameos, Malone is portrayed, as in his aggravating narrative debut, as a self-seeking figure who is at the same time both comic and threatening. Perhaps the most salient instance of this occurs in volume 2, chapter 5, where it becomes apparent that his personal ambitions reach beyond mere demands for extra 'bread'. Here Malone strives to ingratiate himself into the lucrative affections of the property-owning Shirley by offering her 'a huge bunch of cabbage-roses ... in full blow'. To the chagrin of the would-be 'lady's man', this unwieldy floral tribute is no more seductive than the toilette which finds him meticulously 'gloved and scented, with his hair oiled and brushed to perfection'. As well as unintentionally amusing their recipient, Malone's wretched 'red cabbages' elicit a more serious contempt for the monetary motives which spur their presentation. Looking down at the flowers on her 'purple satin lap', Shirley is unable to hide her 'laughing face':

> he was made a joke of – his gallantry, his chivalry were the subject of a jest for a petticoat – for two petticoats – Miss Helstone too was smiling. Moreover, he felt he was seen through, and Peter grew black as a thunder-cloud. When Shirley looked up, a fell eye was fastened on her: Malone, at least, had energy enough to hate: she saw it in his glance. (p. 299)

Apart from the metonymic mockery of its jesting 'petticoats', this passage is notable for the way in which it short-circuits the Irish 'hate' it senses. While Shirley goes on, in the novel's whispered next sentence, to promise Caroline that Malone is 'worth a scene, and shall have it, if he likes, one day' (p. 299), the scene itself never materializes, as if his retributive 'energy' were being denied a concrete narrative outlet.

   This containment of the 'thunder-cloud' into which Malone ominously transforms himself anticipates *Shirley*'s valedictory last chapter, with its pointed refusal to divulge the enigmatic circumstances of the curate's expulsion from an unaccommodating Yorkshire. In contrast to 'the final fates' of other 'personages' in the novel, 'the catastrophe of [Malone's] life' remains tantalizingly untold. Even were it revealed, 'the touching tale of [his] deeds and destinies' would be rejected, the narrator insists, by 'a discriminating public', for whom 'plain facts' – whatever they may be – 'will not digest' (p. 632). As *Shirley* thus 'cut[s] the parson' in a more editorial sense than that fantasized by the knife-wielding Mrs Gale, it also avenges the young Abraham for the loss of the earlier 'spice-cake'. Just as Malone is partly responsible for the rapid disappearance of this coveted comestible, so he in turn is subjected to an equally 'premature and sudden vanishing ... from the stage of Briarfield parish'. This completes the circle of his effacement begun in the novel's first chapter. Here, though, it is not just the disagreeable signs of Malone's Irishness which are eclipsed: he himself is gobbled up *en masse* into an impenetrable narrative void.

Malone's abrupt exit from the narrative does not leave Briarfield long without religious guidance, since 'another Irish curate, Mr. Macarthey' is rapidly installed as his 'successor', doing 'as much credit to his country' as the finally mysterious Malone 'had done it discredit' (p. 634). Brontë's shuffling of the theological pack at the end of *Shirley* might be of no real note, were it not that it is curiously suggestive of the kind of status which the Famine occupies in relation to the novel as a whole. Like Malone himself, the Famine is something whose exclusion is only a prelude to its return in a distorted form. One of the ways in which this pattern is manifest is in terms of the Anglo-Irish conflicts over food with which *Shirley* opens and in which Malone is, of course, directly involved. Another is the conflict between workers and masters with which the novel continues.

Class and corporeality

As well as being figured as a 'meal', *Shirley* itself contains a text which is represented in comparable terms, William Shakespeare's *Coriolanus*. This text first enters Brontë's novel in volume 1, chapter 6 as an 'old English book' (p. 89) which Caroline gives Robert to read during one of their tender *soirées* at Hollow's cottage, Robert's home:

> The very first scene in 'Coriolanus' came with smart relish to his intellectual palate, and still as he read he warmed. He delivered the haughty speech of Caius Marcius to the starving citizens with unction; he did not say he thought his irrational pride right, but he seemed to feel it so. Caroline looked up at him with a singular smile. (p. 91)

The 'very first scene' of Shakespeare's play which Robert so relishes – while enjoying the 'warlike portions' (p. 91) rather less – is one in which, as this passage hints, issues of food and hunger are paramount. The scene in question dramatizes a confrontation between the citizens, 'all resolved rather to die than to famish'[12] and the Roman state which, in the person of Coriolanus in particular, is responsible, the citizens believe, for the dearth of food from which they suffer. As befits *Shirley*'s own corporeal preoccupations, the scene is marked, also, by an extended allegorical reflection on the Roman body politic, whose 'senators' are figured by Menenius as a 'good belly',[13] while the citizens themselves are represented as 'mutinous members'.[14]

As Caroline recognizes, Robert's fascination with the figure of Coriolanus is a narcissistic one. If Shakespeare's dramatic hero is 'a very dog to the commonality',[15] Robert himself (whose 'hunger', at one point, is described as 'canine' [p. 63]), is perceived to be 'the detestation' of 'the neighbourhood' (p. 15) and 'the man most abominated'. Robert's unpopularity stems directly from the new programme of mechanization he has embraced, which renders the workers at Hollow's mill redundant in ever greater numbers, exposing them and their families, as a consequence, to poverty and hunger. They require the labour, which Robert is no longer either able or willing to provide, in order to feed themselves, subsisting only upon the stale biblical tropes which define their destitution: 'so the unemployed underwent their destiny – ate the bread, and drank the waters of affliction' (p. 31). This situation repeatedly erupts into a violence which becomes increasingly personalized. By the end of the novel's second chapter, the 'hellish machinery' Robert wants to introduce in order to accelerate the cloth-manufacturing process at the mill has been 'shivered to smash on Stilbro' Moor' (p. 33), as the wasted frames of the workers wreck the mechanical 'frames' (p. 15) which are the inhuman cause of their suffering. At the novel's rough mid-point, the mill itself undergoes a spectacular if ineffectual assault perpetrated by 'the famished and furious mass of the Operative Class' against the 'Middle Rank' (p. 344) and, at the end of volume 3, chapter 7, Robert himself is seriously injured in an assassination attempt, carried out by the 'mad Calvinist and Jacobin weaver' (p. 237), Michael Hartley.

While Robert is explicitly likened to Coriolanus in the text (p. 131), there is one key difference between the two figures. Coriolanus is identified with Rome, the imperial state of which the citizens are themselves a part, while Robert, by contrast, is a 'furriner' (p. 134), whose face displays 'a most anti-British and anti-

Yorkshire look' (p. 51). His differences, both visual and aural, are insisted upon from an early point in the narrative:

> He is what you would probably call, at first view, rather a strange-looking man; for he is thin, dark, sallow; very foreign of aspect. . . . His manner of speaking displeases; he has an outlandish accent, which, notwithstanding a studied correctness of pronunciation and diction, grates on a British, and especially on a Yorkshire ear.
>
> Mr. Moore, indeed, was but half a Briton, and scarcely that. He came of a foreign ancestry by the mother's side, and was himself born, and partly reared, on a foreign soil. A hybrid in nature, it is probable he had a hybrid's feeling on many points – patriotism for one. (pp. 27–8)

Robert's hybridity complicates the power relations within the novel. Economically superior to the 'frame-breakers', he will always be deemed racially inferior to these 'starved ragamuffins' (p. 41) as a result of 'a foreign ancestry' which not only vitiates his claim to Englishness but also makes him 'unpatriotic' (p. 201): unlike the war-hungry Coriolanus, Robert constantly wishes and indeed agitates for an end to England's military struggle against the French, whose language he speaks fault-lessly, so that the commercial opportunities the conflict has blocked can be reopened.[16]

In addition to this, Robert's status as 'semi-foreigner' (p. 31) has an important bearing on the ways in which the presence of the Famine in Brontë's text is construed. One of the most contentious questions raised by the Famine is the question of blame and, espe-cially, the nature of English involvement in the disaster taking place so close to home. The English were not, of course, responsi-ble for the onset of the Famine: it was, initially at least, a natural phenomenon. Nor were they by any means indifferent to it. Equally, though, they were directly implicated in the event and its horrific consequences, implementing 'measures, half-measures and non-measures', as Terry Eagleton puts it, which 'despatched hun-dreds of thousands to their needless deaths'.[17] As with the dinner-table scene at *Shirley*'s beginning, this situation is at once echoed and reversed. The Famine is both masked and revealed in the novel's representation of the conflict between worker and master as 'a struggle about money, and food, and life' (p. 342), in which the starvation of the working-class male body is consistently em-phasized. At the same time, though, the body in question is an

English one, suffering at the hands of an unyielding master who is 'a perfect outcast on ... the cliffs of Albion' (p. 134). This pattern of English suffering and foreign oppression has its pointed supplement in the co-option of Malone – complete with his 'loaded pistols' and flagrantly ethnic 'shillelagh' (p. 10) – into the master's service when the attack on the mill is originally feared in volume 1, chapter 2. Here he is once again associated with food, exchanging his weapons for cooking utensils. While he and Robert await the onslaught from workers whose 'sight [is] dim with famine' (p. 30), Malone nonchalantly prepares a supper of 'mutton-chops'. As he cooks, the 'fat spits' at him and 'burn[s]' his 'hand' (p. 26), as if offering a reproach for the self-interested nature of his political allegiances.

The balanced irony of Robert's unconcern for the workers' plight is that he himself ultimately comes to partake of the corporeal sufferings he has inflicted upon them. Following his attempted murder by Hartley, Robert is taken, 'pallid, lifeless, helpless' (p. 562), to the Yorke household, where he is nursed by the dram-drinking, pipe-smoking 'ogress' (p. 573), Zillah Horsfall. For the convalescent Robert, this masculinized working-class female is a rebarbative and intimidating figure: 'he hate[s] the sight of her rough bulk, and dread[s] the contact of her hard hands'. A 'sort of giantess' (p. 566) whose 'breadth ... height ... bone, and ... brawn' (p. 565) enable her to make light of Robert's own 'six feet' and 'manly thews and sinews', Zillah 'turn[s] him in his bed as another woman would have turned a babe in its cradle' (p. 566). Such displays of strength are doubly significant. On the one hand, they suggest a reversal of class relations as they prevail within the novel at large, as Zillah establishes over her infantilized patient precisely the control which the novel's insurgent but emasculated 'body of rioters' (p. 356) cannot. On the other, Zillah's care defines her as a 'terror of the male imaginary',[18] symbolically overturning the traditional gender hierarchies which appear, elsewhere in *Shirley*, to be so inflexible.

Prodigious as they are, Zillah's man-handling powers are aggrandized still further by the 15-year-old Martin Yorke, who embellishes the harsh realities of her sick-room routines with mischievous imaginings of his own. In his estimation, Zillah is 'a woman as round and big as [the] largest water-butt – a rough, hard-favoured old girl'. As he goes on to claim in a sensationalized conversation with the anxious Caroline:

'It is my belief she knocks him about terribly in that chamber. I listen at the wall sometimes when I am in bed, and I think I hear her thumping him. You should see her fist: she could hold half a dozen hands like yours in her one palm. After all, notwithstanding the chops and jellies he gets, I would not be in his shoes. In fact, it is my private opinion that she eats most of what goes up on the tray to Mr. Moore. I wish she may not be starving him.' (p. 572)

Whether Martin's final allegation that Zillah is 'starving' her charge by siphoning his food into her own muscular body is anything but 'flummery' (p. 570) is less relevant than the indisputably atrophied condition to which Robert is reduced during the period of his illness. Taking on the look of a 'wasted figure' (p. 580), 'long skeleton' (p. 590) and 'pale, grim phantom ... more pitiable than formidable' (p. 604), he reproduces in his own 'exhausted frame' (p. 565) the very bodily condition of those whom his self-centred industrial schemes have brought low. The oppressor doubles the oppressed.

Shirley's articulation of class conflict in terms of a bodily emaciation visited upon worker and master alike has a significance which extends beyond a Brontëan critique of mid nineteenth-century industrial capitalism. As is also the case with the portrayal of the voracious Malone, the representation of such conflict is overdetermined, accreting to itself an additional meaning as the covert sign of a particularly anguished moment in Ireland's history which is not directly acknowledged in the novel. At the same time, these figurings of class struggle mirror *Shirley*'s depiction of gender conflict, as the latter emerges, in its turn, as a further site for the Famine's inscription.

Figures of female resistance

As Shirley points out, one reason for such conflict is that men 'do not read' their female counterparts 'in a true light'. The patriarchal gaze, in her eyes, is a divisive or polarizing one. It is confined to a repertoire of incurious stereotypes which construct the 'good woman' as 'a queer thing, half doll, half angel' and invariably reduce the 'bad woman' to 'a fiend' (p. 352). The acuity of Shirley's reading of the male misreading of women is something Brontë's novel bears out in the foreshortened tale of Mary Cave, dead wife to the Briarfield Rector, Matthewson Helstone,

Caroline's uncle. The domestic sorrows of this 'girl of living marble',[19] who seems to be 'stillness personified' and is 'beautiful as a monumental angel' (p. 52), are commemorated in volume 1, chapter 4:

> Nature never intended Mr. Helstone to make a very good husband, especially to a quiet wife. He thought, so long as a woman was silent, nothing ailed her, and she wanted nothing. If she did not complain of solitude, solitude, however continued, could not be irksome to her. If she did not talk and put herself forward, express a partiality for this, an aversion to that, she had no partialities or aversions, and it was useless to consult her tastes. He made no pretence of comprehending women, or comparing them with men: they were a different, probably a very inferior order of existence; a wife could not be her husband's companion, much less his confidant, much less his stay. *His* wife, after a year or two, was of no great importance to him in any shape; and when she one day, as he thought, suddenly – for he had scarcely noticed her decline – but as others thought, gradually, took her leave of him and of life, and there was only a still beautiful-featured mould of clay left, cold and white, on the conjugal couch, he felt his bereavement – who shall say how little?   (p. 53; emphasis in original)

Helstone is not a 'good husband' to his 'quiet wife' because he is not a good reader of the signs she proffers him, misconstruing her 'silent' and uncomplaining demeanour as contentment and compliance with her lot. This degree of interpretative error suggests that, even were he to have 'noticed' Mary's bodily 'decline' in the first place, Helstone would not have appreciated its significance. Yet the different senses fused together in the word 'decline' itself – which can mean both 'deterioration' and 'refusal' – provide a clue as to the nature of the affliction in question here. Mary's 'sickness' (p. 53) is not just physical but also political, a form of female protest directed against Helstone himself, the patriarchal order he so blithely embodies and the so-called '"duties of woman"' (p. 81) to which she is beholden as wife and potential mother.

As feminist scholarship has extensively demonstrated, one of the ways in which female illness and patriarchal protest most commonly intersect is in the condition of anorexia nervosa. Although anorexia does not enter Victorian medical discourses as a diagnostic term until the early 1870s,[20] several critics have none the less discerned the early traces of its presence in Brontë's novel. For Rod Edmond, for example, *Shirley* constitutes 'probably the longest, most detailed study of wasting illness in nineteenth-century writing',[21] the 'conspicuous symptom' of such illness being, he goes on to note, 'a refusal or inability to eat',[22] which 'seems to be a form of anorexic suicide'.[23] Similarly, Deirdre Lashgari argues that the 'Individual eating disorders' which interlard the novel's accounts of class strife approximate to an anorectic logic and form 'part of a much larger picture, in which a dysfunctional society starves women, literally and metaphorically, and women internalize that dis/order as self-starvation'.[24] While it remains unclear whether or not Caroline's aunt strictly qualifies as one of Lashgari's disorderly eaters, the corporeal complaints by which Caroline herself is persistently beset certainly place her within that category. Yet the 'pale face and wasted figure' characterizing Caroline's appearance for much of the novel – together with an 'appetite' which is steadily 'diminished' (p. 192) – are not just the signs of a proto-anorectic crisis. As well as broadly linking the leisured middle-class female to *Shirley*'s hungry and idle working-class men, these somatic ailments constitute another means by which the Famine makes its secret mark upon the body of the text.

According to 'rumours ... in the neighbourhood' at least, one 'supposed cause' (p. 53) of Mary's demise is yearning for the lost love of Helstone's rival, Hiram Yorke, whose 'absorbing passion' (p. 52) she unaccountably rejects. At first glance, it seems that Caroline's 'strange sufferings' (p. 243) are likewise attributable exclusively to a 'broken heart' (p. 53). Her romantic tribulations begin in volume 1, chapter 7, when Robert abruptly revokes his desire for her, repressing the amatory 'phrenzy' which he regards as a betrayal of his industrial ambitions and the hyperbolic harbinger of 'downright ruin' (p. 96). Reinvesting his affections in the mill, described as his 'lady-love' (p. 342) and the 'machines' which are 'his grim, metal darlings' (p. 384), 'bonnie Robert' (p. 104) adopts a manner towards his 'eager girl' (p. 105) which is 'anything but lover-like' (p. 104). While Caroline is prevented by an iniquitous set of gender conventions from making her 'Sweetheart' (p. 257) answerable for such changefulness, Brontë's narrator is under no such veto. Herself evidently as much stung by Robert's 'sharp cross' as Caroline, she extemporizes with a bitter eloquence both upon the conventions themselves and the female pain to which they lead:

> A lover masculine so disappointed can speak and urge explanation; a lover feminine can say nothing: if she did the result would be

shame and anguish, inward remorse for self-treachery. . . . Take the
matter as you find it: ask no questions; utter no remonstrances: it is
your best wisdom. You expected bread, and you have got a stone;
break your teeth on it, and don't shriek because the nerves are martyrized: do not doubt that your mental stomach – if you have such
a thing – is strong as an ostrich's – the stone will digest.   (p. 105)

The generalized 'lover feminine' of this passage faces a predicament bleak indeed, able, as she is, to 'say nothing', nor even
'shriek' when her 'nerves are martyrized' by male indifference.
Caroline, however, is more resourceful than the stifled abstraction
whom the narrator summons forth. In response to the metaphorical hunger to which Robert subjects her – feeding her pitiless
'stone' instead of 'bread' – she performs starvation upon herself,
displaying the secret outrage of 'her famished heart' (p. 252) as
corporeal spectacle. So severe are the demands of this self-imposed
regime that when she sits down to breakfast with her uncle
towards the end of volume 1, Caroline is, to his eye, a virtual
'ghost': she has already become 'white-cheeked and miserable-
looking'. Her 'flesh [has] wasted' and she is 'drooping, colourless,
and thin' (p. 189).

Robert's rejection of Caroline threatens to place her in the un-
enviable position of the old maid, Miss Mann, sexually remain-
dered within the world of the novel by dint of a physical
'plainness' (p. 181) not to patriarchal tastes. Like Caroline, de-
prived by her stonewalling paramour of even 'a drop and crumb'
of emotional 'nourishment' – which, were it only given, would be
enjoyed as much as a 'generous feast' or 'banquet' (p. 252) – Miss
Mann craves an 'appreciation and affection' whose perpetual
abeyance leaves her 'corpse-like' and 'ahungered and athirst to
famine', thinning her hopes, in Brontë's archaic phrase, into an
'extenuated spectre' (p. 180). Yet there is a crucial difference
between these two superfluous female figures, manifested textually in terms of the language of stone deployed in the passage cited
above. When Robert turns against her, Caroline 'turn[s] upon
herself' (p. 107), flagrantly sculpting her own body into an effigy
of protest against the hard usage she has received. Miss Mann,
conversely, negotiates her sexual hunger by targeting the patriarchal order which is its source, and is reputed by the narrator once,
for example, to have fixed Robert with a 'dread and Gorgon gaze'
(p. 179). This action, 'quite equal to anything Medusa could do',
is strikingly apposite in its effects, both prefiguring and reversing

Robert's maltreatment of Caroline by disquieting him with the feeling that 'something stony' has been introduced into the 'texture' of his 'flesh' (p. 178).

In the end, though, the disappointment of unreciprocated desire only partially explains Caroline's bodily trials and the rapidly escalating 'nightmare of her life' (p. 395), functioning as an allegory for larger dissatisfactions. For Helstone, his niece's self-consumption is an enigma. As if seeing in Caroline a re-enactment of his deceased wife's malady, he exclaims:

> 'These women are incomprehensible. They have the strangest knack of startling you with unpleasant surprises. To-day you see them bouncing, buxom, red as cherries, and round as apples; to-morrow they exhibit themselves effete as dead weeds, blanched and broken down. And the reason of it all? that's the puzzle.' (p. 189)

In contrast to Helstone's bafflement here, articulated in a delectably ironic language of 'red ... cherries' and 'round ... apples', *Shirley* itself is rather more attuned to the 'reason' underlying the degeneration which leaves Caroline 'blanched and broken down'. In another crass attempt at resolving 'the puzzle' of female bodily illness, Helstone speculates that it is Caroline's habit of sucking the lead in the pencils she uses when painting 'which is poisoning [her]'. For the novel, however, it is less the 'deleterious' chemical properties of these 'colour cakes' which are the problem, than the cosy patriarchal assumption that the stereotypically feminine accomplishments represented by Caroline's 'tinting work' (p. 193) can adequately nourish and sustain the middle-class female subject.

In making such an assumption, Helstone confirms the 'gulf' Caroline senses 'between her own mind and his' (p. 102). She longs repeatedly for an 'occupation' (p. 71) which will give her a degree of financial independence, is even prepared to take the 'painful step' of becoming a governess (despite Shirley's stigmatizing and stock Brontëan assertion that she should 'Better be a slave at once' [p. 241]) and, on occasion, engages in daydreams of gender crossing by wishing 'nature had made her a boy instead of a girl' (p. 77). Her uncle, for his part, considers Caroline's quest for 'earthly employment' (p. 391) to be pointless, since, as his ward, she is already accorded everything she could feasibly require: 'her meals, her liberty [and] a good house to live in' (p. 189). As an antidote to such misguided aspirations, he urges her to 'stick to the needle – learn shirt-making and gown-making, and pie-crust-making' (p. 98), attainments which, he vaguely promises, will turn her into 'a clever woman some day' (pp. 98–9). To this humdrum programme of minor skills he adds the marginally more stimulating acquisition of the French language, which Caroline studies with Hortense Moore, Robert's sister, at Hollow's cottage. It is only when his national pride is publicly affronted by Robert's self-serving opposition to the war against Napoleon that Helstone comes close, albeit unwittingly, to formulating an insight into the unedifying effects which his own domestic pedagogy is having upon its reluctant pupil. Banning Caroline from further instruction from Hortense on the grounds that French is 'bad and frivolous' and its literature 'highly injurious ... to weak female minds', Helstone roundly condemns the 'fashion' (p. 168) of teaching the language to women in general: in his opinion, it is 'like feeding a rickety child on chalk and water-gruel' (p. 169).

Caroline's meditation upon 'the wide and deep chasm' separating herself from her uncle is tellingly bound up with reflections on 'the half-remembered image of her own father'. This 'sinister' (p. 102) figure, whom she last sees 'as a dead man in his coffin' (p. 103), is at the disorientating centre of a troubled childhood memory:

> She recollected – a dark recollection it was – some weeks that she had spent with him in a great town somewhere, when she had had no maid to dress her or take care of her; when she had been shut up, day and night, in a high garret-room, without a carpet, with a bare uncurtained bed, and scarcely any other furniture; when he went out early every morning, and often forgot to return and give her her dinner during the day, and at night, when he came back, was like a madman, furious, terrible; or – still more painful – like an idiot, imbecile, senseless. (pp. 102–3)

Just as the reduction of Caroline's health to 'pallor, debility, and emaciation' (p. 191) eerily replicates the fate of Helstone's late wife, so the care she receives from her uncle entails another repetition: it is simply a more refined, or insidious version of the paternal neglect meted out to her in the 'high garret-room' of a lonely past, where 'dinner' is routinely omitted. Yet the gendered and metaphorical forms of enclosure and starvation structuring Caroline's 'domestic relations' (p. 216) with her uncle at 'the gray

Rectory' (p. 389) are far from unique. As she herself complains in the course of a long interior monologue towards the end of volume 2, these conditions prevail within the nation at large, created and maintained by the 'Men of England' (p. 392), who keep their 'girls' minds narrow and fettered' and refuse them 'scope and work' (p. 393).

One of the parting shots in Caroline's inward appeal to these conspiring patriarchs is a warning that the failure to 'alter these things' (p. 392) will render England's 'daughters' 'still ... a plague and a care' (p. 393). These words prove to be prophetic, fleshed out, as they are, by Caroline herself, whose eating disorder is suddenly compounded and intensified, in the opening two chapters of volume 3, by the dramatic contraction of cholera. This corporeal turn for the worse has a particular resonance in the context of *Shirley*'s submerged engagement with the Famine, since cholera was one of a number of diseases which the disaster brought in its wake, instilling in its victims, in Carleton's phrase, a 'tenfold terror'.[25] But what is striking about the treatment of this second threat to Caroline's already 'fading girlhood' (p. 431) is the way the novel breaks or at least mystifies the very link to the Famine which the eruptive textual presence of this condition works to suggest. In a letter to Margaret Wooler of 31 March 1848, Brontë invokes the symptomatology of cholera to figure the prospect of revolutionary violence in Ireland as a disease played out upon the body of the nation in 'spasms, cramps and frenzy-fits'.[26] In *Shirley*, by contrast, the malaise which takes hold of Caroline, transforming 'palatable food' into 'ashes and sawdust' (p. 421), does not carry an Irish connotation, but is driven back into its Oriental provenance. It is represented variously as one of 'the poisoned exhalations of the East', 'covering white Western isles' and 'dimming the lattices of English homes with ... Indian plague' (p. 421) and, later, is a deadly 'breath' drawn from 'Asiatic deserts' which 'parch[es] Caroline's lips and fever[s] her veins'. In a textual strategy similar to the initial defacement of Malone's Irishness, Brontë's novel rids itself of the Famine by robustly projecting 'the livid cholera-tint' and 'pale malaria-haze' (p. 444) which contaminates it into more distant colonial spaces.

In due course, Caroline overcomes the cholera attack, her recovery aided in large measure by the ministrations of another woman, as it is melodramatically revealed that her 'self-elected nurse' (p. 423), Mrs Pryor, is the mother who had originally abandoned her in childhood. This momentous if belated maternal return not only bestows upon Caroline 'All the love' she has 'needed, and not tasted, from infancy' (p. 322) but also heralds a more general recuperation, as her 'colour and ... plump cheeks' (p. 598) begin to re-establish themselves. Between these two pivotal events, however, Brontë opens up a new anatomy of female self-starvation in relation to the initially exuberant and economically powerful Shirley, whose 'masculine ... cognomen' (p. 198) furnishes the novel with its title.

Despite the obvious psychological and social differences between them, one of the qualities Caroline and Shirley hold in common is an unswerving commitment to the respective objects of their desire: just as 'all [Caroline's] universe' is permanently 'pent' in Robert (p. 111), so Shirley remains constant in her quest for 'a *master*' (p. 552; emphasis in original), 'one who makes [her] sincerely feel that he is [her] superior' (p. 219). Shirley's faith in the existence of this elusive paragon forms the ground for her serial rejection of the three suitors who offer themselves to her in the novel's latter stages – Robert himself, Samuel Fawthrop Wynne and the poetically inclined Sir Philip Nunnely, who fails singularly to charm his potential spouse with the impromptu 'syllabub sonnets' he repeatedly 'whip[s] up' for her (p. 619). It is evidently only in Louis that Shirley finds the exacting criteria of male mastery adequately met and her search brought, accordingly, to an end.

The double wedding with which Brontë's novel closes – of Shirley to Louis and a fully rejuvenated Caroline to Robert – suggests a final narrative capitulation to the conventions of 'romance' so teasingly resisted at the novel's outset. For Shirley especially, however, there are numerous signs that marriage is not necessarily synonymous with fulfilment, sexual or otherwise, and that her eventual husband is not quite as masterful as she would have him be. In a parallel with the misunderstandings between Helstone and Caroline, Shirley's own uncle, Mr Sympson, is sorely limited as a reader of his niece. In volume 3, chapter 4, for example, he receives Shirley's resolution 'to esteem – to admire – to *love*' before marriage as if it were spoken in 'an unknown tongue' (p. 473; emphasis in original) and, some four chapters later, is similarly unable to decipher her intentions towards Nunnely, finding her face to be as 'inscrutable ... as the writing on the wall to Belshazzar' (p. 547). There is none the less a certain truth in

Sympson's claim that Shirley is 'vastly inconsistent' (p. 551) in her romantic preferences. Even towards Louis, her behaviour is marked by 'strange alternations of cool reserve and docile respect', as she one moment 'sweep[s] past him in all the dignity of the monied heiress' and the next 'accost[s] him as abashed school-girls are wont to accost their stern professors' (p. 479). These fluctuations are nowhere more tersely underlined than in a passage recorded in the diary which Louis begins to keep in volume 3. Invited by the diarist to give an assessment of his facial appearance, Shirley obliges with a volte-face of her own:

> 'It looks like a god of Egypt: a great sand-buried stone head; or rather I will compare it to nothing so lofty: it looks like Tartar: you are my mastiff's cousin: I think you as much like him as a man can be like a dog.' (pp. 619–20)

This is a startling metamorphosis, as Shirley flips Oriental 'god' into domestic 'dog', turning her supposed master into a mastiff, over whom she, of course, is mistress. In thus likening Louis to the saucily named Tartar, she not only reminds the reader of the 'canine hunger' to which Louis's brother is sometimes prone but also inflects his newly diminished status with a racial edge: as the narrator quietly observes, one of Tartar's more striking features is 'his negro muzzle' (p. 386).

The unsettling of Louis's entitlement to the position of master effected by the explicit comparison to Tartar is supplemented in terms of the rather more circuitous similarities established between Shirley's suitor and another dog, Phoebe. As Shirley confides to Louis in volume 3, chapter 5, Phoebe is for her a bane, inflicting a bite upon her 'white arm' (p. 508) which, she believes, has infected her with rabies and will cause her to 'be seized with hydrophobia, and die raving mad' (p. 511). Although the bite turns out to be entirely 'innocuous' (p. 610), Shirley's traumatized response to the more harrowing alternative possibility is to stop eating, producing her own less efflorescent version of Caroline's symptoms: her 'face' becomes 'thin', 'her large eye ... hollow' (p. 498) and she has a 'wasted little hand', whose 'fore-finger' is unable to wear the 'ring' which Louis attempts to fasten upon it (p. 507). As Lashgari has noted, both the canine wound Shirley sustains and the self-starvation it immediately occasions are not to be dismissed merely as eccentric or irrelevant textual details but seen, rather, as performing an important symbolic function.[27]

Shirley may not suffer the 'terrors' (p. 509) of hydrophobia and insanity but she gives herself up to one who has both a worryingly 'liquid name' (p. 631) and, like her other suitors, the capacity 'to torment [her] with ... maddening scruples' pertaining to 'such sordid things as money, or poverty, or inequality' (p. 624). These deft points of overlap between Louis and Phoebe endow Shirley's self-starvation with a significance in excess of the viral fears which are its overt trigger, suggesting it to be a coded or displaced expression of the patriarchal resistance more visibly incarnated in Caroline. In Robert's mouth-wateringly inclusive vision, at least, Louis can only benefit the community into which marriage to Shirley will assimilate him. As he tells Caroline in the novel's final chapter, his brother 'is of the "pâte" generally approved, "bon comme le pain" – daily-bread for the most fastidious; good for the infant and the aged, nourishing for the poor, wholesome for the rich' (pp. 643–4). Whether Louis can be so willingly cannibalized by his 'future wife' (p. 643) remains, however, an open question.

In contrast to their working-class male counterparts, *Shirley*'s middle-class women – Mary Cave, Caroline and Shirley herself – endure a form of starvation which is, in the first instance at least, figurative rather than literal, the product of the male order which hems them in. These respective predicaments meet, accordingly, with different responses from those who are their victims. *Shirley*'s working-class male responds to his starvation by means of his insurgency, turning violence out towards the middle-class master. The middle-class female, on the other hand, directs violence upon herself, transforming a figurative into a literal starvation and politicizing the body as the site of patriarchal protest. Yet while the modes of resistance to power might differ according to context – class or gender – they are united in their status as textual vehicles for the return of the colonial. Whether the body in question is male or female, working-class or middle-class, its hunger externally imposed or self-inflicted, it is freighted with the same haunting burden.

This is equally the case for the visions of migration which steal into the novel's latter stages. These, in their way, are just as fanciful as the fleeting glimpse of Ireland offered by Rochester in *Jane Eyre*. Yet they not only share something of the frivolity which characterizes the truncated Irish imaginings of the earlier text, but also mark a furtive return to – or return of – Ireland itself. No more than *Shirley*'s representations of the body, can they be disentangled, in other words, from the historical moment in which Brontë's novel is located.

Circles of migration

Shirley is a fiercely regional text, insisting upon the specificity of its location with particular force in the description of the workers' attack on Robert's mill. The ecstasy of destruction which breaks the mill's 'windows' – 'every pane of every lattice' – into 'shattered and pounded fragments' is succeeded by a cry whose sound is unmistakable. As the narrator puts it, in her own echoing staccato: 'A yell followed this demonstration – a rioters' yell – a North-of-England – a Yorkshire – a West-Riding – a West-Riding-clothing-district-of-Yorkshire rioters' yell' (p. 343). But the novel's regionalism is interwoven with more worldly perspectives. Such a combination of the local and the global emerges, for example, in the quasi-ethnographic account of the 'Jew's basket' given in volume 1, chapter 7. This curious 'utensil' (p. 74) which, for the casually anti-Semitic Robert, is appropriately named and represents, for Caroline, 'an awful incubus', is 'dedicated', the narrator explains:

> to the purpose of conveying from house to house a monster collection of pincushions, needle-books, card-racks, work-bags, articles of infant-wear, &c. &c. &c., made by the willing or reluctant hands of the Christian ladies of a parish, and sold perforce to the heathenish gentlemen thereof, at prices unblushingly exorbitant. The proceeds of such compulsory sales are applied to the conversion of the Jews, the seeking up of the ten missing tribes, or to the regeneration of the interesting coloured population of the globe.   (p. 112)

The 'Jew's basket' plays a double part. On the one hand, it subjugates Caroline and other women to the drudgery of crafting the trivial domestic items which go into it. Yet on the other, the grossly inflated profits from the sale of these homespun sundries are channelled into a range of colonial and missionary projects designed for the apparent betterment of another 'monster collection', whose members include 'Jews' and 'the ten missing tribes', as well as 'the interesting coloured population of the globe'. The form

taken by one of the restrictions placed upon the female subject in
Shirley tacitly involves her in the oppression of the racial other.

In contrast to the 'Christian ladies' stitched into their places by
the 'heathenish gentlemen' whom they so shamelessly fleece,
Brontë's novel moves briefly, on a number of occasions, into the
very colonial spaces and futures towards which the 'phantom-
basket' (p. 113) motions. One of the ways it does this is by means
of what might be called its vignettes of migration. Two of the
more peculiar of these occur in the course of the courtship
between Shirley and Louis, the first in volume 3, chapter 3. Here
Shirley collaborates with Louis in the project of reinventing herself
beyond the stilted compass of middle-class English femininity:

> 'Oh, for rest under my own vine and my own fig-tree! Happy is the
> slave-wife of the Indian chief, in that she has no drawing-room duty
> to perform, but can sit at ease weaving mats, and stringing beads,
> and peacefully flattening her picaninny's head in an unmolested
> corner of her wigwam. I'll emigrate to the western woods.'
> Louis Moore laughed.
> 'To marry a White Cloud or a Big Buffalo; and after wedlock to
> devote yourself to the tender task of digging your lord's maize-field,
> while he smokes his pipe or drinks fire-water.'   (p. 468)

Shirley's effortless caricature of life in 'the western woods' is an
ironic one. Even as she reimagines herself as 'the slave-wife of [an]
Indian chief', the envisaged escape from 'drawing-room duty' only
reproduces other conditions of domestic incarceration. After all,
the slave-wife's occupation of 'weaving mats, and stringing beads'
is not very far removed from that of the women who expend their
labours and their lives in preparing the materials swallowed up by
the seemingly insatiable 'Jew's basket'.

This strange migration fantasy recurs, in a different form, in the
novel's penultimate chapter. Here Louis's diary records an exchange with Shirley in which the brothers Moore are cast by her
in the role of pioneers:

> 'You two might go forth homeless hunters to the loneliest western
> wilds; all would be well with you. The hewn tree would make you a
> hut, the cleared forest yield you fields from its stripped bosom, the
> buffalo would feel your rifle-shot, and with lowered horns and
> hump pay homage at your feet.'
> 'And any Indian tribe of Black-feet, or Flat-heads, would afford
> us a bride, perhaps?'

'No (hesitating): I think not. The savage is sordid: I think, – that is, I *hope*, – you would neither of you share your hearth with that to which you could not give your heart.'

'What suggested the wild West to your mind, Miss Keeldar?' (p. 613; emphasis in original)

This passage to some degree reverses the previous one. Now it seems the 'savage' is not an object of identification – something which Shirley might aspire to be – but 'sordid' and reified as an impersonal 'that'. The prospect of interracial desire, between Anglo-European adventurer and Native American 'bride', is not idealized here, but regarded as transgressive and unthinkable (as in the Ashanti narratives). This is somewhat ironic since both Shirley herself and Caroline are attracted to men whose racial pedigree renders them 'outcast and alien' (p. 38), albeit to a lesser degree than the Native American. The further irony of this passage emerges around the term 'savage'. Shirley applies this to the native subject and yet the text shows that savagery belongs more properly to her two fraternal frontiersmen. These 'homeless hunters' violently turn a natural environment to their own civilizing ends as they chop down trees, clear forest, shoot buffalo and have the power to appropriate the native woman for sexual pleasure and domestic oppression alike.

The larger significance of these two passages is that they suggest the paradoxical circularity of migration in *Shirley*. Just as the novel opens by obscuring the Irishness of Malone's 'face' with a 'North-American-Indian sort of visage', so its later narrative excursions into 'the wild West' point back, by the same token, towards the Famine and the diaspora to which it gave rise, concealing and revealing Ireland in the same gesture. This simultaneous play of concealment and revelation is perceptible, equally, in terms of corporeality, as the diverse bodies circulating in the novel both mask and disclose the traces of the history in which *Shirley* is enmeshed. Such a history, in other words, occupies the position of a kind of textual unconscious. Like the spectre of slavery in *Jane Eyre*, it is something unspeakable whose role is none the less determinate, entering into and shaping the very field of representation from which it is excluded.

The connections between Brontë's fiction and Ireland – so incidental to *Jane Eyre* and yet so integral to *Shirley* – are also evident to some degree in *Villette*, the novel which was to appear in

Shirley's wake. *Villette* holds less in common with its immediate predecessor, however, than *The Professor* and has, of course, long been recognized as marking a return to and reworking of Brontë's first novel. Yet if there is a sense of *déjà vu* (or *déjà lu*) between the two texts, there are also some striking differences and innovations. *Villette* does indeed reopen some of the questions already raised in *The Professor* – concerning itself with the relationships between sexuality, nation and race, for example, and the issue of slavery – but it approaches such topics from its own formally distinctive and ultimately more adventurous angles.

6

'A Thing Double-Existent': Foreigners and Slaves in *Villette*

> A woman is a foreign land.
>
> Coventry Patmore, 'The Angel in the House', Book II,
> Line 223

> Not read Mrs. Stowe's book! But you *must*. Her book is quite a sign of the times, and has otherwise an intrinsically considerable power. For myself, I rejoice in the success both as a woman and a human being. Oh, and is it possible that you think a woman has no business with questions like the question of slavery. Then she had better use a pen no more.
>
> Elizabeth Barrett Browning, letter to Anna Jameson,
> 12 April 1853[1]

> In her nightmare, always the same, she saw herself changed into a sugar statue, which the Frenchmen of France were slowly eating far far away at the other end of the world, first breaking off her fingers, so thin and long that they seemed unreal.
>
> André Schwarz-Bart, *A Woman Named Solitude*, p. 96

As a rewriting of *The Professor* from the perspective of a first-person female narrator, *Villette* clearly marks a significant departure from the male-centred stance adopted in the earlier text. Yet such a difference should not be allowed to obscure the continuities between the two novels. While Lucy Snowe comes to replace William Crimsworth as Brontë's narrator in *Villette*, the tale she tells displays traits which make her as much his counterpart as his opposite. In Lucy's vision of things, as in Crimsworth's before her, sexuality is racialized and race is sexualized. For the similarly repressed and xenophobic male and female narrators who bookend Brontë's brief career as novelist, desire, in other words, is a problem which constantly menaces their mutual sense of Englishness and is best solved by being projected onto the figure of the foreigner.

In its linkage of repressed sexuality with a generalized hostility towards the foreigner, *Villette* looks back towards *The Professor*, while at the same time restaging the materials of the earlier text from another viewpoint. This play of sameness and difference, continuity and change also informs the novel's more complex treatment of 'the question of slavery', as Barrett Browning calls it. As in *The Professor*, slavery provides an easy lexicon with which to organize and articulate other fields of experience, and the rights and wrongs of its deployment for such purposes are even, at various junctures in the novel, openly the source of reflection and debate. In contrast to *The Professor*, however, the question of slavery in *Villette* is more than just a controversy of figuration. What Brontë adds to the question is an intertextual dimension, as her novel engages with Harriet Beecher Stowe's *Uncle Tom's Cabin* (1852) and Jacques-Henri Bernardin de Saint-Pierre's *Paul and Virginia* (1788), texts respectively implicated in the histories of American slavery and French colonialism. While neither of these works has to date been placed in critical dialogue with *Villette*, their presence in Brontë's writing is less unexpected than it might seem. In engaging with Stowe's novel, for example, Brontë simultaneously reopens the issue of American slavery previously touched on via the allusion to Jim Crow in 'Caroline Vernon', and briefly invoked in this book's third chapter as a counterpoint to the racial figurings of *The Professor*. In engaging with *Paul and Virginia*, on the other hand, Brontë enters into a negotiation with a history already present in *Villette* in the form of Guadeloupe, still a French colonial possession, of course, until five years prior to *Villette*'s publication.

Figuring the foreigner

Following her initial appointment at the 'Pensionnat de Demoiselles'[2] as 'nursery-governess' (p. 81) to Madame Beck's three daughters, Lucy provides a brief description of the woman, Mrs Sweeny, whom she has displaced. The sketch is not flattering:

> Beside a table, on which flared the remnant of a candle guttering to waste in the socket, a coarse woman, heterogeneously clad in a broad-striped showy silk dress and a stuff apron, sat in a chair fast asleep. To complete the picture, and leave no doubt as to the state of matters, a bottle and an empty glass stood at the sleeping beauty's elbow.   (p. 68)

Lucy goes on to supplement this 'remarkable tableau' (p. 68) with a more detailed résumé of Mrs Sweeny's employment history. In the course of her account, it rapidly transpires that this 'heroine of the bottle' is not quite what she claims to be – 'an English lady in reduced circumstances', who has 'had the bringing-up of the son and daughter of a marquis' (p. 70). While there is 'no doubt' as to Mrs Sweeny's dissipated condition, her drunkenness is, for Lucy, just as certainly the index of national origins: 'I need hardly explain to the reader', she announces, 'that this lady was ... a native of Ireland' (p. 70). In making this statement, Lucy briefly courts a narrative version of the redundancy to which her arrival at Madame Beck's school has consigned her ill-disciplined predecessor, while at the same time recalling the Irish preoccupations of *Shirley*, of which Mrs Sweeny would herself appear to be a poorly accommodated 'remnant'.

The stereotypically Irish inebriation of this migrant from Brontë's previous novel mocks her persona as 'English lady', even as Mrs Sweeny's assumption of such a persona is, ironically, the sign of an equally stereotypical Irish duplicity. These two stereotypes of Irishness are compounded by a third, in the shape of Mrs Sweeny's implicitly felonious 'possession' of 'a wardrobe of rather suspicious splendour', whose 'chief item' is '*a real Indian shawl*' (p. 70; emphasis in original). As well as being pointedly authentic, this flamboyant Oriental fetish complements and extends the primary textual focus on Mrs Sweeny's self-fashioning as Englishwoman, suggesting a capacity for rather more daring and exotic experiments in racial transvestism.

Despite her eye-catching attire and striking line in self-fabrication, 'the intolerable Mrs. Sweeny' (p. 72) has elicited little attention from critics of *Villette*, giving rise to contradictory readings on the rare and fleeting occasions when her presence is acknowledged. For Sandra M. Gilbert and Susan Gubar, Mrs Sweeny should be seen as one of the narrator-heroine's many doubles. She is a 'counterfeiter', who 'reminds us that Lucy too hides her passions behind her costume'.[3] For Terry Lovell, by contrast, the relationship between the two figures is one of antithesis, with Mrs Sweeny as 'false pretender' to the 'bona fide *Englishwoman*'.[4] Gilbert and Gubar exhibit little interest in the 'nationalist bearings'[5] of *Villette* which galvanize the more culturally grounded Lovell. Even so, their recognition of Mrs Sweeny as Lucy's double remains useful, not least in its implication that Lovell's opposition between false and genuine Englishwomen is itself something of a pretence. After all, one of *Villette*'s more radical insights is that the 'English reserve' (p. 303) of its protagonist is itself a sham, an ideological fiction, albeit a powerful one, forged at the intersections between early Victorian discourses of gender, race and class. Like Mrs Sweeny, Lucy is not what she seems: the chimerical coherence of her identity – 'next day I was again Lucy Snowe' (p. 119) – is sustained only by the repression of those 'passions' (whether emotional or sexual) which threaten to disrupt it, breaking 'the whole repose of [her] nature' (p. 119).

Lucy's acts of self-repression can sometimes be extreme. The most literally stunning example of this occurs in chapter 12, in the aftermath of a 'thunderstorm' which temporarily awakens within her the mysterious 'being [she is] always lulling' (p. 109). Here Lucy invokes a lurid biblical tale of female murder in order to dramatize a struggle with desires unspecified:

> I did long, achingly, then and for four-and-twenty hours afterwards, for something to fetch me out of my present existence, and lead me upwards and onwards. This longing, and all of a similar kind, it was necessary to knock on the head; which I did, figuratively, after the manner of Jael to Sisera, driving a nail through their temples. Unlike Sisera, they did not die: they were but transiently stunned, and at intervals would turn on the nail with a rebellious wrench; then did the temples bleed, and the brain thrill to its core.   (pp. 109–10)

One of the subtler effects of this passage is to place its reader in a position analogous to that of Sisera himself, who, in Brontë's source-text, is duped by Jael into thinking that she will protect him from his enemies.[6] The passage offers nothing like the sweet resolution of subjective turmoil which might be anticipated from the earlier use of the word 'lulling'. Instead it maps the spaces of what Dr John will later diagnose as Lucy's 'long-continued mental conflict' (p. 249) in a language of aggression and pain which is as brutal as it is precise.

Villette is not solely concerned, however, with plotting the ideologically constructed nature of middle-class English femininity and the acts of self-repression on which it is predicated. If such acts entail considerable violence, there is another kind of violence abroad in Brontë's novel, articulated in a recurrent vision of the foreigner which is highly negative, not to say pathological. Such a vision evolves as much from Brontë's commentaries on her two brief periods of residence, in the early 1840s, at the Pensionnat Heger in Brussels, as from *The Professor*. The cutting tone of Brontë's reflections on this 'foreign venture'[7] is typified in a letter to Ellen Nussey, written in July 1842:

> If the national character of the Belgians is to be measured by the character of most of the girls in this school, it is a character singularly cold, selfish, animal and inferior – they are besides very mutinous and difficult for the teachers to manage – and their principles are rotten to the core.[8]

The strain of xenophobia in this letter pervades *Villette* from first to last and is even insinuated into the novel's two main fictional place-names. The 'great capital of the great kingdom of Labassecour' (p. 55) is not so great, since 'Villette'/Brussels means 'little town', just as 'Labassecour'/Belgium self-mockingly translates itself into English as 'farm-' or 'poultry-yard'.

In its fluctuation between the psychic predicaments of its central figure and the larger question of 'national character', *Villette* would seem to constitute a rather fractured project, as if such splits were the thematic equivalent to the novel's nervous switches between realist and Gothic modes. The novel's psychic and national concerns are not quite as hopelessly estranged from one another as they might appear, however, as is initially suggested in the course of the narrative transition from England to 'the continent of Europe' (p. 56). At the end of chapter 6, Lucy completes her Channel crossing by arriving at night at the primevally named port of Boue-Marine (meaning 'sea-mud'). This moment is doubly significant. As well as looking forward to the concern with surveillance which will become so prominent in the novel as a whole,[9] Lucy's initial impressions of Europe construct it as a place of multiple menace. As she puts it, 'the lights of the foreign sea-port town, glimmering round the foreign harbour', confront her 'like unnumbered threatening eyes' (p. 57).

This identification of the foreign with a sense of incalculable danger is developed in the following chapter. Here Lucy makes another nocturnal arrival, this time at Villette itself, and struggles to retrieve her trunk from the conductor of the stage-coach on which she has been travelling. Hampered in her efforts by an inability to speak the French which 'the whole world' seems to be 'now gabbling' (p. 61) around her, she receives assistance from 'a true young English gentleman' (p. 63). Lucy is clearly attracted to this intercessional figure – later revealed to be Dr John – whose appearance is 'good enough for a prince' (p. 62) and whose 'frank tread' (p. 63) provides a sound contrast to 'the gliding step foreigners practise' (p. 338). Yet the fairy-tale promise of this brief encounter is not fulfilled. Less chivalrous than he is supposed to be, Dr John chaperons Lucy across a park which 'it is too late and too dark for a woman to go through … alone', but eventually leaves her to make her own way towards the English-speaking inn he has recommended. '[H]urrying fast through a magnificent street and square' (p. 63), Lucy finds herself abruptly swayed off course:

> Just as I passed a portico, two moustachioed men came suddenly from behind the pillars; they were smoking cigars, their dress implied pretensions to the rank of gentlemen, but, poor things! they were very plebeian in soul. They spoke with insolence, and, fast as I walked, they kept pace with me a long way. At last I met a sort of patrol, and my dreaded hunters were turned from the pursuit; but they had driven me beyond my reckoning: when I could collect my faculties, I no longer knew where I was; … puzzled, out of breath, all my pulses throbbing in inevitable agitation, I knew not where to turn. It was terrible to think of again encountering those bearded, sneering simpletons; yet the ground must be retraced.   (p. 64)

While this accidental crossing of paths culminates in disorientation – 'I no longer knew where I was' – there is a sense in which the very account of it is also somewhat wayward, a distinctly Gothic product of the 'overheated and discursive imagination' (p. 12) Lucy so questionably disavows. The 'two moustachioed men' are demonized into 'dreaded hunters', as urban space becomes a labyrinthine site of sexual 'pursuit', complete with crudely phallic 'pillars' and 'cigars' and a female body left 'puzzled' and 'out of breath', with 'all [its] pulses throbbing'. In refiguring her 'sneering simpletons' as sexual predators, Lucy ironically partakes of that 'suspicious nature so far misled by its own inventions' (p. 119) which she later attributes to Madame Beck. At the same time, she offers a panic-ridden narrative whose logic is strangely circular or claustral. The transgressive desire (for Dr John) which Lucy, as middle-class Englishwoman, must repress, is subjected to a double alienation. As well as being projected onto the foreigner, it is translated into the form of male sexual threat, simultaneously rendering Lucy's flight from her imaginary pursuers a covert flight from herself.

The double alienation of Lucy's desire in this early scene – it is channelled through the foreigner and regendered en route – is a process evident elsewhere in *Villette*, as, for example, in Lucy's extraordinary portrait of Zélie St Pierre. This Parisian teacher, introduced in the opening paragraphs of chapter 14, is Madame Beck's deputy at the pensionnat and one of Lucy's main rivals for the affections of the 'professor of literature' (p. 129), Monsieur Paul Emanuel. Zélie is an even more critically marginalized figure than Mrs Sweeny, yet her presence in *Villette* is worth considering in some detail. Part of her importance, for Lucy at least, is that she fully vindicates the essentialist distinctions between the 'continental' and 'the insular "female"' (p. 79) upon which Lucy's identity as proper Englishwoman is so reliant:

> [Zélie] was ... externally refined – at heart, corrupt – without a creed, without a principle, without an affection: having penetrated the outward crust of decorum in this character, you found a slough beneath. . . .
> [She] was prodigal and profligate (in disposition, that is: as to action, I do not know). That latter quality showed its snake-head to me but once, peeping out very cautiously. A curious kind of reptile it seemed, judging from the glimpse I got; its novelty whetted my curiosity: if it would have come out boldly, perhaps I might philosophically have stood my ground, and coolly surveyed the long thing from forked tongue to scaly tail-tip; but it merely rustled in the leaves of a bad novel; and, on encountering a hasty and ill-advised demonstration of wrath, recoiled and vanished, hissing. She hated me from that day.
> This Parisienne was always in debt; her salary being anticipated by expenses – not only in dress, but in perfumes, cosmetics, confectionery, and condiments. . . . She mortally hated work, and loved what she called pleasure; being an insipid, heartless, brainless dissipation of time. (pp. 126–7)

Here Zélie emerges, ironically, as no more 'pure-minded' (p. 143) than the 'girls of almost every European nation' (p. 82) whom she teaches. What is notable about this vituperative passage is the different discourses it enlists in order to establish the reprehensibility of its subject. As the passage begins, the reader is offered an archaeology of the foreigner, with Lucy excavating Zélie's decorous 'outward crust' to find 'a slough beneath'. This archaeological idiom in turn gives way to a zoological one, as the initial tropes of 'penetrated' 'crust' and hidden mire are cast off in favour of an extended reptilian metaphor. Lucy's venomous deployment of this second rhetorical strategy is just as 'curious' as the 'profligate' sexuality it refigures, since the 'snake-head' and 'long thing' she would like to view 'from forked tongue to scaly tail-tip' have a coarsely phallic resonance. These frail euphemisms would not be out of place among 'the leaves of [the] bad novel' which Zélie is caught reading, but their greater significance consists in the way they firmly rearticulate Zélie's 'pleasure' in the language of male desire. This is an effect also discernible in the concluding account of Zélie's self-inflicted financial difficulties. While her state of permanent 'debt' accrues from the purchase of stereotypically feminine luxuries – 'perfumes, cosmetics, confectionery, and condiments' – her 'prodigal' outlays recall the circulation of money in Victorian medical discourses, and *The Professor*, as a metaphorical means of representing a male sexual economy. As in the previous encounter with her 'dreaded hunters', Lucy's repressed sexuality is transposed onto the figure of a foreign other, who gives it back to her in a strangely male guise.

Villette's invective against the foreigner is not restricted merely to a continental horizon. At one point, it moves further afield in the direction of the Orient, as if Lucy were seeking to effect a fuller displacement or projection of the sexuality she cannot acknowledge in herself. This Oriental shift, also characteristic of *The Professor*, occurs in chapter 19, in Lucy's dramatic set-piece confrontation, in one of Villette's 'picture-galleries' (p. 198), with the painting of the 'huge, dark-complexioned gipsy-queen' (p. 200), Cleopatra. As well as replicating the outlandish bodily proportions of its subject in its 'pretentious size', 'this picture' is, it seems, sufficiently self-admiring as to take on Cleopatra's regal status by 'consider[ing] itself the queen of the collection' (p. 199) of which it is a part. Lucy, however, refuses to validate the painting's inflated self-regard, debunking it with a scathing review:

It represented a woman, considerably larger, I thought, than the life. I calculated that this lady, put into a scale of magnitude suitable for the reception of a commodity of bulk, would infallibly turn from fourteen to sixteen stone. She was, indeed, extremely well fed: very much butcher's meat – to say nothing of bread, vegetables, and liquids – must she have consumed to attain that breadth and height, that wealth of muscle, that affluence of flesh. She lay half-reclined on a couch: why, it would be difficult to say; broad daylight blazed round her; she appeared in hearty health, strong enough to do the work of two plain cooks; she could not plead a weak spine; she ought to have been standing, or at least sitting bolt upright. She had no business to lounge away the noon on a sofa. She ought likewise to have worn decent garments; a gown covering her properly, which was not the case: out of abundance of material – seven-and-twenty yards, I should say, of drapery – she managed to make inefficient raiment. Then, for the wretched untidiness surrounding her, there could be no excuse. Pots and pans – perhaps I ought to say vases and goblets – were rolled here and there on the foreground; a perfect rubbish of flowers was mixed amongst them, and an absurd and disorderly mass of curtain upholstery smothered the couch and cumbered the floor. On referring to the catalogue, I found that this notable production bore name 'Cleopatra.'   (pp. 199–200)

'[T]his notable production' takes its place in *Villette* as the Oriental counterpart to the 'remarkable tableau' of Mrs Sweeny delineated in chapter 8. At the same time, as Jill. L. Matus has argued, it participates in a nineteenth-century Western patriarchal tradition of pictorial representation in which the figure of Cleopatra comes to function 'as the acme of exotic Oriental sexuality'.[10] Lucy's resistance to the picture of 'the indolent gipsy-giantess' (p. 202) – dismissed as 'on the whole an enormous piece of claptrap' (p. 200) – is thus also a critique of the larger male-driven body of Orientalist conventions on which the composition draws.

It is not just the painterly Orientalism exhibited in the work of 'the artist of the Cleopatra' (p. 258) which incurs Lucy's displeasure here. As she gazes at his creation, 'examining, questioning, and forming conclusions' (p. 198), Lucy becomes less exercised by the painting's aesthetic deficiencies than the personal flaws of the 'dusk and portly Venus of the Nile' (p. 205) whom it represents. These flaws, it would appear, are numerous. In the first instance, they pertain to Cleopatra's 'bulk', which, Lucy 'calculate[s]', places her somewhere between 'fourteen' and 'sixteen stone' in weight. Such 'mighty brawn' (p. 258) implicitly results from the overconsumption of 'very much butcher's meat' and other foods and 'liquids', items perhaps contributory to the untimely languor with which Cleopatra 'lounge[s] away the noon on a sofa'. Each of these expressions of bodily ill-discipline is, of course, a loosely coded signifier of sexual appetite, a pattern maintained in Cleopatra's perverse failure to contain her own flesh within the ample 'material' at her disposal. This long inventory of faults is brought to an end only by a new complaint, directed not at Cleopatra's hypersexualized body but the randomized and neglected space which that body inhabits, with its 'Pots and pans ... roll[ing] here and there' and its 'perfect rubbish of flowers'. Yet the final sign of Cleopatra's domestic disarray suggests a certain blurring between poor housekeeping and corporeal mismanagement, as it becomes difficult to distinguish the 'curtain upholstery smother[ing] the couch' from the couch's slothful occupant: each is its own 'disorderly mass'.

Lucy's *ad feminam* indictment of Cleopatra's sexual and domestic abandon rewards further consideration. As Matus points out, the 'plumpness and lassitude' (and indeed 'slovenliness') characterizing Lucy's Cleopatra are also qualities stereotypically ascribed in Victorian social and medical discourses to the figure of the prostitute.[11] This is an observation supported by the repeated metaphorical association of Cleopatra's corporeality with forms of economic exchange and prosperity: she is 'a commodity of bulk', possessing both 'wealth of muscle' and 'affluence of flesh'. '[H]alf-reclined on a couch', she is presented in 'the posture of a whore',[12] whose 'business' is evidently thriving.

As uncorseted Oriental prostitute, Cleopatra could hardly offer a more startling alternative to the straight-laced norms of the middle-class English femininity with which Lucy identifies, however ambivalently. But as much as she is Lucy's opposite, Cleopatra is also her uncanny double, literally embodying the sexuality Lucy denies in herself. *Villette* teases its readers with this parallel in chapter 38, where Lucy gives an opium-tinctured account of the 'festal night' (p. 454) on which Labassecour celebrates its independence from its oppressors. These annual rituals of national self-definition are as peculiar as they are extravagant. Intended as 'a commemoration of patriotic sacrifice' (p. 460), they entail a different kind of surrender. The Labassecouriens' sense of their own nationhood proves to be a surprisingly fragile thing, dissolving in the moment of its assertion, to be rebuilt in the image of another realm. Europe is briefly Orientalized, as Lucy is seemingly transported to 'a land of enchantment' (p. 453). Here for a while she becomes caught up in that weird 'mix of Afro-Egyptian images', which demarcates, as Isobel Armstrong has noted, 'the primal scene of [Brontë's] early writing':[13]

> a garden most gorgeous, a plain sprinkled with coloured meteors, a forest with sparks of purple and ruby and golden fire gemming the foliage; a region, not of trees and shadow, but of strangest architectural wealth – of altar and of temple, of pyramid, obelisk, and sphynx; incredible to say, the wonders and the symbols of Egypt teemed throughout the park of Villette.   (p. 453)

Despite being 'drugged to the brink of frenzy' (p. 456), Lucy 'quickly recognize[s]' this exotic vision for the charade it is, even as her 'inevitable discoveries' do not 'quite … undermine the marvel of [the] night'. The 'solemn fragments' of ancient Egyptian culture which she beholds are traceable to origins homely enough, composed, as they are, from mere 'timber … paint, and … paste-board'.

The Labassecouriens' assimilation of such Oriental 'spectacles, decorations, and illuminations' – which even extend to include 'the image of a white ibis, fixed on a column' – into their 'great fête' (p. 453) provides an appropriate context for Lucy's less conspicuous identifications with her Egyptian other, Cleopatra. As she jostles among both 'peasantry' and 'decent burghers … dressed in their best' (p. 454), Lucy makes a small adjustment to her own working-class garb, designed to ensure that her clandestine presence in Villette's crowded 'summer-park' (p. 450) is not detected:

> My straw-hat passed amidst cap and jacket, short petticoat, and long calico mantle, without, perhaps, attracting a glance; I only took the precaution to bind down the broad leaf gipsy-wise, with a supplementary ribbon; and then I felt safe as if masked.   (p. 454)

Lucy's modest sartorial prophylaxis ironically reveals as much as it 'mask[s]', as the decision to wear her 'straw-hat' 'gipsy-wise' suggests a Cleopatran doubling.

To be doubled with Cleopatra is necessarily also to take on another 'mantle', that of the prostitute. Lucy's positioning in this role is something at which *Villette* hints in the ambiguous scene in which she attends 'a grand concert in the open air' (p. 454). As she strives to remain anonymous among the concert-goers, Lucy finds herself situated, like Cleopatra, as a spectacle or 'study' for the male gaze, falling, specifically, under the 'scrutiny' (p. 457) of

Dr John. In the earlier gallery-scene, Dr John shuns the self-flaunting Cleopatra, defining her, somewhat loosely, as a 'mulatto' who is 'little to [his] liking' (p. 206). Here, by contrast, he takes a special interest in the rather more obscure figure before him, complete with its 'straw-hat and closely-folded shawl' (p. 455):

> Why, if he *would* look, did not one glance satisfy him? why did he turn on his chair, rest his elbow on its back, and study me leisurely? He could not see my face, I held it down; surely, he *could* not recognize me; I stooped, I turned, I *would* not be known. He rose, by some means he contrived to approach, in two minutes he would have had my secret; my identity would have been grasped between his never tyrannous, but always powerful hands. There was but one way to evade or to check him. I implied, by a sort of supplicatory gesture, that it was my prayer to be let alone. . . . He looked, but he desisted. He shook his handsome head, but he was mute. He resumed his seat, nor did he again turn or disturb me by a glance, except indeed for one single instant, when a look, rather solicitous than curious, stole my way.   (p. 457; emphases in original)

This is an uncertain passage, whose meanings hinge upon the nature of the motivations underlying Dr John's unsated 'glance' and anticipated 'approach'. Is Lucy correct in assuming that, despite her efforts at concealment, Dr John has 'recognize[d]' her? Or is it that, as Armstrong speculates, he has 'mistaken [her] for a prostitute'[14] (or park woman) and 'come[s] forward with the intention of accosting her'?[15] Either way, Lucy blocks Dr John's rapid advance with the 'supplicatory gesture' which both preserves her incognito and releases her from the compromising position in which she has been slyly placed by the text: in an odd transposition of roles, it is not, in the end, her own 'look' which is 'solicitous', but Dr John's. Lucy 'evade[s]' the frame of male fantasy here, even as her language works to uncover the sexual nature of the 'secret' she withholds. The fearful vision in which she imagines the truth of her 'identity ... grasped between [Dr John's] always powerful hands' is couched in something close to wanton innuendo.

The projection of desire onto the figure of the foreigner is as regular a ritual in *Villette* for Lucy as it is for Crimsworth in *The Professor*. It could be further demonstrated, for example, in terms of Lucy's relationship to the spectral 'black and white nun', who habitually returns to haunt the formerly conventual site of Madame Beck's school, where she had originally been 'buried alive, for some sin against her vow', by 'a monkish conclave of the drear middle ages'. As numerous critics have noted, the mysterious 'legend' (p. 106) attached to this striking Gothic revenant makes her the perfect double for Lucy, who is forced constantly to repress the very desires of which the nun's returns are the fearful symbolic expression.[16] If *Villette*'s nun is the purveyor of a disavowed sexuality, however, she possesses other functions as well. In particular, her presence marks a reopening of the question of slavery, articulated in the form of a dialogue with Stowe's *Uncle Tom's Cabin*, the first of *Villette*'s two main intertexts.[17]

Transatlantic Gothic

Although *Villette* and *Uncle Tom's Cabin* might seem, at first glance, to have little to do with one another, Brontë herself implicitly brings the two texts together, albeit as antitheses. She does this in a letter of 30 October 1852, written to her publisher, George Smith, at a time when *Villette* was 'not finished yet'.[18] Here Brontë sets out a brief anticipatory apologia for the text on which she is working, specifically contrasting her own fictional practices with those of Stowe, whose novel had appeared some seven months earlier:

> You will see that 'Villette' touches on no matter of public interest. I cannot write books handling the topics of the day; it is of no use trying. Nor can I write a book for its moral. Nor can I take up a philanthropic scheme, though I honour philanthropy; and voluntarily and sincerely veil my face before such a mighty subject as that handled in Mrs. Beecher Stowe's work, 'Uncle Tom's Cabin.' To manage these great matters rightly, they must be long and practically studied – their bearings known intimately, and their evils felt genuinely; they must not be taken up as a business matter, and a trading speculation. I doubt not, Mrs. Stowe had felt the iron of slavery enter into her heart, from childhood upwards, long before she ever thought of writing books. The feeling throughout her work is sincere, and not got up.[19]

In describing how the act of reading *Uncle Tom's Cabin* metaphorically prompts her 'voluntarily and sincerely' to 'veil [her] face', Brontë produces a variety of effects. First, she signals her sense of the deference due to the issue of slavery which dominates Stowe's novel, but which seems so far removed from the narrative terrains traversed by her own. Secondly, she indicates a desire to block out the 'topics' Stowe 'handl[es]' so adroitly, perhaps even instantly erasing them in the euphemism which dextrously refigures slavery as an oxymoronic 'mighty subject'. Thirdly and most significantly, she looks directly back towards the very nun whose ghostly appearance repeatedly disrupts *Villette*'s realist surfaces, her identity always blanked out by a 'white face-cloth' (p. 254). As this last effect suggests, Brontë's response to Stowe's novel is formulated in terms which ironically recall *Villette*'s main Gothic personage. The solemn and unusual trope of the veiled authorial face thus not only doubles the vehemently anti-Catholic Brontë with her own religious spectre. It also works to establish that spectre as an implicit link in a surreptitious inter-textual chain binding *Villette* to *Uncle Tom's Cabin* and, in particular, to 'the old ghost legend'[20] of racial and sexual conflict which begins to surface in the closing chapters of Stowe's novel.

A good starting point from which to trace out the submerged concatenation of Brontë's 'ghost story' (p. 106) with Stowe's is provided in chapter 22 of *Villette*. Here Lucy retreats 'into the deep, black, cold garret' (p. 243) at the top of the pensionnat, in order to read a letter from Dr John, whose promised 'shape' has 'haunted [her] brain in its very core for seven days past' (p. 238). Despite being 'firm, substantial [and] satisfying' in its feel, the communiqué proves, once unsealed in the attic, to be disappointingly 'flimsy' (p. 239) in its contents: it is 'simply good-natured – nothing more'. While Lucy none the less claims that she has been made to feel 'happier than most queens in palaces' and is indeed 'deeply blessed' (p. 244) by the possession of the letter, the text suggests a profound dismay. The sexual desires for Dr John which Lucy censors in herself are not only glancingly signalled in the allusion to the palatial Cleopatra. They are also figured in the sudden advent of another 'shape', rather more spectacularly 'haunting' than that attributed to Dr John's prosaic missive:

> Are there wicked things, not human, which envy human bliss? Are there evil influences haunting the air, and poisoning it for man? What was near me? ...
> Something in that vast solitary garret sounded strangely. Most surely and certainly I heard, as it seemed, a stealthy foot on that floor: a sort of gliding out from the direction of the black recess haunted by the malefactor cloaks. I turned: my light was dim; the room was long – but, as I live! I saw in the middle of that ghostly

chamber a figure all black or white; the skirts straight, narrow, black; the head bandaged, veiled, white.

Say what you will, reader – tell me I was nervous, or mad; affirm that I was unsettled by the excitement of that letter; declare that I dreamed: this I vow – I saw there – in that room – on that night – an image like – a NUN. (pp. 244–5; ellipsis in original)

As this demonic passage indicates, *Villette*'s typographically elevated 'NUN' proves to be as uncontainable a figure in her death as in her life. She surges up through the crypt of Brontë's loosening syntax in an act of defiance analogous to the sexual transgression which had been the tacit cause of her entombment in the first place. Her posthumous resistance to the patriarchal authority of Catholicism serves as a timely reminder to Lucy that the repression of desire is only a prelude to its inevitable and terrifying return.

Just as Lucy's 'gaunt nun' (p. 255) refuses to be contained by the dictates of Catholicism, so she is not entirely restricted to the symbolic duties of being a signifier for female desire – whether repressed, as in Lucy's case, or unruly, as in her own. This is something which *Villette* itself suggests in the typically Brontëan manoeuvre which figures Catholicism in terms of slavery. Lucy's description, in chapter 14, of the daily rituals of religious indoctrination performed at the pensionnat is a particularly pertinent example of this familiar rhetorical operation:

A strange, frolicsome, noisy little world was this school: great pains were taken to hide chains with flowers: a subtle essence of Romanism pervaded every arrangement: large sensual indulgence (so to speak) was permitted by way of counterpoise to jealous spiritual restraint. Each mind was being reared in slavery. (p. 127)

The problems attendant upon the slave metaphor have been discussed in detail in Chapters 2 and 3 of this book and require no further elaboration. What does need to be noted here, however, is the way in which the return of the metaphor in the context of Catholicism invests *Villette*'s errant nun with a new symbolic potential. The logical implication of the metaphor is to establish a certain correspondence between the nun's acts of defiance and those of a rebel slave. The corollary to this oblique rhetorical transformation of nun into slave is that the Gothic narrative of white female oppression in which she participates takes on an additional racial dimension, moving beyond the feminist critical frameworks usually placed around it.

As if to underscore this point, the passage cited above features an echo at once blatant and recherché of *Uncle Tom's Cabin*, as the 'little world' of the pensionnat becomes caught in a wider and rather less 'frolicsome' vision. The seductive practice of 'hid[ing] chains with flowers' is not exclusive to the 'Romanism' whose 'subtle essence' suffuses Madame Beck's school. It is also characteristic of the sentimentalized but still disciplinary regime favoured by Augustine St Clare, one of the slave-masters to whom the eponymous hero of Stowe's novel is subjected. As Stowe's narrator reviews Tom's odyssey through the mournful 'valley of slavery' at the beginning of chapter 40, she describes the period of his ownership under the ironically cultivated St Clare as one, precisely, when 'generous hands concealed his chains with flowers' (*UTC*, p. 354). Brontë's female Gothic is, it turns out, as much haunted by America's slave narrative as is the pensionnat by the 'nun of the attic' (p. 470).

In the end, *Villette*'s 'sable-robed, snowy-veiled woman' (p. 297) turns out to be a 'phantom' (p. 470) in more senses than one. As both Lucy and her 'reader' finally learn, the nun's ghostly presence is nothing but a mischievous 'spectral disguise', concocted by Colonel Alfred de Hamal. De Hamal utilizes the pensionnat's 'legend of the nun' (p. 474) as a stratagem by which to infiltrate its grounds in order to carry out his secret assignations with the 'vain coquette' (p. 87), Ginevra Fanshawe, with whom he eventually elopes and then goes on to marry. The romantic subterfuge is officially disclosed only towards the end of Brontë's novel, in Ginevra's letter celebrating her 'moonlight flitting and runaway match' (p. 475). It is, however, something at which the text hints even in the moment of the nun's initial stepping forth. In the passage already cited from chapter 22, the reference to the 'malefactor cloaks' from which the nun seems to 'glid[e] out' is a flirtatious nod in De Hamal's direction. It cryptically reveals his status as the figure quite literally behind the ruse of the resurrected nun: 'malefactor' = 'male factor'.

De Hamal's self-serving appropriation of the nun's story forms the final respect in which Brontë's novel intersects with *Uncle Tom's Cabin*. In Stowe's text, the role of ghostly impersonator falls to Cassy, enslaved quadroon mistress to the Louisiana planter and 'southern grotesque',[21] Simon Legree. For Cassy, though, it is not a dead nun but a dead slave who becomes the subject of impersonation. This slave's narrative is intimately tied to a Gothic location both akin to but ultimately more menacing than *Villette*'s 'haunted grenier' (p. 255):

> The garret of the house that Legree occupied, like most other garrets, was a great, desolate space, dusty, hung with cobwebs, and littered with cast-off lumber. . . . Altogether, it was a weird and ghostly place; but, ghostly as it was, it wanted not in legends among the superstitious negroes, to increase its terrors. Some few years before, a negro woman, who had incurred Legree's displeasure, was confined there for several weeks. What passed there, we do not say; the negroes used to whisper darkly to each other; but it was known that the body of the unfortunate creature was one day taken down from there, and buried; and, after that, it was said that oaths and cursings and the sound of violent blows, used to ring through that old garret, and mingled with wailings and groans of despair. (*UTC*, p. 346)

Like De Hamal to Lucy, Cassy 'play[s] ghost' (*UTC*, p. 353) to Legree. In an inspired dialectical reversal, she manipulates this *sotto voce* account of black female oppression to her own 'purpose' (*UTC*, p. 346) in a bitter 'game' (*UTC*, p. 350) of hide-and-seek which turns the 'terrors' of slavery back upon their perpetrator. Installing herself in the 'fatal garret' (*UTC*, p. 366), Cassy exploits the 'superstitious excitability … so great in Legree' (*UTC*, p. 346) by masquerading as the scandalized spirit of the 'unfortunate creature' whom he had gradually beaten to death, 'Some few years before'. Already in the grip of a powerful racial guilt, Legree mistakes the somewhat clichéd 'tall figure in a white sheet' who 'glide[s] about [his] house' (*UTC*, p. 366) for the retributive ghost of his mother, whose earnest attempts 'to win him from a life of sin' (*UTC*, p. 323) he has rebutted. Despite this misrecognition, Cassy's 'ghostly disguise' (*UTC*, p. 367) achieves its objective. As well as sealing Legree's psychological disintegration and death, it enables Cassy's 'liberation' from her oppressor, together with 'that of her fellow-sufferer' (*UTC*, p. 346), the 15-year-old Emmeline, Legree's next intended sexual victim.

That *Villette* should enter into a transatlantic exchange with *Uncle Tom's Cabin* is not wholly surprising, given the existence of other connections between Brontë and Stowe, whether these be spookily biographical or more conventionally literary. As Gilbert and Gubar point out, Stowe claimed, for example, to have been visited by Brontë's 'spectral presence' and 'did not seem particularly incredulous that her ghostly guest [had] crossed the

Atlantic'.[22] For Diane Roberts, on the other hand, *Uncle Tom's Cabin* 'shows [its] debt to ... Brontë in the narrative of Cassy, the "madwoman" who eventually masters the master from her attic'.[23] In Roberts's reading, Cassy can be compared to Bertha Mason of *Jane Eyre*, another figure born from the conjunction of Gothic and racial/racist discourses. As Roberts notes, however, one of the differences between the two women is that Cassy's rage towards Legree ensures her survival, while Bertha's towards Rochester results only in her destruction.[24]

What is striking about the revisionary sequence uniting these three texts – *Jane Eyre*, *Uncle Tom's Cabin* and *Villette* – is its repetitiveness. The acts of ghostly impersonation at the Gothic centres of *Villette* and *Uncle Tom's Cabin* rely alike upon the requisition of stories buried in the past – whether a nun's or a slave's – to meet specific needs in the present. Such strategic requisitions in turn characterize Stowe's initial response to Brontë and Brontë's counter-response to Stowe, as each exhumes the other's writing for her own ends. In a further repetition, the intertextual relationships established between *Jane Eyre* and *Uncle Tom's Cabin*, on the one hand, and *Uncle Tom's Cabin* and *Villette*, on the other, are predicated upon cross-racial analogies which are difficult to sustain. Roberts's claim that Cassy is a reincarnation of Bertha is questionable, since, for all the maltreatment meted out to her by Rochester, Bertha is herself a plantocratic subject, profiting from a West Indian version of the slavery by which Cassy is victimized in America. Similarly, the intertextual doubling of Brontë's nun with Stowe's battered 'negro woman' brings together orders of female oppression whose linkage is compromised, if not fully undone, by the stubbornly constructed realities of racial difference. The critical distinction between the predicaments of Cassy and Bertha undercuts Brontë's conviction that 'Stowe had felt the iron of slavery enter into her heart ... long before she ever thought of writing books'. Equally, the problematic nature of the intertextual nun/slave analogy in *Villette* confirms Brontë's misgiving that she herself is unable 'To manage these great matters rightly'.

In its subterranean dialogue with *Uncle Tom's Cabin*, *Villette* expands the question of slavery beyond the framework initially established in *The Professor* and more fully developed in *Jane Eyre*: drawing narratives of white and black female oppression into parallel with one another, it reconfigures the troubled politics of metaphor as an equally uneasy politics of intertextuality. *Uncle*

Tom's Cabin is not *Villette*'s only intertext, however, Brontë's novel engaging also with Bernardin's *Paul and Virginia*. This text, located in an eighteenth-century French rather than a nineteenth-century American abolitionist literary tradition, becomes increasingly important as *Villette* moves into its final stages. In *Villette*'s third volume, in particular, its materials are strikingly appropriated by Brontë and transformed into a sentimental melodrama, in which colonial exploitation and ill-starred love – as in the original – go hand in hand.

Rewriting *Paul and Virginia*

In a postscript to a letter written to Heger from Haworth on 24 October 1844, Brontë catalogues the miscellaneous textual gifts received from her former teacher and unresponsive beau during the period 'when [she] was still in Brussels':

> I have just had bound all the books that you gave me. . . . I take pleasure in looking at them – they make quite a little library – First there are the complete works of Bernardin de St. Pierre – the Pensées of Pascal – a book of verse, two German books – and (something worth all the rest) two speeches, by Professor Heger – given at the Prize Distribution of the Athénée Royal.[25]

While these freshly 'bound' volumes afford their owner a decidedly tart visual 'pleasure', it is doubtful whether all of them would make an entirely gratifying read. Amongst the 'books' included in Brontë's 'little library', there is one text rather more likely to induce a bittersweet response in Heger's 'devoted pupil', writing without word from her distant correspondent for some 'six months'.[26] This is Bernardin's *Paul and Virginia*, summarized by Margaret Smith, in her notes to Brontë's letter, as 'a highly popular sentimental romantic tale of parted lovers'.[27] Unnamed but implied in Brontë's literary inventory, this narrative of constancy maintained against the trials of separation resonates ironically with the emotionally defeated circumstances in which the letter to Heger is composed.

If Bernardin's novel is a 'sentimental romantic tale', it is also a colonial one, having, as Anna Neill notes, a 'precise geographical and historical setting'.[28] This is the island of Mauritius, annexed by the French in 1715 and worked by them as a slave colony until

1810, when the Île de France, as it had been renamed, came under British rule. It is in this colonial space, located off Africa's East Coast, that *Paul and Virginia*'s eponymous male and female protagonists are born and grow up together, the respective Creole offspring of two socially outcast Frenchwomen, the peasant Margaret and the aristocratic Madame de la Tour. While these 'children of nature'[29] gradually become sexually attracted to one another in the course of their adolescence, their simple happiness is blighted by the intervention of Madame de la Tour's aunt – 'rich, old and a great bigot' (*PV*, p. 14) – who demands that the 15-year-old Virginia come to Paris to be educated and splendidly married, promising 'the inheritance of her whole fortune' (*PV*, p. 48) in exchange. Virginia is obliged by economic and familial considerations to comply with this project, but resists the upper-class metropolitan persona in which her aunt attempts to imprison her and resolves to return home. The 'melancholy narration' (*PV*, p. 99) climaxes in a 'day of horror' (*PV*, p. 86), as Virginia is drowned in a shipwreck, close to the shores of her native land. Paul, her grief-stricken lover, dies two months afterwards.

This Mauritian love story provides a broad framework within and against which Brontë plots her own colonial romance in *Villette*'s third volume. At this point in the narrative, the tenor of Lucy's relationship to Monsieur Paul alters dramatically, as the reciprocal animosity which marks their earlier interactions gives way to a mood of increasing intimacy and accord. As with Bernardin's budding couple, however, the mutual hopes of Brontë's more mature would-be lovers are threatened and, in the end, comprehensively dashed by external forces. Madame de la Tour's 'hard-hearted' (*PV*, p. 14) aunt is resurrected in Brontë's text in the even more baleful shape of Madame Walravens, whose 'desperate ill-humour' (p. 391) is both fully reflected in her bodily deformity and recalls the 'malignant dispositions' characterizing the 'mind' of her intertextual counterpart (*PV*, p. 15). This avaricious, malevolent and decrepit 'hunchback' (p. 460) conspires with Madame Beck and the Catholic priest, Père Silas, to block Monsieur Paul's intended marriage to Lucy, just as, 20 years earlier, she had interdicted his wedding to her now deceased granddaughter and 'saint in Heaven' (p. 394), Justine Marie. Neither of these actions is mere caprice. Madame Walravens thwarts Monsieur Paul's aspiration towards Justine Marie's 'well-dowered hand' on the basis of class prejudice, when his initially attractive 'worldly prospects' (p. 392) meet with an abrupt downturn. She frustrates him again, with respect to Lucy, in the name of her own dormant colonial economy. Monsieur Paul 'cannot marry' (p. 447) his beloved because he is 'bound for the West Indies' (p. 440), corralled by Madame Walravens and her equally self-interested cohorts into rejuvenating the fortunes of the slave plantation which she 'possesse[s]' (p. 461) at Basseterre in Guadeloupe – historically, of course, a French colony, but imaginatively reallocated in *Villette* to Labassecour. Brontë's novel thus replays the triangular conflicts of Bernardin's, while steering the earlier narrative in an altogether different direction. It retains the pathetic conceit of lovers torn asunder, even as it subjects Monsieur Paul to a colonial exile which reverses the trajectory of Virginia's banishment to Europe.

Devoted lover that he is, Monsieur Paul naturally writes to Lucy during his three years' absence in Guadeloupe (the same amount of time, incidentally, as Virginia spends in Paris). The manner in which his letters are produced is as generous as the correspondence is punctual, appearing, as it does, 'By every vessel'. As Lucy gratefully recalls, Monsieur Paul, 'wrote as he gave and as he loved, in full-handed, full-hearted plenitude. He wrote because he liked to write; he did not abridge, because he cared not to abridge.' Such epistolary candour stands in marked contrast to *Villette*'s own censoriousness with regard to the realities of the location, 'far away beyond seas, in an Indian isle' (p. 494), into which Lucy's bountiful correspondent is reluctantly cast. Although Monsieur Paul takes up his commission in Guadeloupe at a time before France finally outlawed slavery within its colonial dominions in 1848, the racial terrors in which he is necessarily implicated are carefully finessed by Brontë's novel. This sustained silence concerning the precise circumstances of Monsieur Paul's colonial agency both aligns *Villette* with *Paul and Virginia* and places the two texts at odds with one another. It might be said that, despite its author's abolitionist politics, *Paul and Virginia* practises its own colonial mystifications, as the main interracial relationships in the novel are represented in remarkably idyllic terms. The violent racial hierarchies on which slavery is predicated are frequently occulted by a rhetoric of empathy, as in those moments when the two slaves, Mary and Domingo, are touched by the occasional sadnesses of their white owners. As the 'old man' (*PV*, p. 2) who relays Paul and Virginia's story to Bernardin's primary narrator explains:

> 'whenever melancholy took possession of any member of this little society, the rest endeavoured to banish painful thoughts rather by sentiment than by arguments. Margaret exerted her gaiety; Madame de la Tour employed her mild theology; Virginia, her tender caresses; Paul, his cordial and engaging frankness; even Mary and Domingo hastened to offer their succour, and to weep with those that wept.' (*PV*, p. 35)

There are other moments in Bernardin's text, however, when the limits to this blithely inclusive vision are brought sharply into focus. '[T]his little society', bound together by the egalitarianism of fellow-feeling, tells only half the truth of the colonial dispensation depicted in *Paul and Virginia*. Its bleak antitype is scored into the margins of the text in the transitory narratives of other black subjects less comfortably assimilated into the white order of things than Mary and Domingo. The suicidal fugitive slave whom Paul and Virginia, at one point, find wandering close to their 'habitation' (*PV*, p. 18) is no more able to liberate herself from the 'possession' of her master than she can escape the signs of his racial privilege, disported in the 'deep scars' he has carved into her 'wasted' body with his whips. When Paul and Virginia return this 'Unhappy woman' to her owner with the plea that he pardon her attempted flight, their naive request is not granted. As Domingo subsequently informs these 'good white people' (*PV*, p. 18), the runaway is merely subjected to further discipline and punishment. She is exhibited on her master's plantation 'with her feet chained to a block of wood, and an iron collar with three hooks fastened round her neck' (*PV*, p. 24).[30]

Yet even as *Villette* censors the violent truths of slavery which occasionally blot *Paul and Virginia*'s otherwise halcyon pastoral vision, they run beneath its surface none the less, rebelliously returning in distorted forms. Prior to their mutual mellowing, Monsieur Paul and Lucy are locked together in a series of fraught confrontations which discreetly re-enact the invisible power relationships played out among and within the 'persons not named [and] circumstances not defined' (p. 463) of colonial Guadeloupe. In a scene in chapter 21, for example, Lucy catches Monsieur Paul spying upon her as she struggles inwardly with the tearful realization that her love for Dr John will never be openly expressed, much less requited. Her indignation at the invasive presence whose 'fixed gaze ... hit[s] right against [her] own glance' (p. 231) turns her 'mournful' condition into a 'mutinous' one, precipitating a one-sided exchange of views:

> 'I see on your cheek two tears which I know are hot as two sparks, and salt as two crystals of the sea. While I speak you eye me strangely. Shall I tell you of what I am reminded while watching you?'
> 'Monsieur, I shall be called away to prayers shortly; my time for conversation is very scant and brief at this hour – excuse –'
> 'I excuse everything,' he interrupted; 'my mood is so meek, neither rebuff nor, perhaps insult could ruffle it. You remind me, then, of a young she wild creature, new caught, untamed, viewing with a mixture of fire and fear the first entrance of the breaker-in.' (p. 232)

The 'wild creature' here conjured up by Monsieur Paul is equivocally located somewhere between the animal and the human. Such taxonomic ambiguity serves an important function, closing down the disturbing image of Lucy as virgin slave to Monsieur Paul as sexually violating master which it simultaneously opens up. Ironically, though, the blurring of the animal/human distinction which characterizes this passage points back towards the very context it helps to obscure, since slaves are routinely figured in colonial discourse in bestial terms.

The encipherment of colonial slavery in the passage just cited is particularly acute in chapter 34. As Lucy comes slowly to understand, the series of 'little incidents' (p. 393) which take place at this point in the novel is not arbitrary. Rather, it is meticulously crafted by 'the secret junta' (p. 460) of Madame Walravens *et al.* as part of the plan to impede Lucy's marriage to Monsieur Paul. At the same time, Brontë's chapter is itself put together just as cunningly as are the conspiratorial events unfolding within it. Although it begins nearly 60 pages before *Villette* makes its initial – and strikingly rushed – triple reference to '"Basseterre in Guadaloupe [sic]"' (p. 441), the chapter contains a cluster of anticipatory clues as to the destination to which Monsieur Paul's 'long voyage' (p. 439) will lead him. The first of these is the 'pretty basket' which Lucy is asked by Madame Beck to deliver to Madame Walravens as a gift. With its 'hothouse fruit ... reposing amongst the dark green, wax-like leaves, and pale yellow stars' of a mysterious 'exotic plant' (p. 386), such an offering seems well suited to the owner of a textually 'sequestered' 'West-Indian estate', which it is Monsieur Paul's task to make 'largely productive' (p. 461) once again. It is equally appropriate that Lucy's errand should take her 'deep into the old and grim Basse-Ville' (p. 387) where Madame Walravens is domiciled. Like the 'malefactor' of chapter 22, the name given to this quarter of Villette is a cryptogram. It glances silently towards Basseterre (as does 'Labassecour' indeed), just as the dual role of Madame Walravens as romantic 'obstruction' (p. 389) and colonial mistress by proxy is encrypted in the conundrum of her surname, whose letters felicitously unscramble into 'warn' and 'slave'. Even the description of the crone who grudgingly admits Lucy across the 'inhospitable threshold' of Madame Walravens's dwelling is not without a trace of the sea-borne colonial project into which Monsieur Paul is co-opted: as Lucy notices, this 'cantankerous' figure wears 'sabots more like little boats than shoes' (p. 388).

The largest element in these patterns of colonial prolepsis is the early evening storm which erupts shortly before Lucy is treated by Père Silas to the 'little romantic narrative' (p. 392) of Monsieur Paul's allegedly undying love for Justine Marie:

> Down washed the rain, deep lowered the welkin; the clouds, ruddy a while ago, had now, through all their blackness, turned deadly pale, as if in terror. . . . the gleams of lightning were very fierce, the thunder crashed very near; this storm had gathered immediately above Villette; it seemed to have burst at the zenith; it rushed down prone; the forked, slant bolts pierced athwart vertical torrents; red zig-zags interlaced a descent blanched as white metal: and all broke from a sky heavily black in its swollen abundance.   (p. 390)

'[T]his storm' is not just a natural phenomenon but also a kind of cryptography or oblique sky-writing, offering yet another coded colonial forecast. By dint of its 'red zig-zags', the violent atmosphere evoked in this passage itself becomes 'interlaced' with a different but directly related moment of turbulence. In chapter 38, Lucy recalls how her sleep is regularly interrupted by the twisting dream of her lover's impending overseas departure. '[R]oused with a start', she wakes repeatedly, at this late juncture in the novel, to find the two words which have come to dominate her existence – 'Basseterre' and 'Guadaloupe' – seemingly 'pronounced over [her] pillow' and running 'athwart the darkness around and before [her], in zig-zag characters of red or violet light' (p. 441).

Although it may be 'gathered immediately above Villette', Brontë's storm is already drifting elsewhere.

As well as looking forward to Monsieur Paul's colonial destiny, the storm carries out another function, underlining the radical conjunction between the worlds of Labassecour and Guadeloupe, metropole and colony, with the riches amassing to the one dependent upon the slaves exploited in the other. As Lucy enters the Basse-Ville, she also delves into its recent history, noting the difference between the region's former 'wealth and greatness' and its currently impoverished condition – itself a mirroring of the desuetude into which Madame Walravens's colonial holdings have lapsed. Yet the terms in which Lucy represents the storm's onset suggest the incipient return of past prosperity, as the pavement beneath her feet becomes 'slowly darken[ed]' by 'drops' of rain, each of which is 'almost as large as a five-franc piece' (p. 387). This monetary comparison is developed in the description of the storm proper, in which the rainfall intensifies into 'a descent blanched as white metal'. The language of money deployed here is also, however, a language crackling with the sufferings and the terrors of slavery. Whether it be 'white' or, as at an earlier point, 'a mass of black-blue' (p. 387), Brontë's racially tempered and gradated 'metal' combines with the 'forked, slant bolts' of lightning to evoke the disciplinary paraphernalia to which the slave's body is ordinarily subjected. These two languages are fused with particular force in the image of the 'swollen abundance' disgorged from Brontë's lowering 'sky'. If this image suggests the 'Indian fortune' (p. 466) which it is 'the origin and the object' (p. 461) of Monsieur Paul's colonial mission to procure, it simultaneously registers the exorbitant bodily pain of the slaves whose labours are the 'fortune''s source.

The storm of chapter 34 has its more powerful sequel in the 'tempest' (p. 495) which presides over *Villette*'s final paragraphs:

> That storm roared frenzied for seven days. It did not cease till the Atlantic was strewn with wrecks: it did not lull till the deeps had gorged their full of sustenance. Not till the destroying angel of tempest had achieved his perfect work, would he fold the wings whose waft was thunder – the tremor of whose plumes was storm.
>
> Peace, be still! Oh! a thousand weepers, praying in agony on waiting shores, listened for that voice, but it was not uttered – not uttered till, when the hush came, some could not feel it: till, when the sun returned, his light was night to some!

> Here pause: pause at once. There is enough said. Trouble no
> quiet, kind heart; leave sunny imaginations hope. Let it be theirs to
> conceive the delight of joy born again fresh out of great terror, the
> rapture of rescue from peril, the wondrous reprieve from dread, the
> fruition of return. Let them picture union and a happy succeeding
> life.
>
> Madame Beck prospered all the days of her life; so did Père Silas;
> Madame Walravens fulfilled her ninetieth year before she died.
> Farewell.   (pp. 495–6)

Spread across 'seven days', this 'frenzied' storm takes on a divine
energy and puts it into reverse, as the biblical creation myth is
itself recreated in a 'perfect work' which leaves 'the Atlantic
strewn with wrecks'. Given its magnitude, it is unlikely that even
as formidable a figure as Lucy's 'Christian Hero' (p. 398) could
withstand such devastation. Monsieur Paul's watery apocalypse is
intimated here, accordingly, both in terms of his name's conspicuous absence from the roll-call of *Villette*'s cursory penultimate
sentence and the way in which the flow of Brontë's narrative as a
whole is so violently suspended. Lucy's invitation to the reader to
'picture union and a happy succeeding life' is a challenge indeed,
to which 'sunny imaginations' of only the most dazzlingly self-
blinded calibre could ever be equal.

Villette's tumultuous conclusion brings Brontë's confabulation
with Bernardin full circle. If Monsieur Paul leaves for Guadeloupe
aboard the buoyantly allusive '"Paul et Virginie"' (pp. 466, 479),
his perilous homeward passage is just as clearly modelled on the
shipwreck which fatally intercepts Bernardin's heroine as she
voyages back from France to Mauritius aboard the *Saint-Géran*.
In Bernardin's text, Virginia's death results as much from her in-
terpolation by eighteenth-century protocols of feminine conduct
as from the hurricane which pulls her ship to pieces. In what Chris
Bongie calls 'an egregious display of virtue',[31] she refuses to
disrobe before the naked sailor, 'strong as Hercules' (*PV*, p. 86),
who is poised to help her swim towards her own 'waiting shores',
on which a 'crowd of people ... accompanied by their negroes'
(*PV*, p. 83) has assembled. In contrast to the missing body of
Monsieur Paul, Virginia's 'corpse' is later discovered on a beach,
its 'countenance' cosmeticized by 'the pale violets of death' which
are 'blended on her cheek with the blush of virgin modesty' (*PV*,
p. 87). If internal evidence makes it hard to dredge up anything
resembling a conventional fairy-tale ending from the debris of

Villette's desperate last moments, the difficulties are compounded when the novel's intertextual relation to *Paul and Virginia* is given its due.

As well as exerting a significant influence on the way in which *Villette*'s ending is to be read, *Paul and Virginia* has implications for the novel as a whole, highlighting, in particular, the ironic dissonance between *Villette*'s thematic and formal elements, as between the novel's narrator-heroine and its author. On the one hand, Lucy strives, following the glaringly supremacist Crimsworth of *The Professor*, once again, to maintain a difference between herself as Englishwoman and the foreigners whom she encounters in the course of the novel – whether they be her 'dreaded hunters', Zélie, Cleopatra or indeed the Gothic nun, *inter alia*. Yet she is located, in the end, in a narrative hybridized by virtue of its reliance upon a fiction drawn from the very continental culture which she herself is so keen to condemn.

More broadly, the hybridizing presence of Bernardin's novel in *Villette* – like that of Stowe's 'American book'[32] – provides another sign of the shackling to which Brontë subjects her own imagination from the time of *The Professor* onwards. Like the ubiquitous and seemingly inexhaustible slave trope, each of these texts has a double-edged function in *Villette*. Each brings back, while at the same time containing, the visions of racial conflict and colonial encounter which were once so nonchalantly the stuff of Brontë's early writings and which her later novels are able neither fully to accommodate nor fully to censor.

Conclusion

'When my children were very young, when, as far as I can remember, the oldest was about ten years of age, and the youngest
about four, thinking that they knew more than I had yet discovered, in order to make them speak with less timidity, I deemed
that if they were put under a sort of cover I might gain my end;
and happening to have a mask in the house, I told them all to
stand and speak boldly under cover of the mask.'
                    Patrick Brontë, letter to Elizabeth Gaskell, undated[1]

A conclusion could do worse than begin with a gesture of valediction. In her 'Farewell to Angria' (1839), Brontë writes of the
difficulties entailed in extrapolating herself from the colonial
fictions created and explored by her own imagination in the
course of the previous ten years. Drawing on a vocabulary which
is a blend of geography and weather, Brontë recognizes the need
'to quit for a while that burning clime where [she] has sojourned
too long' and enter 'a cooler region', in which 'the coming day, for
a time at least, is subdued in clouds'.[2] Equally, though, she is at
pains to stress that the projected transition from old to new
fictional terrains will not be smooth: 'It is no easy thing,' she
confides, 'to dismiss from my imagination the images which have
filled it so long.'[3]

   Brontë's sense of the potential problems involved in exchanging
the imaginative homeland of her early colonial writings for an as
yet undefined alternative fictional milieu – the problem, precisely,
of saying 'so long' – is well grounded. The 'images' she strives to
block out, forget or obscure are endowed with a captivating
power, invariably linked to racial conflicts which express themselves in terms of physical or sexual violence. Among the repertoire of such troublingly addictive 'images', for example, there
is 'the ghastly exhibition' of Quamina's 'severed ... head'[4] which

appears in 'A Leaf from an Unopened Volume' (1834) or, again, the evocation of Quamina basking rapaciously 'in the bower of Zamorna's lady!'[5] in 'Well, here I am at Roe Head' (1836). Yet it is not only the better established 'images' which possess the capacity to entrench themselves in the 'imagination' struggling to be free of them: those most freshly engendered seem even more capable of resisting their creator's self-decolonizing impulses, their increased stubbornness directly related to an increased monstrosity. One particularly striking example of the monstrous colonial 'images' Brontë was producing at the same time as she was urging their banishment occurs in *Stancliffe's Hotel*, a novella dated 28 June 1838, just a year or so prior to the writing of 'Farewell to Angria'. In this text (published for the first time in 2003), Brontë includes a remarkable conversation between Charles Townshend, who is the text's narrator, and Sir William Percy, Northangerland's second son. As the conversation proceeds, the self-venerating Percy proudly informs a sceptical Townshend of his recent role in the seemingly interminable war against the Ashanti, as it has been widely reported, so he claims, in the press:

> Have you not seen in every newspaper: 'The exertions of the 10th Hussars in the east under their Colonel Sir William Percy continue unabated. The efforts made by that Gallant Officer to extirpate the savages are beyond all praise. Scarce a day passes but five or six are hung under the walls of Dongola'? Then again: 'A signal instance of vengeance was exhibited at Katagoom last week, by order of Sir William Percy. A soldier had been missing some days from his regiment stationed at that place. His remains were at length found in a neighbouring jungle, hideously mangled, and displaying all the frightful mutilation of Negro slaughter. Sir William instantly ordered out two of the fiercest and keenest hounds in his leashes. They tracked up the murderers in a few hours. When seized, the blood-stained wretches were sunk up to the neck in the deep mire of a carr-brake. Sir William had them shot through the head where they stood, and their bodies merged in the filth which afforded them such a suitable sepulchre.'[6]

This passage qualifies as one of the most extreme visions of racial conflict in Brontë's work, as colonizer and colonized are rendered barely recognizable by the violence which each perpetrates upon the other: the white male body of the 'missing' soldier suffers 'all the frightful mutilation of Negro slaughter', while the black 'bodies' of his 'murderers' are reduced, in their turn, to sepulchral 'filth'. Such indeed are the horrors of this 'signal instance' of colonial violence that they have to be carefully displaced into another scene of writing (the 'newspaper') and are defensively ironized by Townshend, shortly afterwards, as 'glorious toil'.

Lest they 'continue unabated', such visions need to be 'extirpate[d]', and it is to the labour of their forgetting that Brontë's novels are dedicated, setting themselves, as they do, in England and Belgium/Labassecour – those welcomingly underheated 'regions' invoked at the end of 'Farewell to Angria'. The novels do not just institute a certain distance between Brontë and the fiery colonial origins of her own writing, however. They also provide allegories of the imaginative self-exile which they represent. As Monsieur Paul whirls to his Atlantic death at the end of *Villette*, he takes with him those bitter tales of slavery in Guadeloupe which might otherwise have soured the 'fruition of [his] return'.[7] He becomes, as he drowns, the ultimate Brontëan figure for the generalized muzzling to which both *Villette* and the novels prior to it subject their various colonial histories. In addition to this, Monsieur Paul's death mirrors that earlier departure for (rather than from) the colonies which is recorded at the outset to *The Professor*. Like Monsieur Paul's, the voyage undertaken by William Crimsworth's 'old friend' leads only into mystery and silence, yielding no subsequent narrative enlightenment: 'What has become of him since I know not.'[8]

As this book has argued throughout, that which the novels expel or cast out from themselves tends, however, always to return in different forms, as if Brontë were indeed speaking, or writing, to recall her father's well-known subterfuge, 'under cover of [a] mask'. The death of Monsieur Paul is itself a case in point. The storm which kills off Madame Walravens's colonial emissary is not just an especially dramatic meteorological event, but also a figure for the kind of black vengeance rather more openly displayed upon the 'hideously mangled' body of the ambushed colonial 'soldier' featured in *Stancliffe's Hotel*.[9] Although the slaves of Guadeloupe make no appearance in *Villette*, their distant discontent is written, just the same, in what the novel calls the 'signs of the sky'.[10]

Silenced and masked as they are, it is perhaps to be expected that questions of colonialism in Brontë's novels have not to date been adequately addressed by criticism. In *Jane Eyre*, of course, the critical unmasking of colonialism is now a fine art, albeit one owing much, in the end, to the postcolonial iconoclasm of Jean Rhys's *Wide Sargasso Sea* (1966), in which the story of Brontë's novel is retold from the perspective of Bertha Mason. With Brontë's other novels, by contrast, the possibilities for postcolonial analysis have been much less fully recognized. This book has sought to give a more comprehensive account than hitherto of such possibilities by distributing its gaze more evenly across all four novels and drawing attention to the connections between them. It has also sought to strike a greater balance than is customary between the novels and the many neglected writings which precede and inform them, emphasizing, once again, the patterns of continuity and transformation by which the earlier and later phases of Brontë's authorial career are hinged together. The book cannot claim to be the last word on Brontë's intricate, surprising and sophisticated relationship to colonialism, but perhaps constitutes, more modestly, the first word in a new dialogue with the questions to which that relationship gives rise.

Notes

INTRODUCTION

1. For a succinct recent critique of Gaskell's construction of the Brontës along these lines, see Juliet Barker, 'The Haworth Context', in *The Cambridge Companion to the Brontës*, ed. Heather Glen (Cambridge: Cambridge University Press, 2002), p. 30: 'In her *The Life of Charlotte Brontë* Mrs Gaskell portrayed the Brontës as victims of an abnormal childhood and upbringing, suffering an involuntary exile from civilisation, society and friendships in the barbarous isolation of Haworth. . . . She could not have been more wrong.'

2. Elizabeth Gaskell, *The Life of Charlotte Brontë*, ed. Elisabeth Jay (Harmondsworth: Penguin, 1997), p. 70.

3. Elisabeth Jay, 'Introduction' to ibid., p. ix.

4. The terms of this vision are broadly echoed, for example, in the opening lines of an anonymous sonnet published in *Brontë Society Transactions* in 1940. These lines not only apostrophize Brontë herself, but her two sisters, Emily and Anne, also: 'Pale Sisters! reared amid the purple sea / Of windy moorland, where, remote, ye plied / All household arts, meek, passion-taught and free / Kinship your joy and Fantasy your guide!' Cited in Patsy Stoneman, 'The Brontë Myth', in Glen, *The Cambridge Companion*, p. 214. See also Richard Offor, writing in the same journal, six years later. The Brontë sisters, in his opinion, owe 'less than any other great writers to contemporary currents of religious and political opinion, and more perhaps than any to gifts descending direct to them from heaven with no human intermediary'. Cited in Sally Shuttleworth, *Charlotte Brontë and Victorian Psychology* (Cambridge: Cambridge University Press, 1996), p. 19. As Shuttleworth later points out, 'Such investment in notions of intuitive genius can be found in early feminist readings' of Brontë, and also, she suggests, in John

Maynard's *Charlotte Brontë and Sexuality* (Cambridge: Cambridge University Press, 1984). See Shuttleworth, *Charlotte Brontë and Victorian Psychology*, p. 251, note 2.

5. Gayatri Chakravorty Spivak, 'Three Women's Texts and a Critique of Imperialism', *Critical Inquiry*, 12 (1985), 243.

6. Ibid., p. 248.

7. These critics include, most notably: Laura E. Donaldson, 'The Miranda Complex: Colonialism and the Question of Feminist Reading', *Diacritics*, 18: 3 (1988), 65–77; Suvendrini Perera, *Reaches of Empire: The English Novel from Edgeworth to Dickens* (New York: Columbia University Press, 1991), pp. 79–102; Firdous Azim, *The Colonial Rise of the Novel* (London and New York: Routledge, 1993), pp. 172–97; Joyce Zonana, 'The Sultan and the Slave: Feminist Orientalism and the Structure of *Jane Eyre*', *Signs*, 18 (1993), 592–617; Susan Meyer, *Imperialism at Home: Race and Victorian Women's Fiction* (Ithaca, NY, and London: Cornell University Press, 1996), pp. 60–95; and Sue Thomas, 'The Tropical Extravagance of Bertha Mason', *Victorian Literature and Culture*, 27 (1999), 1–17.

8. For major instances of the critical exploration of this question outside the precincts of *Jane Eyre*, see Azim, *The Colonial Rise of the Novel*, pp. 109–71; Meyer, *Imperialism at Home*, pp. 29–59; and Cannon Schmitt, *Alien Nation: Nineteenth-Century Gothic Fictions and English Nationality, 1797–1897* (Philadelphia, PA: University of Pennsylvania Press, 1997), pp. 76–106.

9. *Charlotte Brontë: Juvenilia, 1829–1835*, ed. Juliet Barker (Harmondsworth: Penguin, 1996), p. 270.

10. This volume famously sold only two copies during its first year of issue. It did at least make a minor stir within contemporary literary circles, eliciting favourable reviews in the *Athenaeum* and, in particular, *Critic*. For a detailed account of Brontë's drive towards the publication of *Poems*, the collection's immediate critical reception and the shifts in her own evaluation of the project, see Juliet Barker, *The Brontës* (London: Phoenix, 1995), pp. 478–99.

11. For a comprehensive and illuminating discussion of the vexed but formative relationship between Brontë and Heger, see *The Belgian Essays: Charlotte Brontë and Emily Brontë*, ed. and trans. Sue Lonoff (New Haven, CT, and London: Yale University Press, 1996), pp. xxi–lxxxvi.

12. Elizabeth Gaskell, letter to George Smith, 13 August 1856, in *The Letters of Mrs Gaskell*, ed. J. A. V. Chapple and Arthur Pollard (Manchester: Manchester University Press, 1966), p. 403 (emphasis in original).

13. Edward W. Said, *Culture and Imperialism* (London: Vintage, 1994), p. xiii.

CHAPTER 1: MISCEGENATION IN THE ASHANTI NARRATIVES

1. Cited in *The Letters of Charlotte Brontë, with a Selection of Letters by Family and Friends*, ed. Margaret Smith, 2 vols to date (Oxford: Clarendon Press, 1995–), vol. I, p. 144.

2. Elizabeth Gaskell, letter to George Smith, in *The Letters of Mrs Gaskell*, ed. J. A. V. Chapple and Arthur Pollard (Manchester: Manchester University Press, 1966), p. 398.

3. Bette London, *Writing Double: Women's Literary Partnerships* (Ithaca, NY, and London: Cornell University Press, 1999), p. 35.

4. Elizabeth Gaskell, *The Life of Charlotte Brontë*, ed. Elisabeth Jay (Harmondsworth: Penguin, 1997), p. 69.

5. Christine Alexander, *The Early Writings of Charlotte Brontë* (Oxford: Basil Blackwell, 1983), p. 5.

6. Sally Shuttleworth, *Charlotte Brontë and Victorian Psychology* (Cambridge: Cambridge University Press, 1996), p. 111.

7. London, *Writing Double*, p. 30. For an approach similar to London's, see Carol Bock, '"Our Plays": the Brontë Juvenilia', in *The Cambridge Companion to the Brontës*, ed. Heather Glen (Cambridge: Cambridge University Press, 2002), pp. 34–52.

8. See, for example, 'Mission from Cape Coast Castle to Ashantee', a two-part article which appeared in *Blackwood's Edinburgh Magazine*, 5 (May and June 1819), 175–83 and 302–10; 'Geography of Central Africa. Denham and Clapperton's Journals', *Blackwood's*, 19 (June 1826), 687–709; and 'The British Settlements in Western Africa', *Blackwood's*, 26 (September 1829), 341–50. A brief but useful overview of the intertextual relationships between Brontë's early work and *Blackwood's* is provided in Christine Alexander, 'Africa as Play in the Childhood of the Brontës', *Journal of African Travel Writing*, 6 (1999), 5–15.

9. Ratchford, cited in Bock, '"Our Plays"', p. 34.

10. For critical accounts which privilege the colonial and racial elements in Brontë's early writings, see Firdous Azim, *The Colonial Rise of the Novel* (London and New York: Routledge, 1993), pp. 109–46; and Susan Meyer, *Imperialism at Home: Race and Victorian Women's Fiction* (Ithaca, NY, and London: Cornell University Press, 1996), pp. 29–59. For an earlier, less theoretical,

but valuable analysis of these elements, rich in historical detail, see Christopher Heywood, 'Africa and Slavery in the Brontë Children's Novels', *Hitotsubashi: Journal of Arts and Sciences*, 30 (1989), 75–89.

11. The adventurers named in the subtitle to this narrative are generally recognized to be textualized versions of that legendary troop of toy soldiers whose thrilling invasion of her domestic space is recorded by Brontë as a defining moment in 'The History of the Year' (1829):

> Papa bought Branwell some soldiers from Leeds. When Papa came home it was night and we were in bed, so next morning Branwell came to our door with a box of soldiers. Emily and I jumped out of bed and I snatched up one and exclaimed, 'This is the Duke of Wellington! It shall be mine!' When I said this, Emily likewise took one and said it should be hers. When Anne came down she took one also. Mine was the prettiest of the whole and perfect in every part. Emily's was a grave-looking fellow. We called him 'Gravey'. Anne's was a queer little thing, very much like herself. He was called 'Waiting Boy'. Branwell chose 'Bonaparte'. (Charlotte Brontë, 'The History of the Year', in *An Edition of the Early Writings of Charlotte Brontë*, ed. Christine Alexander, 2 vols to date [Oxford: Blackwell, 1987–], vol. I, p. 5)

12. Charlotte Brontë, 'A Romantic Tale [or The Twelve Adventurers]', in Alexander, *Edition*, vol. I, p. 10.

13. Ibid., p. 12.

14. Ibid., p. 11.

15. Charlotte Brontë, 'Lo! stretched beneath the clust'ring palm', lines 57–8, in 'A Fragment', in Alexander, *Edition*, vol. I, p. 330.

16. Charlotte Brontë, 'A Day Abroad', in Alexander, *Edition*, vol. II, part 2, p. 122.

17. Ibid., p. 123.

18. Charlotte Brontë, 'Passing Events', in *Charlotte Brontë: Five Novelettes*, ed. Winifred Gérin (London: Folio, 1971), p. 38.

19. Robert Southey, letter to Brontë, 12 March 1837, in Smith, *Letters*, vol. I, p. 166.

20. Charlotte Brontë, 'A Leaf from an Unopened Volume', in Alexander, *Edition*, vol. II, part 1, p. 326. Subsequent references to this work are incorporated in the text and given in parenthesis after quotations.

21. Meyer, *Imperialism at Home*, p. 53.

22. In the imagined future time in which this tale is set, Zamorna has assumed the suitably self-aggrandizing alias of 'the Emperor Adrian,

surnamed the Magnificent' (p. 325). As is standard critical practice, however, he is referred to by his original name throughout the reading of the text included in this chapter.

23. Frantz Fanon, *Black Skin, White Masks*, trans. Charles Lam Markmann, Foreword by Homi K. Bhabha (London: Pluto Press, 1986), p. 159 (emphasis in original).

24. Sigmund Freud, 'Fetishism' (1927), in *On Sexuality*, ed. and trans. Angela Richards, Pelican Freud Library, vol. 7 (Harmondsworth: Penguin, 1977), p. 353.

25. Meyer, *Imperialism at Home*, p. 46.

26. Peter Stallybrass and Allon White, cited in Robert J. C. Young, *Colonial Desire: Hybridity in Theory, Culture and Race* (London and New York: Routledge, 1995).

27. Charlotte Brontë, 'Well, here I am at Roe Head', ed. Christine Alexander, in *Jane Eyre*, ed. Richard J. Dunn, 2nd edition (New York and London: W. W. Norton, 1987), p. 410. Subsequent references to this work are incorporated in the text and given in parenthesis after quotations.

28. Brontë's representation of Quamina in this passage bears some comparison with the portrayal of the colonized male subject in Fanon's *The Wretched of the Earth*. Quamina's invasion of a white female space seems to occur precisely at the epochal moment when, as Fanon puts it, the 'native decid[es] to embody history in his own person [and] surges into the forbidden quarters'. See Frantz Fanon, *The Wretched of the Earth*, trans. Constance Farrington, Preface by Jean-Paul Sartre (Harmondsworth: Penguin, 1990), p. 31. Similarly, the rapacious dreams Brontë attributes to Quamina can be likened to those jubilant visions of material and sexual appropriation Fanon outlines earlier in his book:

> The look that the native turns on the settler's town is a look of lust, a look of envy; it expresses his dreams of possession – all manner of possession: to sit at the settler's table, to sleep in the settler's bed, with his wife if possible. The colonized man is an envious man . . . there is no native who does not dream at least once a day of setting himself up in the settler's place. (Fanon, *Wretched*, p. 30)

29. Homi K. Bhabha, *The Location of Culture* (London and New York: Routledge, 1994), p. 72.

30. Ibid., p. 73.

31. Charlotte Brontë, 'Caroline Vernon', in Gérin, *Charlotte Brontë: Five Novelettes*, p. 285. Subsequent references to this work are incorporated in the text and given in parenthesis after quotations.

32. Alexander, *Early Writings*, p. 195.

33. Charles Lamb, cited in Ruth Cowhig, 'Blacks in English Renaissance Drama and the Role of Shakespeare's Othello', in *The Black Presence in English Literature*, ed. David Dabydeen (Manchester: Manchester University Press, 1985), p. 16.

34. Samuel Taylor Coleridge, cited in Cowhig, 'Blacks in English Renaissance Drama', p. 17.

35. Perhaps the most famous exception to this general racist convention is the African American actor, Ira Aldridge, who first played Othello at the Theatre Royal, Covent Garden in April 1833. For a discussion of Aldridge in this role and the intensely hostile reviews which he received, see Cowhig, 'Blacks in English Rennaissance Drama', pp. 18–21.

36. Sam Dennison, *Scandalize My Name: Black Imagery in American Popular Music* (New York and London: Garland, 1982), p. 45.

37. Ted Olson, 'Jim Crow', in *The Oxford Companion to African American Literature*, ed. William L. Andrews, Frances Smith Foster and Trudier Harris (New York and Oxford: Oxford University Press, 1997), pp. 398–9.

38. H. L. Malchow, *Gothic Images of Race in Nineteenth-Century Britain* (Stanford, CA: Stanford University Press, 1996), p. 3.

CHAPTER 2: COLONIALISM IN THE POETRY AND BELGIAN ESSAYS

1. Charlotte Brontë, *The Professor*, ed. Margaret Smith and Herbert Rosengarten (Oxford: Clarendon Press, 1987), p. 3.

2. Ibid., p. 3.

3. Charlotte Brontë, 'The African Queen's Lament', in *An Edition of the Early Writings of Charlotte Brontë*, ed. Christine Alexander, 2 vols to date (Oxford: Blackwell, 1987–), vol. II, part 1, p. 3. Subsequent references to this work are incorporated in the text and given in parenthesis after quotations.

4. As Alexander usefully points out, these misdemeanours are elaborated upon in Brontë's 'The Green Dwarf' (1833). At the beginning of its sixth chapter, this narrative exposes the contradictions in Quamina's position as Wellington's adopted 'son' and 'slave' and goes on to describe how 'the young prince' struggles to break the 'gilded fetters' (Alexander, *Edition*, vol. II, part 1, p. 178) in which he is reared:

> Since his fifteenth year [Quamina] had been accustomed to take long excursions by himself among the mountains and forests of Ashantee, for the

purpose, as he said, of hunting the wild animals that abound there. But subsequent events showed that his real employment during these expeditions was discovering and prompting to rebellion the hidden tribes of Africans, who, after the destruction of Coomassie and the slaughter of King Quamina, had concealed themselves in fastnesses inaccessible to any but a native of the country.   (Alexander, *Edition*, vol. II, part 1, p. 179)

5. Ibid., p. 179.

6. Firdous Azim, *The Colonial Rise of the Novel* (London and New York: Routledge, 1993), p. 130.

7. Isobel Armstrong, *Victorian Poetry: Poetry, Poetics and Politics* (London and New York: Routledge, 1993), p. 324.

8. Charlotte Brontë, 'The Letter', in *The Poems of Charlotte Brontë*, ed. Tom Winnifrith (Oxford: Basil Blackwell, 1984), p. 47 (line 75). Subsequent references to this poem are incorporated in the text and given in parenthesis after quotations.

9. Ronald Hyam, *Empire and Sexuality: The British Experience* (Manchester and New York: Manchester University Press, 1991), p. 1.

10. Winnifrith, *Poems*, p. 355.

11. Charlotte Brontë, 'Passion', in Winnifrith, *Poems*, p. 55 (line 23). Subsequent references to this poem are incorporated in the text and given in parenthesis after quotations. The reference to 'Indus' borders' replaces that to 'Spain's sierras' which features in the 1841 version of the poem (also at line 23). For a full listing of the variations between the poem's earlier and later drafts, see Winnifrith, *Poems*, pp. 355–6.

12. 'The Campaign of the Sutlej', in *Blackwood's Edinburgh Magazine*, 59 (May 1846), 625.

13. John Sheehan, 'The Campaign of the Sutlej', line 1. Cited in *The White Man's Burdens: An Anthology of British Poetry of the Empire*, ed. Chris Brooks and Peter Faulkner (Exeter: University of Exeter Press, 1996), p. 172.

14. Ibid., lines 11 and 31.

15. Hyam, *Empire and Sexuality*, p. 89.

16. *Blackwood's*, 59 (May 1846), p. 633.

17. Ibid., p. 625.

18. Juliet Barker, *The Brontës* (London: Phoenix, 1995), p. 451.

19. Charlotte Brontë, 'The Missionary', in Winnifrith, *Poems*, p. 67 (lines 1–2). Subsequent references to this poem are incorporated in the text and given in parenthesis after quotations.

20. The overworked space of the missionary's soul is reminiscent of the empty terrestrial regions which seem so to appeal to the 'never-resting Europe' celebrated at the end of Thomas Carlyle's *Chartism* (1839). Although the solicitous vision with which Carlyle concludes his book is of migration not to India but Canada, it resonates suggestively with the violent programme of spiritual recultivation imagined at the outset to Brontë's poem, literalizing her metaphors: 'does not … a whole vacant Earth, as it were, call to us, Come and till me, come and reap me!', Carlyle importunes, 'a world where Canadian forests stand unfelled, boundless Plains and Prairies unbroken with the plough'. Cited in Suvendrini Perera, *Reaches of Empire: The English Novel from Edgeworth to Dickens* (New York: Columbia University Press, 1991), p. 54.

21. The story of Jephtha's sacrifice of his daughter is recounted in Judges, xi: 29–40.

22. The transformation of Christ's bodily fluids, one into another, to which Brontë alludes here is described in Luke, xxiii: 44: 'And being in an agony he prayed more earnestly: and his sweat was as it were great drops of blood falling down to the ground.'

23. While it is possible to read this fire-proof image in terms of *sati*, its more immediate associations are, of course, biblical. See Daniel, iii: 19–30, in which Nebuchadnezzar persecutes the dissident figures of Shadrach, Meshach and Abed-nego by casting them into 'the burning fiery furnace' (iii: 21), only to learn how they are insulated from physical suffering by means of faith: 'upon [their] bodies the fire had no power, nor was an hair of their head singed' (iii: 27).

24. See Alexander, *Edition*, vol. II, part 2, pp. 193 and 343.

25. Charlotte Brontë, 'Sacrifice of an Indian Widow', in Lonoff, *The Belgian Essays*, p. 2. Subsequent references to this work are incorporated in the text and given in parenthesis after quotations.

26. Ania Loomba, *Colonialism/Postcolonialism* (London and New York: Routledge, 1998), p. 168.

27. William Cavendish Bentinck, 'Sati Regulation XVII, AD 1829 of the Bengal Code, 4 December 1829', in *Imperialism & Orientalism: A Documentary Sourcebook*, ed. Barbara Harlow and Mia Carter (Oxford: Blackwell, 1999), p. 93.

28. Ibid., p. 94.

29. Margery Sabin, 'The Suttee Romance', *Raritan: A Quarterly Review*, 11: 2 (1991), 7.

30. Sandra M. Gilbert and Susan Gubar, *The Madwoman in the Attic: The Woman Writer and the Nineteenth-Century Literary Imagination* (New Haven, CT, and London: Yale University Press, 1979), p. 25.

31. Perera, *Reaches of Empire*, p. 92.

32. Sabin, 'The Suttee Romance', p. 5.

33. Lonoff, *The Belgian Essays*, p. 9.

CHAPTER 3: SLAVERY AND SEXUALITY IN *THE PROFESSOR*

1. Charlotte Brontë, *The Professor*, ed. Margaret Smith and Herbert Rosengarten (Oxford: Clarendon Press, 1987), p. 5. Subsequent references to this work are incorporated in the text and given in parenthesis after quotations.

2. Firdous Azim, *The Colonial Rise of the Novel* (London and New York: Routledge, 1993), p. 163.

3. Macaulay's 'Minute' is reprinted in full in *Imperialism & Orientalism: A Documentary Sourcebook*, ed. Barbara Harlow and Mia Carter (Oxford: Blackwell, 1999), pp. 56–62. It is, as the editors note, 'a critical and much cited contribution to the debate on the respective roles of Indian and English traditions in the issues of government and instruction' (p. 62). For a detailed analysis of this debate and, in particular, the role of English literature as an instrument of colonial power, see Gauri Viswanathan, *Masks of Conquest: Literary Study and British Rule in India* (New York: Columbia University Press, 1989).

4. The institutions of British and American slavery were formally eradicated by means of legislation carried out during the course of the nineteenth century. The transatlantic slave trade was outlawed by both Britain and America in 1807, with full emancipation of slaves in British colonies eventually brought about between 1834 and 1838. Slavery in America was finally abolished by the Emancipation Proclamation in 1863 and the Thirteenth Amendment in 1865.

5. For Brontë's own humorous yet caustic account of the blighted quest for publication of her 'martyrized M.S.', see her letter to George Smith of 5 February 1851, in *The Letters of Charlotte Brontë, with a Selection of Letters by Family and Friends*, ed. Margaret Smith, 2 vols to date (Oxford: Clarendon Press, 1995–), vol. 2, pp. 572–3. The phrase cited appears on p. 572.

6. Penny Boumelha, *Charlotte Brontë* (Hemel Hempstead: Harvester Wheatsheaf, 1990), p. 38.

7. Ibid., p. 38.

8. See Eric Cheyfitz, *The Poetics of Imperialism: Translation and Colonization from 'The Tempest' to Tarzan* (New York and Oxford: Oxford University Press, 1991), p. 36.

9. See, for example, Marx's comments, in *Capital*, that 'Liverpool waxed fat on the slave-trade. This was its method of primitive accumulation. ... The veiled slavery of the wage-workers in Europe needed, for its pedestal, slavery pure and simple in the new world.' Cited in Peter Fryer, *Aspects of Black British History* (London: Index Books, 1993), p. 12. See also Frantz Fanon, who both echoes and expands Marx's understated figuration of Europe as a body bloated by its own colonial gormandizing:

> For in a very concrete way Europe has stuffed herself inordinately with the gold and raw materials of the colonial countries: Latin America, China and Africa. From all these continents, under whose eyes Europe today raises up her tower of opulence, there has flowed out for centuries towards that same Europe diamonds and oil, silk and cotton, wood and exotic products. Europe is literally the creation of the Third World. The wealth which smothers her is that which was stolen from the under-developed peoples. The ports of Holland, the docks of Bordeaux and Liverpool were specialized in the Negro slave-trade, and owe their renown to millions of deported slaves. (Frantz Fanon, *The Wretched of the Earth*, trans. Constance Farrington, Preface by Jean-Paul Sartre [Harmondsworth: Penguin, 1990], p. 81)

10. Macaulay's phrase (which strikingly figures race in terms of class) appears in a speech on parliamentary reform of 2 March 1831 and is cited in Robin Blackburn, *The Overthrow of Colonial Slavery, 1776–1848* (London and New York: Verso, 1988), p. 448.

11. In his Jamaican diary entry for 9 April 1818, Matthew Lewis provides a graphically non-fictional version of the kind of colonial domination to which Brontë's Juanna looks forward, while at the same time making the female the object rather than agent of abuse. 'I have not passed six months in Jamaica', Lewis writes, 'and I have already found on one of my estates a woman who had been kicked in the womb by a white book-keeper, by which she was crippled herself, and on another of my estates another woman who had been kicked in the womb by another book-keeper, by which he had crippled the child. ... and thus, as my two estates are at the two extremities of the island, I am entitled to say, from my own knowledge (*i.e.* speaking *literally*, observe), that "white book-keepers kick black women in the belly *from one end of Jamaica to the other*."' See Matthew Lewis, *Journal of a West India Proprietor, Kept during a Residence in the Island of Jamaica*, ed. Judith Terry (Oxford: Oxford University Press, 1999), p. 241 (emphases in original).

12. Frederick Douglass, *Narrative of the Life of Frederick Douglass, An American Slave, Written by Himself*, ed. William L. Andrews and William S. McFeely (New York and London: W. W. Norton, 1997), p. 47.

13. Ibid., p. 42.

14. Ibid., p. 50.

15. Frederick Douglass, *The Frederick Douglass Papers*, ed. John W. Blassingame (New Haven, CT, and London: Yale University Press, 1979), vol. I, p. 317.

16. The politically charged nature of the figure of the 'Maroon' is noted, in a brief consideration of this passage, by Susan Meyer in *Imperialism at Home: Race and Victorian Women's Fiction* (Ithaca, NY, and London: Cornell University Press, 1996), p. 61, note 5. As Meyer explains: 'Every slave plantation colony in the West Indies had its "maroons," roaming communities of runaway slaves who had banded together and survived in the uncultivated areas of the colony. The Jamaican maroons were particularly successful and particularly threatening to the British colonists.'

17. This example is also discussed, along similar lines, in Meyer, *Imperialism at Home*, p. 62.

18. Heather Glen, 'Introduction' to Charlotte Brontë, *The Professor*, ed. Heather Glen (Harmondsworth: Penguin, 1989), p. 11.

19. A similar point is made by Sally Shuttleworth in *Charlotte Brontë and Victorian Psychology* (Cambridge: Cambridge University Press, 1996), p. 127. For a useful overview of the Foucauldian elements running through *The Professor* as a whole, see Glen, 'Introduction', pp. 18–19.

20. Steven Marcus, *The Other Victorians: A Study of Sexuality and Pornography in Mid-Nineteenth-Century England* (London: Weidenfeld and Nicolson, 1966), p. 13.

21. Ibid., p. 22.

22. Shuttleworth, *Charlotte Brontë and Victorian Psychology*, p. 132.

23. Glen, 'Introduction', p. 13.

24. Sigmund Freud, 'Negation' (1925), in *On Metapsychology: The Theory of Psychoanalysis*, ed. Angela Richards, trans. James Strachey, Pelican Freud Library, vol. 11 (Harmondsworth: Penguin, 1984), p. 438.

25. Boumelha, *Charlotte Brontë*, p. 41.

26. See Azim, *The Colonial Rise of the Novel*, pp. 155–6 and Shuttleworth, *Charlotte Brontë and Victorian Psychology*, pp. 141–4. For an excellent related reading of 'Hypochondria' in *The Professor* as a condition born of sexual malaise and anxieties about the early Victorian construction of masculinity in general, see Jane Wood, *Passion and Pathology in Victorian Fiction* (Oxford: Oxford University Press, 2001), pp. 83–9.

27. Shuttleworth, *Charlotte Brontë and Victorian Psychology*, p. 141.

28. These assumptions are not unique to thinkers in the English medical tradition, who include Henry Maudsley and Robert P. Ritchie, as well as Acton. They are also to be found in two popular French texts, both in translation in Britain at the time when Brontë was working on *The Professor*. The first of these is Léopold Deslandes's *Manhood: The Causes of its Premature Decline, with Directions for its Perfect Restoration* (1843) and the second, Claude François Lallemand's *A Practical Treatise on the Causes, Symptoms, and Treatment of Spermatorrhoea* (1847). As Shuttleworth notes, Deslandes's work was 'one of the regulars in the advertising columns of the Leeds newspapers' with which Brontë would have been familiar (p. 273, note 25). Lallemand, on the other hand, was an influence on Acton, as noted in *Embodied Selves: An Anthology of Psychological Texts, 1830–1890*, ed. Jenny Bourne Taylor and Sally Shuttleworth (Oxford: Clarendon Press, 1998), p. 209. Such intellectual cross-currents clearly place the oppositions which Brontë's novel sets up between English and continental masculinities in a somewhat ironic light.

29. Stephen J. Greenblatt, 'Improvisation and Power', in *Literature and Society*, ed. Edward W. Said (Baltimore, MD, and London: Johns Hopkins University Press, 1980), p. 80.

30. William Shakespeare, *Othello*, IV.iii.18–20, in *William Shakespeare: The Complete Works*, ed. Alfred Harbage (New York: Viking Press, 1977), p. 1050.

CHAPTER 4: SLAVERY AND THE POLITICS OF METAPHOR IN *JANE EYRE*

1. Sandra M. Gilbert and Susan Gubar, *The Madwoman in the Attic: The Woman Writer and the Nineteenth-Century Literary Imagination* (New Haven, CT, and London: Yale University Press, 1979), p. 338. In this respect, Gilbert and Gubar at once repeat, while also transvaluing, the contemporary Victorian response to Brontë's novel as a radical or subversive text. Such a response is typified by Elizabeth Rigby in an article in *The Quarterly Review*, 84 (December 1848): 'We do not hesitate to say that the tone of the mind and thought which has overthrown authority and violated every code human and divine abroad, and fostered Chartism and rebellion at home, is the same which has also written *Jane Eyre*.' Cited in *The Brontës: The Critical Heritage*, ed. Miriam Allott (London: Routledge & Kegan Paul, 1974), pp. 109–10. For readings which argue that *Jane Eyre* involves a containment rather than an

affirmation of female transgression, see Bette London, 'The Pleasures of Submission: *Jane Eyre* and the Production of the Text', *English Literary History*, 58 (1991), 195–213; and Kathryn Sutherland, '*Jane Eyre*'s Literary History: the Case for *Mansfield Park*', *English Literary History*, 59 (1992), 409–40.

2. Gilbert and Gubar, *The Madwoman*, p. 338. As is evident from the very title of their book, *Jane Eyre* certainly provides the 'pattern' or paradigm for the feminist poetics which *The Madwoman in the Attic* itself seeks to formulate: along with Brontë's other novels, it occupies a 'central position' in Gilbert and Gubar's analytic schema, generating 'new ways in which all nineteenth-century works by women can be interpreted' (p. xii). See also pp. 77–9.

3. Ibid., p. 339. The ascription of 'hunger, rebellion, and rage' to Brontë is Matthew Arnold's. It is made, in relation to the recently published *Villette*, in a letter to John Forster of 14 April 1853. See *Letters of Matthew Arnold, 1848–1888*, ed. George W. E. Russell, 2 vols (London and New York: Macmillan, 1895), vol. I, p. 29.

4. The tendency of 'narrowly ... race-blind interpretations' to construct *Jane Eyre* as a feminist epic of self-realization is discussed by Penny Boumelha in *Charlotte Brontë* (Hemel Hempstead: Harvester Wheatsheaf, 1990), p. 60.

5. For greater detail on this point, see Susan Meyer, *Imperialism at Home: Race and Victorian Women's Fiction* (Ithaca, NY, and London: Cornell University Press, 1996), p. 68.

6. Gilbert and Gubar, *The Madwoman*, p. 360.

7. Such differences none the less reappear in the linguistic tensions of the very critical formulation which seeks to deny them, Bertha being not only Jane's 'truest' but also her 'darkest double'. Elaine Showalter makes the analogous comment that Bertha's death constitutes for Jane a symbolic destruction of 'the dark passion of her own psyche'. See Elaine Showalter, *A Literature of Their Own: British Women Novelists from Brontë to Lessing* (London: Virago, 1978), p. 122.

8. William Shakespeare, *The Tempest*, I.ii.309–10, in *William Shakespeare: The Complete Works*, ed. Alfred Harbage (New York: Viking Press, 1977), p. 1377.

9. Laura E. Donaldson, 'The Miranda Complex: Colonialism and the Question of Feminist Reading', *Diacritics*, 18: 3 (1988), 66.

10. Charlotte Brontë, *Jane Eyre*, ed. Margaret Smith (Oxford and New York: Oxford University Press, 1998), p. 4. Subsequent references to

this work are incorporated in the text and given in parenthesis after quotations.

11. See Brontë's letter of 28 January 1848 to W. S. Williams, in *The Letters of Charlotte Brontë, with a Selection of Letters by Family and Friends*, ed. Margaret Smith, 2 vols to date (Oxford: Clarendon Press, 1995–), vol. 2, p. 22. The circumstances of Thackeray's marriage are documented in Gordon N. Ray, *Thackeray: The Uses of Adversity, 1811–1846* (London: Oxford University Press, 1955), pp. 250–77. See also Gilbert and Gubar's comments on Thackeray's marriage (*The Madwoman*, pp. 680–1, note 23).

12. Jane is figured in similar terms at Thornfield, where she not only engages in what Rochester calls 'governessing slavery' (p. 283) but is also looked upon, as governess, as part of an 'anathematized race' (p. 186).

13. Eric Cheyfitz, *The Poetics of Imperialism: Translation and Colonization from 'The Tempest' to Tarzan* (New York and Oxford: Oxford University Press, 1991), p. 35.

14. Aristotle, cited in Paul Ricœur, *The Rule of Metaphor: Multi-Disciplinary Studies in the Creation of Meaning in Language*, trans. Robert Czerny et al. (Toronto and Buffalo, NY: University of Toronto Press, 1977), p. 13.

15. See Quintilian, *The Institutio Oratoria of Quintilian*, trans. H. E. Butler, 4 vols (Cambridge, MA: Harvard University Press, 1976), vol. III, p. 303.

16. Ricœur, *The Rule of Metaphor*, p. 19.

17. Patricia Parker, *Literary Fat Ladies: Rhetoric, Gender, Property* (London and New York: Methuen, 1987), p. 36.

18. As, for example, in St John Rivers's relationship to Rosamond Oliver: 'His chest heaved once, as if his large heart, weary of despotic constriction, had expanded, despite the will, and made a vigorous bound for the attainment of liberty' (p. 384). Against his 'large heart''s struggles for 'liberty', St John is always 'preparing some iron blow of contradiction, or forging a fresh chain to fetter [it]' (p. 393). These labours of self-enslavement find apotheosis in the form of his 'missionary's career' (p. 414).

19. Jane herself is oddly to be discovered, at the end of volume 1, chapter 15, 'standing in a pool' (p. 158) made by the water she uses to extinguish the fire Bertha lights in an attempt to burn the sleeping Rochester in his bed.

20. Gilbert and Gubar, *The Madwoman*, p. 360 (emphasis in original).

21. Ibid., p. 361.

22. This count includes Bertha's attempted strangulation of Rochester at the end of volume 2 (pp. 307–8). Consistent with Bertha's marginalization throughout *Jane Eyre*, the ambiguous drama of her final moments – setting fire to Thornfield and finally leaping to her death before the advancing Rochester – is presented from an obscure narrative perspective. It is a story told to Jane by one of the novel's more recherché figures, Rochester's father's butler (pp. 448–52).

23. Adrienne Rich, *On Lies, Secrets and Silence: Selected Prose, 1966–1978* (London: Virago, 1980), p. 99.

24. Meyer, *Imperialism at Home*, p. 67 (emphasis in original).

25. Ibid., p. 71. As James Walvin notes, an example of just such anticipated violence, particularly disturbing to the colonizers in its scale, occurs in the 'Baptist War' of 1831–2 as 'slaves in Jamaica erupted in the latest of that island's apparently endless slave revolts'. See James Walvin, *Black Ivory: A History of British Slavery* (London: HarperCollins, 1992), p. 265, see also pp. 276–8; and Robin Blackburn, *The Overthrow of Colonial Slavery, 1776–1848* (London and New York: Verso, 1988), pp. 432–3.

26. Donaldson, 'The Miranda Complex', p. 66.

27. See Genesis, xxiv:15–23.

28. Rochester's inadvertent likening of himself to a slave is anticipated by his self-description, during an early conversation with Jane, as 'a man and a brother' (p. 145), a direct Brontëan reference to the seal of the Slave Emancipation Society manufactured by Josiah Wedgwood in 1787. On this point, see R. J. Dingley, 'Rochester as Slave: an Allusion in *Jane Eyre*', *Notes and Queries*, 31 (1984), 66. It should also be juxtaposed with a passage from Robert Walsh's *Notices of Brazil in 1828 and 1829*, a text cited by Thomas Pringle in his 'Supplement to the History of Mary Prince' in order to illustrate the corrupting effects of slavery upon its practitioners. 'I never walked through the streets of Rio', Walsh complains:

> that some house did not present to me the semblance of a Bridewell, where the moans and the cries of the sufferers, and the sounds of whips and scourges within, announced to me that corporal punishment was being inflicted. Whenever I remarked this to a friend, I was always answered that the refractory nature of the slave rendered it necessary, and no house could properly be conducted unless it was practised. But this is certainly not the case; and the chastisement is constantly applied in the very wantonness of barbarity, and would not, and dared not, be inflicted on the humblest wretch in society, if he was not a slave, and so put out of the pale of pity. (Cited in Prince, *The History of Mary Prince*, p. 61)

29. See also, among further instances, Jane's description of the goodnight kiss ritually conferred upon her by St John as 'a seal affixed to [her] fetters' (p. 419) or, again, the rhetorical question concerning marriage which she directs towards Diana, St John's sister: 'Would it not be strange, Die, to be chained for life to a man who regarded one but as a useful tool?' (p. 438).

30. Such an expanded frame of reference answers to the pattern of historical change. As Blackburn notes: 'by the 1820s and 1830s a thoroughgoing reorientation of Britain's imperial interests was already well underway' (p. 434), towards the Orient and particularly India.

31. Suvendrini Perera, *Reaches of Empire: The English Novel from Edgeworth to Dickens* (New York: Columbia University Press, 1991), p. 79.

32. As, for example, in terms of Jane's imagination of the silent conflict within St John between desire for Rosamond and Christian vocation: 'He seemed to say, with his sad and resolute look, if he did not say it with his lips, "I love you. ... If I offered my heart, I believe you would accept it. But that heart is already laid on a sacred altar: the fire is arranged round it. It will soon be no more than a sacrifice consumed"' (p. 387). There are clear verbal echoes here of the Orientalized language of self-denial informing Brontë's 'The Missionary'.

33. Cheyfitz, *The Poetics of Imperialism*, pp. 35–6, 89–90.

34. It is quite fitting that it should be this particular text which is the object of translation here. Its title, when translated into English as *The Robbers*, is a reminder of the processes by which Rochester comes to acquire his wealth and hence, also, the colonial past from which Jane had sought to escape. The remark of the Rivers's old housekeeper, Hannah, as she apologizes for having initially misconstrued the destitute Jane as a beggar, produces a similar effect: 'I was quite mista'en in my thoughts of you: but there is so many cheats goes about, you mun forgie me' (p. 360).

35. Carolyn Williams, 'Closing the Book: the Intertextual End of *Jane Eyre*', in *Victorian Connections*, ed. Jerome J. McGann (Charlottesville, VA: University Press of Virginia, 1989), p. 61.

36. Ibid., p. 85, note 2.

37. Rich, *On Lies, Secrets and Silence*, p. 97.

38. See Gilbert and Gubar, *The Madwoman*, pp. 369–71; Pat Macpherson, *Reflecting on Jane Eyre* (London and New York: Routledge, 1989), p. 117; and Sutherland, '*Jane Eyre*'s Literary History', pp. 434–5.

CHAPTER 5: EMBODYING THE IRISH FAMINE IN *SHIRLEY*

1. Charlotte Brontë, *Jane Eyre*, ed. Margaret Smith (Oxford and New York: Oxford University Press, 1998), p. 263.

2. Terry Eagleton, *Heathcliff and the Great Hunger: Studies in Irish Culture* (London and New York: Verso, 1995), p. 23. Despite its contemporaneity with Brontë's first three novels and her own Irish extraction indeed (her father was born to working-class parents in County Down), the Famine's precise relationship to Brontë's writings remains largely unelaborated by criticism. There are, however, two notable exceptions to this ironic and anomalous silence. See Elsie Michie, 'From Simianized Irish to Oriental Despots: Heathcliff, Rochester and Racial Difference', *Novel*, 25 (1992), 125–40; and Susan Schorn, 'Punish Her Body to Save Her Soul: Echoes of the Irish Famine in *Jane Eyre*', *Journal of Narrative Technique*, 28 (1998), 350–65. For comprehensive historical studies of the Famine, see: Cecil Woodham-Smith, *The Great Hunger: Ireland, 1845–1849* (London: Hamish Hamilton, 1962); Peter Gray, *The Irish Famine* (London: Thames and Hudson, 1995); Colm Tóibín and Diarmaid Ferriter, *The Irish Famine: A Documentary* (London: Profile Books, 2001); and James S. Donnelly, Jr, *The Great Irish Potato Famine* (Stroud: Sutton, 2002).

3. Michie, 'From Simianized Irish', p. 125.

4. Charlotte Brontë, *Shirley*, ed. Herbert Rosengarten and Margaret Smith (Oxford and New York: Oxford University Press, 1998), pp. 5–6. Subsequent references to this work are incorporated in the text and given in parenthesis after quotations.

5. Other critical analyses to have placed varying degrees of emphasis on this constellation of concerns and its symbolic and political implications include: Sandra M. Gilbert and Susan Gubar, *The Madwoman in the Attic: The Woman Writer and the Nineteenth-Century Literary Imagination* (New Haven, CT, and London: Yale University Press, 1979), pp. 372–98; Janet Gezari, *Charlotte Brontë and Defensive Conduct: The Author and the Body at Risk* (Philadelphia, PA: University of Pennsylvania Press, 1992), pp. 90–124; Deirdre Lashgari, 'What Some Women Can't Swallow: Hunger as Protest in Charlotte Brontë's *Shirley*', in *Disorderly Eaters: Texts in Self-Empowerment*, ed. Lilian R. Furst and Peter W. Graham (Pennsylvania, PA: Pennsylvania State University Press, 1992), pp. 141–52; and Sally Shuttleworth, *Charlotte Brontë and Victorian Psychology* (Cambridge: Cambridge University Press, 1996), pp. 183–218. Illuminating as these readings often are – Lashgari's in particular – the broadly feminist approach they share can be restrictive. The critics in question here are sensitive to the

analogies which *Shirley* traces out between the respective hungers of working-class men and middle-class women, but none of them looks beyond this nexus of relationships towards the colonial history which underpins it.

6. For accounts specifically devoted to this aspect of the Famine, see David Fitzpatrick, *Oceans of Consolation: Personal Accounts of Irish Migration to Australia* (Ithaca, NY, and London: Cork University Press, 1994); and Edward Laxton, *The Famine Ships: The Irish Exodus to America, 1846–51* (London: Bloomsbury, 1996).

7. 'The Tide of Emigration to the United States and to the British Colonies', *Illustrated London News*, 6 July 1850. Cited in Gray, *The Irish Famine*, p. 1.

8. Brontë, *Jane Eyre*, p. 308.

9. Michie, 'From Simianized Irish', p. 125.

10. Ibid., p. 128.

11. Malone's muscularity, supported elsewhere, for example, by the allusion to his 'athletic Irish legs' (p. 279), distinguishes him from those anonymous and implicitly waif-like compatriots of his who are dispersed into the novel's margins. The first of these emerges in the course of Shirley's conjectures as to the various 'soothsayers' she would decide to 'consult' in order to divine her romantic fortunes and is casually dehumanized by context. As Shirley tells Caroline, these assorted oracles not only include the 'little Irish beggar that comes barefoot to [her] door', but also a 'mouse that steals out of the cranny in the wainscot; [a] bird that in frost and snow pecks at [her] window for a crumb' and '[a] dog that licks [her] hand and sits beside [her] knee' (p. 218). The second appears as the narrator muses upon the different ways in which an 'Irish girl' and her metropolitan counterpart characteristically negotiate hardship, the one predictably represented as far less fastidious and resourceful than the other: 'That British love of decency will work miracles: the poverty which reduces an Irish girl to rags is impotent to rob the English girl of the neat wardrobe she knows necessary to her self-respect' (p. 296).

12. William Shakespeare, *Coriolanus*, I.i.3, in *William Shakespeare: The Complete Works*, ed. Alfred Harbage (New York: Viking Press, 1977), p. 1216.

13. Ibid., I.i.143, in Harbage, p. 1217.

14. Ibid., I.i.144, in Harbage, p. 1217.

15. Ibid., I.i.25–6, in Harbage, p. 1216.

16. For an original examination of Robert's hybridity and *Shirley*'s ambivalent construction of images of European otherness as a whole,

see Susie O'Brien, 'Lying Back and Thinking of England: Sex and Nationalism in Charlotte Brontë's *Shirley*', *Frontenac Review*, 10–11 (1993–4), 54–79.

17. Eagleton, *Heathcliff and the Great Hunger*, p. 24.

18. Shuttleworth's formulation, in *Charlotte Brontë and Victorian Psychology*, p. 216.

19. This phrase entails a direct self-borrowing from line 26 of Brontë's 'The Lonely Lady', a poem written in 1837. See *The Poems of Charlotte Brontë*, ed. Tom Winnifrith (Oxford: Blackwell, 1984), p. 203. The generally sepulchral language in terms of which Mary is figured also owes much to this earlier text which at one point, underlines the blankly marmoreal look of its eponymous heroine by suggesting that her face is 'smooth and bright / As sculptured effigy on hallowed tomb' (lines 26–7). Yet if *Shirley* contains echoes of 'The Lonely Lady', this poem is a reworking of Tennyson's 'Mariana' (1830), itself a text looking back to Shakespeare's *Measure for Measure*. Brontë's evocation of Mary in *Shirley* is thus the last in a series of representations whose mutual concern is with the potentially suicidal longings which a patriarchal order can induce within its women. For a brief analysis of Brontë's debt to Tennyson in 'The Lonely Lady', see Isobel Armstrong, *Victorian Poetry: Poetry, Poetics and Politics* (London and New York: Routledge, 1993), pp. 334–5.

20. For discussion of the historical institution of anorexia as a diagnostic category, see Helen Malson, *The Thin Woman: Feminism, Post-Structuralism and the Social Psychology of Anorexia Nervosa* (London and New York: Routledge, 1998), pp. 61–75.

21. Rod Edmond, *Affairs of the Hearth: Victorian Poetry and Domestic Narrative* (London and New York: Routledge, 1988), p. 193.

22. Ibid., p. 195.

23. Ibid., p. 196.

24. Lashgari, 'What Some Women Can't Swallow', p. 141.

25. Carleton, *The Black Prophet*, p. 210.

26. *The Letters of Charlotte Brontë, with a Selection of Letters by Family and Friends*, ed. Margaret Smith, 2 vols to date (Oxford: Clarendon Press, 1995–), vol. II, p. 48.

27. See Lashgari, 'What Some Women Can't Swallow', pp. 148–9.

CHAPTER 6: FOREIGNERS AND SLAVES IN *VILLETTE*

1. Cited in Sandra M. Gilbert and Susan Gubar, *The Madwoman in the Attic: The Woman Writer and the Nineteenth-Century Literary*

Imagination (New Haven, CT, and London: Yale University Press, 1979), p. 481 (emphasis in original).

2. Charlotte Brontë, *Villette*, ed. Margaret Smith and Herbert Rosengarten, intro. Tim Dolin (Oxford and New York: Oxford University Press, 2000), p. 64. Subsequent references to this work are incorporated in the text and given in parenthesis after quotations.

3. Gilbert and Gubar, *The Madwoman*, p. 409.

4. Terry Lovell, 'Gender and Englishness in *Villette*', in *Political Gender: Texts and Contexts*, ed. Sally Ledger, Josephine McDonagh and Jane Spencer (Hemel Hempstead: Harvester Wheatsheaf, 1994), p. 49 (emphasis in original).

5. Ibid., p. 39.

6. For the dire tale of Sisera's deception by Jael, see Judges, iv: 17–22.

7. Preface to *The Belgian Essays: Charlotte Brontë and Emily Brontë*, ed. and trans. Sue Lonoff (New Haven, CT, and London: Yale University Press, 1996), p. xii.

8. *The Letters of Charlotte Brontë, with a Selection of Letters by Family and Friends*, ed. Margaret Smith, 2 vols to date (Oxford: Clarendon Press, 1995–), vol. I, p. 289.

9. For critical analyses of this aspect of Brontë's novel, see: Joseph A. Boone, 'Depolicing *Villette*: Surveillance, Invisibility, and the Female Erotics of "Heretic Narrative"', *Novel*, 26 (1992), 20–42; Sally Shuttleworth, *Charlotte Brontë and Victorian Psychology* (Cambridge: Cambridge University Press, 1996), pp. 219–42; and Mark M. Hennelly, Jr, '"The Surveillance of Désirée": Freud, Foucault, and *Villette*', *Victorian Literature and Culture*, 26 (1998), 421–40.

10. Jill L. Matus, *Unstable Bodies: Victorian Representations of Sexuality and Maternity* (Manchester and New York: Manchester University Press, 1995), p. 135.

11. Ibid., p. 139.

12. William Shakespeare, *Antony and Cleopatra*, V.ii.221, in *William Shakespeare: The Complete Works*, ed. Alfred Harbage (New York: Viking Press, 1977), p. 1209. Cited in Matus, *Unstable Bodies*, p. 138.

13. Isobel Armstrong, 'Charlotte Brontë's City of Glass', Hilda Hulme Memorial Lecture, 2 December 1992 (London: University of London, 1993), p. 27.

14. Ibid., p. 28.

15. Ibid., p. 29.

16. For more detailed discussion of the processes of doubling between Lucy and the nun, see: Mary Jacobus, 'The Buried Letter: Feminism and Romanticism in *Villette*', in *Women Writing and Writing about Women*, ed. Mary Jacobus (London: Croom Helm, 1979), pp. 48–50; Gilbert and Gubar, *The Madwoman*, pp. 425–6; and Penny Boumelha, *Charlotte Brontë* (Hemel Hempstead: Harvester, 1990), p. 116.

17. For a recent alternative perspective on the intertextual possibilities offered by *Villette*'s nun, see Toni Wein, 'Gothic Desire in Charlotte Brontë's *Villette*', *Studies in English Literature*, 39 (1999), 733–46. In this essay, Wein argues that Brontë rewrites Matthew G. Lewis's *The Monk* (1796) and, in particular, the sexually charged narrative of Beatrice de las Cisternas, the so-called 'Bleeding Nun' who haunts Lewis's novel. In this way, Wein suggests, Brontë is able to correct 'the perverted representations of women' (p. 737) which course through the earlier text, in a complex triple bid to establish herself 'as a woman, as an author, and as an heir to literary conventions' (p. 734). Interesting and persuasive as it often is, Wein's approach is limited by the assumption that the English literary tradition fully accounts for and exhausts the intertextual potential of *Villette*, just as her feminist critical emphasis tends to block out the questions of colonialism, race and slavery in which Brontë's novel, like her work as a whole, is entangled.

18. Elizabeth Gaskell, *The Life of Charlotte Brontë*, ed. Elisabeth Jay (Harmondsworth: Penguin, 1997), p. 389.

19. Ibid., p. 390.

20. Harriet Beecher Stowe, *Uncle Tom's Cabin*, ed. Elizabeth Ammons (New York and London: W. W. Norton, 1994), p. 347. Subsequent references to this work, abbreviated as *UTC*, are incorporated in the text and given in parenthesis after quotations.

21. Karen Halttunen, 'Gothic Imagination and Social Reform: the Haunted Houses of Lyman Beecher, Henry Ward Beecher, and Harriet Beecher Stowe', in *New Essays on Uncle Tom's Cabin*, ed. Eric J. Sundquist (Cambridge: Cambridge University Press, 1986), p. 120.

22. Gilbert and Gubar, *The Madwoman*, p. 444.

23. Diane Roberts, *The Myth of Aunt Jemima: Representations of Race and Region* (London and New York: Routledge, 1994), p. 46.

24. On this point, see ibid., p. 202, note 23.

25. Brontë, in Smith, *The Letters*, vol. I, p. 370.

26. Ibid., vol. I, p. 370.

27. Smith, *The Letters*, vol. I, p. 371, note 9.

28. Anna Neill, 'The Sentimental Novel and the Republican Imaginary: Slavery in *Paul and Virginia*', *Diacritics*, 23: 3 (1993), 38.

29. Jacques-Henri Bernardin de Saint-Pierre, *Paul and Virginia and the Indian Cottage*, trans. Helen Maria Williams (London: William Smith, 1789), p. 40. Subsequent references to this work, abbreviated as *PV*, are incorporated in the text and given in parenthesis after quotations.

30. Bernardin produces a much more extended and graphic eyewitness account of the ordeals and punishments endured by such runaway slaves in his own *Journey to Mauritius* (1773), a text which is part travelogue, part colonial indictment. See, for example, letter 12, 'On Blacks':

> Usually they hide in the forest, where they are hunted by parties of soldiers, Negroes and dogs, with some of the local plantation owners joining in for the fun. They are dragged back like savage beasts. When they cannot be caught, they are shot by rifle, their heads are severed and carried back in triumph to town on the end of sticks. That is what I have seen every week.
>
> When runaway blacks are caught, they have an ear sliced off and are whipped. A second time, they are whipped, their hamstrings are cut and they are put in chains. A third time, they are hanged … .
>
> I have seen them hanged and their bones broken while still alive; they went to their execution joyfully, and suffered without a sound. I saw a woman throw herself from the top of the ladder. They believe that in the next world they will find a happier life and that the Father of men will not treat them unjustly. (Jacques-Henri Bernardin de Saint-Pierre, *Journey to Mauritius*, ed. and trans. James Wilson [Oxford: Signal Books, 2002], p. 130)

31. Chris Bongie, *Islands and Exiles: The Creole Identities of Post/Colonial Literature* (Stanford, CA: Stanford University Press, 1998), p. 105.

32. Gaskell, *The Life of Charlotte Brontë*, p. 388.

CONCLUSION

1. See Elizabeth Gaskell, *The Life of Charlotte Brontë*, ed. Elisabeth Jay (Harmondsworth: Penguin, 1997), p. 47.

2. Charlotte Brontë, 'Farewell to Angria', ed. Christine Alexander, in *Jane Eyre*, ed. Richard J. Dunn, 2nd edition (New York and London: W. W. Norton, 1987), p. 427.

3. Ibid., p. 426.

4. Charlotte Brontë, 'A Leaf from an Unopened Volume', in *An Edition of the Early Writings of Charlotte Brontë*, ed. Christine Alexander, 2 vols to date (Oxford: Blackwell, 1987–), vol. II, part 1, p. 329.

5. Charlotte Brontë, 'Well, here I am at Roe Head', ed. Christine Alexander, in *Jane Eyre*, ed. Dunn, p. 412.

6. Charlotte Brontë, *Stancliffe's Hotel*, ed. Heather Glen (Harmondsworth: Penguin, 2003), p. 27. As well as being a recent Brontëan creation, the disfigured colonial 'soldier' who appears in this passage looks back nostalgically (or perhaps regressively) to the toy army so warmly celebrated in 'The History of the Year' (1829). '[M]issing' in one sense, the 'soldier' is found in another, joining up, once again, with the original company out of which Brontë weaves her first colonial fictions.

7. Charlotte Brontë, *Villette*, ed. Margaret Smith and Herbert Rosengarten, intro. Tim Dolin (Oxford and New York: Oxford University Press, 2000), p. 496.

8. Charlotte Brontë, *The Professor*, ed. Margaret Smith and Herbert Rosengarten (Oxford: Clarendon Press, 1987), p. 14.

9. A similar point is made by Susan Meyer in *Imperialism at Home: Race and Victorian Women's Fiction* (Ithaca, NY, and London: Cornell University Press, 1996), p. 60. Meyer also interestingly links the violent weather system out of which *Villette*'s ending erupts to 'Well, here I am at Roe Head', where, as she puts it, another 'wild storm evokes in [Brontë] the vision of Africans in revolution against white British colonists' (p. 61).

10. Brontë, *Villette*, p. 495.

Select Bibliography

Alexander, Christine, *The Early Writings of Charlotte Brontë* (Oxford: Blackwell, 1983).

Alexander, Christine (ed.), *An Edition of the Early Writings of Charlotte Brontë*, 2 vols to date (Oxford: Blackwell, 1987–).

Alexander, Christine, 'Africa as Play in the Childhood of the Brontës', *Journal of African Travel Writing*, 6 (1999), 5–15.

Armstrong, Isobel, 'Charlotte Brontë's City of Glass', Hilda Hulme Memorial Lecture, 2 December 1992 (London: University of London, 1993).

Armstrong Isobel, *Victorian Poetry: Poetry, Poetics and Politics* (London and New York: Routledge, 1993).

Azim, Firdous, *The Colonial Rise of the Novel* (London and New York: Routledge, 1993).

Barker, Juliet, *The Brontës* (London: Phoenix, 1995).

Barker Juliet (ed.), *Charlotte Brontë: Juvenilia, 1829–1835* (Harmondsworth: Penguin, 1996).

Bentinck, William Cavendish, 'Sati Regulation XVII, A.D. 1829 of the Bengal Code, 4 December 1829', in *Imperialism & Orientalism: A Documentary Sourcebook*, ed. Barbara Harlow and Mia Carter (Oxford: Blackwell, 1999), pp. 93–4.

Bhabha, Homi K., *The Location of Culture* (London and New York: Routledge, 1994).

Blackburn, Robin, *The Overthrow of Colonial Slavery, 1776–1848* (London and New York: Verso, 1988).

Bongie, Chris, *Islands and Exiles: The Creole Identities of Post/Colonial Literature* (Stanford, CA: Stanford University Press, 1998).

Boone, Joseph A., 'Depolicing *Villette*: Surveillance, Invisibility, and the Female Erotics of "Heretic Narrative"', *Novel*, 26 (1992), 20–42.

Boumelha, Penny, *Charlotte Brontë* (Hemel Hempstead: Harvester Wheatsheaf, 1990).

'The British Settlements in Western Africa', *Blackwood's Edinburgh Magazine*, 26 (September 1829), 341–50.

Brontë, Charlotte, 'Farewell to Angria', ed. Christine Alexander, in *Jane Eyre*, ed. Richard J. Dunn, 2nd edition (New York and London: W. W. Norton, 1987), pp. 426–7.

Brontë, Charlotte, *Jane Eyre*, ed. Margaret Smith (Oxford and New York: Oxford University Press, 1998).

Brontë, Charlotte, *The Professor*, ed. Margaret Smith and Herbert Rosengarten (Oxford: Clarendon Press, 1987).

Brontë, Charlotte, *Shirley*, ed. Herbert Rosengarten and Margaret Smith (Oxford and New York: Oxford University Press, 1998).

Brontë, Charlotte, *Stancliffe's Hotel*, ed. Heather Glen (Harmondsworth: Penguin, 2003).

Brontë, Charlotte, *Villette*, ed. Margaret Smith and Herbert Rosengarten, intro. Tim Dolin (Oxford and New York: Oxford University Press, 2000).

Brontë, Charlotte, 'Well, here I am at Roe Head', ed. Christine Alexander, in *Jane Eyre*, ed. Richard J. Dunn, 2nd edition (New York and London: W. W. Norton, 1987) pp. 410–2.

'The Campaign of the Sutlej', *Blackwood's Edinburgh Magazine*, 59 (May 1846), 625–44.

Carleton, William, *The Black Prophet: A Tale of Irish Famine*, intro. John Kelly (1847; Poole: Woodstock Books, 1996).

Chapple, J. A. V. and Arthur Pollard (eds), *The Letters of Mrs Gaskell* (Manchester: Manchester University Press, 1966).

Cheyfitz, Eric, *The Poetics of Imperialism: Translation and Colonization from 'The Tempest' to Tarzan* (New York and Oxford: Oxford University Press, 1991).

Constable, Kathleen, *A Stranger within the Gates: Charlotte Brontë and Victorian Irishness* (Lanham, MD, and Oxford: University Press of America, 2000).

Cowhig, Ruth, 'Blacks in English Renaissance Drama and the Role of Shakespeare's Othello', in *The Black Presence in English Literature*, ed. David Dabydeen (Manchester: Manchester University Press, 1985), pp. 1–25.

Dennison, Sam, *Scandalize My Name: Black Imagery in American Popular Music* (New York and London: Garland, 1982).

Donaldson, Laura E., 'The Miranda Complex: Colonialism and the Question of Feminist Reading', *Diacritics*, 18: 3 (1988), 65–77.

Donnelly, Jr, James S., *The Great Irish Potato Famine* (Stroud: Sutton, 2002).

Douglass, Frederick, *Narrative of the Life of Frederick Douglass, An American Slave, Written by Himself*, ed. William L. Andrews and William S. McFeely (New York and London: W. W. Norton, 1997).

Eagleton, Terry, *Myths of Power: A Marxist Study of the Brontës* (Basingstoke: Macmillan, 1975).

Eagleton, Terry, *Heathcliff and the Great Hunger: Studies in Irish Culture* (London and New York: Verso, 1995).

Fanon, Frantz, *Black Skin, White Masks*, trans. Charles Lam Markmann, Foreword by Homi K. Bhabha (London: Pluto Press, 1986).

Fanon, Frantz, *The Wretched of the Earth*, trans. Constance Farrington, Preface by Jean-Paul Sartre (Harmondsworth: Penguin, 1990).

Fitzpatrick, David, *Oceans of Consolation: Personal Accounts of Irish Migration to Australia* (Ithaca, NY, and London: Cork University Press, 1994).

Freud, Sigmund, 'Fetishism', in *On Sexuality*, ed. and trans. Angela Richards, Pelican Freud Library, vol. 7 (Harmondsworth: Penguin, 1977), pp. 345–57.

Gaskell, Elizabeth, *The Life of Charlotte Brontë*, ed. Elisabeth Jay (Harmondsworth: Penguin, 1997).

'Geography of Central Africa: Denham and Clapperton's Journals', *Blackwood's Edinburgh Magazine*, 19 (June 1826), 687–709.

Gérin, Winifred (ed.), *Charlotte Brontë: Five Novelettes* (London: Folio, 1971).

Gezari, Janet, *Charlotte Brontë and Defensive Conduct: The Author and the Body at Risk* (Philadelphia, PA: University of Pennsylvania Press, 1992).

Gilbert, Sandra M. and Susan Gubar, *The Madwoman in the Attic: The Woman Writer and the Nineteenth-Century Literary Imagination* (New Haven, CT, and London: Yale University Press, 1979).

Glen, Heather (ed.), *The Cambridge Companion to the Brontës* (Cambridge: Cambridge University Press, 2002).

Glen, Heather, *Charlotte Brontë: The Imagination in History* (Oxford: Oxford University Press, 2002).

Gray, Peter, *The Irish Famine* (London: Thames and Hudson, 1995).

Harbage, Alfred (ed.), *William Shakespeare: The Complete Works* (New York: Viking Press, 1977).

Hennelly, Jr, Mark M., '"The Surveillance of Désirée": Freud, Foucault, and *Villette*', *Victorian Literature and Culture*, 26 (1998), 421–40.

Heywood, Christopher, 'Africa and Slavery in the Brontë Children's Novels', *Hitotsubashi: Journal of Arts and Sciences*, 30 (1989), 75–89.

Hyam, Ronald, *Empire and Sexuality: The British Experience* (Manchester and New York: Manchester University Press, 1991).

Jacobus, Mary, 'The Buried Letter: Feminism and Romanticism in *Villette*', in *Women Writing and Writing about Women*, ed. Mary Jacobus (London: Croom Helm, 1979), pp. 48–50.

Kristeva, Julia, *Strangers to Ourselves*, trans. Leon S. Roudiez (New York: Columbia University Press, 1991).

Lashgari, Deirdre, 'What Some Women Can't Swallow: Hunger as Protest in Charlotte Brontë's *Shirley*', in *Disorderly Eaters: Texts in Self-*

Empowerment, ed. Lilian R. Furst and Peter W. Graham (Pennsylvania, PA: Pennsylvania State University Press, 1992), pp. 141–52.

Laxton, Edward, *The Famine Ships: The Irish Exodus to America, 1846–51* (London: Bloomsbury, 1996).

Lewis, Matthew, *Journal of a West India Proprietor, Kept during a Residence in the Island of Jamaica*, ed. Judith Terry (Oxford: Oxford University Press, 1999).

London, Bette, 'The Pleasures of Submission: *Jane Eyre* and the Production of the Text', *English Literary History*, 58 (1991), 195–213.

London, Bette, *Writing Double: Women's Literary Partnerships* (Ithaca, NY, and London: Cornell University Press, 1999).

Lonoff, Sue (ed. and trans.), *The Belgian Essays: Charlotte Brontë and Emily Brontë* (New Haven, CT, and London: Yale University Press, 1996).

Loomba, Ania, *Colonialism/Postcolonialism* (London and New York: Routledge, 1998).

Lovell, Terry, 'Gender and Englishness in *Villette*', in *Political Gender: Texts and Contexts*, ed. Sally Ledger, Josephine McDonagh and Jane Spencer (Hemel Hempstead: Harvester Wheatsheaf, 1994), pp. 37–52.

Macaulay, Thomas Babington, 'Minute on Indian Education', in *Imperialism and Orientalism: A Documentary Sourcebook*, ed. Barbara Harlow and Mia Carter (Oxford: Blackwell, 1999), pp. 56–62.

Macherey, Pierre, *A Theory of Literary Production*, trans. Geoffrey Wall (London: Routledge & Kegan Paul, 1978).

Malchow, H. L., *Gothic Images of Race in Nineteenth-Century Britain* (Stanford, CA: Stanford University Press, 1996).

Malson, Helen, *The Thin Woman: Feminism, Post-Structuralism and the Social Psychology of Anorexia Nervosa* (London and New York: Routledge, 1998).

Marcus, Steven, *The Other Victorians: A Study of Sexuality and Pornography in Mid-Nineteenth-Century England* (London: Weidenfeld and Nicolson, 1966).

Matus, Jill L., *Unstable Bodies: Victorian Representations of Sexuality and Maternity* (Manchester and New York: Manchester University Press, 1995).

Maynard, John, *Charlotte Brontë and Sexuality* (Cambridge: Cambridge University Press, 1984).

Meyer, Susan, *Imperialism at Home: Race and Victorian Women's Fiction* (Ithaca, NY, and London: Cornell University Press, 1996).

Michie, Elsie, 'From Simianized Irish to Oriental Despots: Heathcliff, Rochester and Racial Difference', *Novel*, 25 (1992), 125–40.

'Mission from Cape Coast Castle to Ashantee', *Blackwood's Edinburgh Magazine*, 5 (May and June 1819), 175–83 and 302–10.

Neill, Anna, 'The Sentimental Novel and the Republican Imaginary: Slavery in *Paul and Virginia*', *Diacritics*, 23: 3 (1993), 36–47.

O'Brien, Susie, 'Lying Back and Thinking of England: Sex and Nationalism in Charlotte Brontë's *Shirley*', *Frontenac Review*, 10–11 (1993–4), 54–79.

Olson, Ted, 'Jim Crow', in *The Oxford Companion to African American Literature*, ed. William L. Andrews, Frances Smith Foster and Trudier Harris (New York and Oxford: Oxford University Press, 1997), pp. 398–9.

Patmore, Coventry, 'The Angel in the House', in *The Broadview Anthology of Victorian Poetry and Poetic Theory*, ed. Thomas J. Collins and Vivienne J. Rundle (Ontario: Broadview Press, 1999), p. 757.

Perera, Suvendrini, *Reaches of Empire: The English Novel from Edgeworth to Dickens* (New York: Columbia University Press, 1991).

Prince, Mary, *The History of Mary Prince, a West Indian Slave*, ed. Sarah Salih (Harmondsworth: Penguin, 2000).

Robbe-Grillet, Alain, *Snapshots and Towards a New Novel*, trans. Barbara Wright (London: Calder and Boyers, 1965).

Roberts, Diane, *The Myth of Aunt Jemima: Representations of Race and Region* (London and New York: Routledge, 1994).

Rushdie, Salman, *The Satanic Verses* (London: Viking, 1988).

Sabin, Margery, 'The Suttee Romance', *Raritan: A Quarterly Review*, 11: 2 (1991), 1–24.

Said, Edward W., *Culture and Imperialism* (London: Vintage, 1994).

Saint-Pierre, Jacques-Henri Bernardin de, *Journey to Mauritius*, ed. and trans. James Wilson (Oxford: Signal Books, 2002).

Saint-Pierre, Jacques-Henri Bernardin de, *Paul and Virginia and the Indian Cottage*, trans. Helen Maria Williams (London: William Smith, 1789).

Schmitt, Cannon, *Alien Nation: Nineteenth-Century Gothic Fictions and English Nationality, 1797–1897* (Philadelphia, PA: University of Pennsylvania Press, 1997).

Schorn, Susan, 'Punish Her Body to Save Her Soul: Echoes of the Irish Famine in *Jane Eyre*', *Journal of Narrative Technique*, 28 (1998), 350–65.

Schwarz-Bart, André, *A Woman Named Solitude*, trans. Ralph Manheim (New York: Atheneum, 1973).

Shuttleworth, Sally, *Charlotte Brontë and Victorian Psychology* (Cambridge: Cambridge University Press, 1996).

Smith, Margaret (ed.), *The Letters of Charlotte Brontë, with a Selection of Letters by Family and Friends*, 2 vols to date (Oxford: Clarendon Press, 1995–).

Sollors, Werner, *Neither Black nor White yet Both: Thematic Explorations of Interracial Literature* (New York and Oxford: Oxford University Press, 1997).

Spivak, Gayatri Chakravorty, 'Three Women's Texts and a Critique of Imperialism', *Critical Inquiry*, 12 (1985), 243–61.

Stowe, Harriet Beecher, *Uncle Tom's Cabin*, ed. Elizabeth Ammons (New York and London: W. W. Norton, 1994).

Sutherland, Kathryn, '*Jane Eyre's* Literary History: the Case for *Mansfield Park*', *English Literary History*, 59 (1992), 409–40.

Thomas, Sue, 'The Tropical Extravagance of Bertha Mason', *Victorian Literature and Culture*, 27 (1999), 1–17.

Tóibín, Colm and Diarmaid Ferriter, *The Irish Famine: A Documentary* (London: Profile Books, 2001).

Viswanathan, Gauri, *Masks of Conquest: Literary Study and British Rule in India* (New York: Columbia University Press, 1989).

Walvin, James, *Black Ivory: A History of British Slavery* (London: HarperCollins, 1992).

Wein, Toni, 'Gothic Desire in Charlotte Brontë's *Villette*', *Studies in English Literature*, 39 (1999), 733–46.

Williams, Carolyn, 'Closing the Book: the Intertextual End of *Jane Eyre*', in *Victorian Connections*, ed. Jerome J. McGann (Charlottesville, VA: University Press of Virginia, 1989), pp. 60–87.

Winnifrith, Tom (ed.), *The Poems of Charlotte Brontë* (Oxford: Blackwell, 1984).

Wood, Jane, *Passion and Pathology in Victorian Fiction* (Oxford: Oxford University Press, 2001).

Woodham-Smith, Cecil, *The Great Hunger: Ireland, 1845–1849* (London: Hamish Hamilton, 1962).

Young, Robert J. C., *Colonial Desire: Hybridity in Theory, Culture and Race* (London and New York: Routledge, 1995).

Zonana, Joyce, 'The Sultan and the Slave: Feminist Orientalism and the Structure of *Jane Eyre*', *Signs*, 18 (1993), 592–617.

Index

Note: References to annotated text are indicated as '101 (n3)'; references to Notes as '159 n11'.